Molly

Blake Butler

PRAISE FOR *MOLLY*

"The most immediate feeling of life I've ever had reading a book—a life lived at the desk and out in the world, a life of openness and secrets. 'Make art for me,' Molly wrote to Blake. 'I will read it all.' I breathed along with every word."
—PATRICIA LOCKWOOD

"How to praise a book of such wounded beauty as Blake Butler's phenomenal *Molly*? The same way one would a life lost early: with love and sincerity and anger and wonder and lithely elegant and observant insights that remind us and inspire us, as Butler precisely does, to live and to love ourselves."
—JOHN D'AGATA

"*Molly* is a brilliant and brutal book. Blake Butler fearlessly takes on love and grief and the mysteries of this world and the next."
—EMMA CLINE

"A dark miracle—actual evidence that what we can never know, what we could never imagine about the one we love, is what binds us to them, beyond death."
—MICHAEL W. CLUNE

"I was gripped from the start by this memoir's urgent honesty. Blake Butler turned a story that was almost unspeakable into a narrative at once brutal and loving, broken and solid."
—CATHERINE LACEY

Published in the United States by:
Archway Editions,
a division of powerHouse Cultural Entertainment, Inc.
32 Adams Street, Brooklyn, NY 11201

www.archwayeditions.us

Daniel Power, CEO
Chris Molnar, Editorial Director
Nicodemus Nicoludis, Managing Editor
Naomi Falk, Senior Editor
Caitlin Forst, Contributing Editor

Library of Congress Control Number: 2023937145

ISBN 978-1-64823-037-0

Printed by Toppan Leefung

First edition, 2023

10 9 8 7 6 5 4 3 2

Edited by Chris Molnar
Proofread by José Carpio

Printed and bound in Canada

EDITIONS

Molly

Blake Butler

Archway Editions, Brooklyn, NY

This memoir contains graphic descriptions of suicide, self-harm, and suicidal ideation.

If you are contemplating self-destruction, please tell someone you trust. Immediate counseling is available 24/7 by dialing 1-800-SUICIDE or 988.

A Sunday afternoon in early spring. We'd spent the morning quiet, in separate rooms—me in my office, writing; Molly, my partner, in the guest room, working too, so I believed. Sometimes I'd pass by and see her using her computer or reading from the books piled on the bed where she lay prone or staring off out through the window to the yard. It was warm for March already, full of the kind of color through which you can begin to see the blooming world emerge. Molly didn't want to talk really, clearly feeling extremely down again, and still I tried to hug her, leaning over the bed to wrap my arms around her shoulders as best I could. She brushed me off a bit, letting me hold her but not really responding. I let her be—it'd been a long winter, coming off what felt like the hardest year in both our lives, to the point we'd both begun to wonder if, not when, the struggle would ever slow. I wished there could be something I might say to lift her spirits for a minute, but I also knew how much she loathed most any stroke of optimism or blind hope, each more offensive than the woe alone. Later, while passing in the hallway in the dark, she slipped her arms around me at the waist and drew me close. She told me she loved me, almost a whisper, tender, small. I told her I loved her too, and we held each other standing, a clutch of limbs. I put my head in her hair and looked beyond on through the bathroom where half-muted light pressed at the window as through a tarp. When we let go, she slipped out neatly, no further words, and back to bed. The house was still, very little sound besides our motion. After another while spent working, I came back and asked if she'd come out with me to the yard to see the chickens, watch them scour through the grass for bugs, one of our favorite ways to pass the time. Molly said no, she didn't want to go, but asked if I'd bring one to the bedroom window so she could see— something I often did so many days, an easy way to make her smile. Outside, it was sodden, lots of rain lately, and the birds were restless, eager to rush out of their run. I scooped up Woosh, our Polish hen, my favorite, and brought her over to the window where Molly sat. This time, though, when I approached, Molly didn't move toward us, lift the sash, as she would usually. Even as I smiled and waved, holding Woosh up close against the glass, speaking for her in the hen-voice that I'd made up, Molly's mouth held clamped, her eyes like dents obscured against the glare across the dimness of the room. Woosh began to wriggle, wanting down. The other birds were ranging freely, unattended—which always made me nervous now, as in recent months a hawk had taken favor to our area, often reappearing in lurking circles overhead, waiting for the right time to swoop down and make a meal out of our pets. So I didn't linger for too long at the window, antsy anyway to get on and go for my daily run around the neighborhood, one of the few reasons I still had for getting out of the house. I gripped Woosh by her leg and made it wave, a little goodbye, then hurried on, leaving Molly there looking back out at where I'd just been, onto the lone sapling that she'd planted just last spring so one day she wouldn't have to see the neighbors.

I corralled the chickens to their coop, came back inside. In Molly's office, where I had a closet, I sat across from her while changing clothes. She seemed faraway, distracted, speaking very calmly. She said she'd just finished reading the galley of my next novel, and that she liked the way it ended: with the book's disturbed protagonist suspended in a grim, panopticonic cryostasis, haunted by ads. I felt surprised to hear she'd finished, given her low spirit and how she'd said she found the novel difficult to read because it hurt for her to have to see the pain behind my language, how much I'd been carrying around all this time. I told her I was grateful that she'd made it through, that I wanted to hear more of what she thought after my run, already anxious to get on with it, in go-mode. My reaction seemed to vex her, causing a little back and forth where we both kept misunderstanding what the other had just said, each at different ends of a conversation: for me, the beginning; for her, the end. She remained flat on the bed as I kissed her on the forehead, squeezed her arm, said see you shortly, then proceeded through the house, out the front door. It was a clear afternoon, calmer than usual after many recent days of incessant rain. Coming down the driveway, I took my phone out to put on music I could run to and saw I'd received an email, sent from Molly, according to the timestamp, just after I had left her in the room. *(no subject)*, and in the body, just: *I love you*, nothing else, besides a Word document she'd attached, titled *Folk Physics*, which I knew to be the title of the manuscript of poems she'd been working on the last few months. I stopped short in my tracks, surprised to see she'd sent it to me like that, then and there. Something felt off about it, too out of nowhere—not at all like Molly, or perhaps too much like Molly. I turned around at once and went inside.

During my brief absence, Molly had gotten out of bed, up and about for one of only a few times that whole day. I found her in the kitchen with the lights off, standing as if dazed by my appearance, arms at her sides. The room around us in that moment—dim, traced with a glow, half-hollow where the walls arrange themselves against the black side of my mind—will remain burned in my memory forever as the last time I'd see Molly alive, all prior memory we'd shared in that same space half covered over, like a drowned ship, the last few seconds of *our home*. Molly seemed to clench up as I came near her, letting me put my arm around her once again, but staying loose, confused, on edge. I realize now she must have had the gun on her already, getting ready for the endgame of her plan. She hesitated when I asked her if she'd finished her manuscript, said I was surprised she hadn't mentioned it. Yes, she said, she guessed that it was finished, her diction tight, quiet, just like it had been all that week. A draft at least, like no big deal, still work to be done, always more. I told her I was excited to get to read it either way, that I was proud of her, and I squeezed her closer, just a moment, then let go. She seemed to hover there in front of me a moment, waiting mute for what I'd do next. I asked if after I got finished running, maybe we could go to Whole Foods, pick up some dinner stuff to cook together, maybe watch a movie, have a nice night. She said yes, that sounded good, and I said I'd see her soon, then left her standing in the kitchen in the dark.

———

On my run, I worked my way along the same path I often made around our neighborhood, following its pattern without thought. I don't remember seeing any other people, then or later, though I must have; in retrospect, the smaller details fade to gray around the corridor of time spent rushing forward in the wake of what awaited just ahead. I'd always liked the way the world went narrow in this manner during exercise, leaving nothing else to do but the task at hand, one foot in front of the other, counting down without a number. Near the end of the run, as I did often, I decided to extend my route, turning back around to double back the way I'd just come, adding on an extra half-mile on a path that took me past the entrance to the gardens where Molly and I would often walk in warmer months along a creek, searching for animals. The sidewalks in this part of the neighborhood were cracked and bumpy, requiring specific care not to trip. I pulled my phone out to see how far I'd gone and saw a ping from Twitter telling me that Molly had made a post, just minutes past—a link to a YouTube video of "The Old Revolution" by Leonard Cohen, including her transcription of the song's opening line: "I finally broke into the prison." I liked the tweet and thumbed the link immediately, opening the song to let it play, happy to imagine her selecting the closing soundtrack for my run home, just a couple blocks away now. "Into this furnace I ask you now to venture," Cohen sang, in cryptic lament, coyly backed by a doomy twang. "You whom I cannot betray."

The song was still there with me in my head as I arrived back at our driveway. Looking up from halfway along the path toward our front porch stairs, I saw a shape covering the door's spyhole—a plain white envelope, affixed with tape. My body seized. From early in our relationship I'd had visions of Molly picking up and leaving just like that, deciding on a whim and without warning she preferred to be alone. Running up the steps, already flooding with adrenaline, a pounding pulse, I saw my first name, *Blake*, handwritten in the center of the envelope's face in Molly's script. Immediately, I wailed, devoid of language, too much too fast, real and unreal. Inside the envelope, a two-page letter, printed out. My mind froze on the first lines:

Blake,

I have decided to leave this world.

Then there was nothing but those words—words to which I have no corollary, no distinct definition in that moment, even as simple as they seem. Every sentence I've tried to put here to frame it feels like a doormat laid on blood, an unstoppable force colliding with an intolerable object in slow motion, beyond the need of being named. Before and after.

—

Out of something like an instinct, I forced my eyes along the rest of the letter, not really reading it so much as scanning for a more direct form of information, anything she'd written that might tell me where she was—which, near the end of the second page, I found: *I left my body in the nature area where we used to go walking so I could see the sky and trees and hear the birds one last time.* Then: *I shot myself so it would be over instantly with certainty and no suffering whatsoever.* This time, when I screamed again, it was the only word that I could think of: *No.* I must have sounded like a child jabbed in his guts, squealing. I knew exactly where she meant—I'd run right by it, just minutes before, perhaps a few hundred yards away. I might have even crossed her path had times aligned right, had I known. A sudden frenzy of possible options of what to do next swarmed my brain, none of them quite correct, devised in terror.

—

At the edge of the sidewalk, I stopped and tried to think if I should go inside and get my keys and drive to where she might be, or if I should run there fast as I could, still in my running clothes, already half-exhausted and slick with sweat. Each instant that I didn't do exactly the right thing felt like the last chance, a window closing. Finally, I took off running at full speed along the sidewalk, shouting her name loud as I could, begging her or me or God or whoever else might be able to hear me: *No, please, Molly. Not like this.* No matter what I said, there was no answer; no one on the streets surrounding, zero cars. Ahead, the sidewalk seemed to stretch so far beyond me, no matter how fast or hard I ran, growing longer with every step; all the houses shaped the same as they were always, full of other people in the midst of their own lives. As I ran, I tried to scan her letter, held out before me with both hands, already wadded up in frantic grip, scanning through fragments of despondent logic that felt impossible to connect with any actual moment in the present as it passed. "Everyone's life ends, and mine is over now," she'd written in present tense about the future, which was apparently in the midst of happening right now—or had it already happened? Was there still time? I felt embarrassed, sick to my stomach, to feel my body's power giving out no matter how hard I tried to maintain sprint, forced instead at several points to slow down against the burning in my muscles, sucking for air with everything I thought I knew now on the line.

———

I couldn't find her in the fields. The grass was high and muddy, and my running shoes kept getting stuck, sucking half off me, as I worked my way along unkempt plots of wild grass left overgrown through the winter and the vacant patches where in the spring ahead flowers would bloom. Everything felt blurred, moving much faster all around me than I could parse, more like a livestream of a too-real horror movie than my life. I was still screaming her name, begging her to answer, to be okay, but my voice just disappeared into the strangling silence. I searched the spots where last summer we'd returned daily to watch a mother duck care for her newborn flock; the bank of reeds where frogs would often sing till you got too near; the grown-together pair of trees Molly said she thought would resemble us in our old age someday. I kept calling her number, listening to it ring and ring until the default voicemail recording came back on, asking in an android woman's voice for me to leave a message. Maybe in the memory on Molly's phone now there's a recording of me huffing and howling, just before I really understood that there was no way to go back, that nothing I could say or want or do could reverse what had taken place.

———

The longer she failed to turn up, the more I felt a desperate possibility that it wasn't already too late—that she was out here somewhere, and I could save her. I realized I should call 911, holding the phone to my face while rushing through the mud into the far end of the gardens, clogged with trees. After what seemed endless ringing, an operator's voice came on the line, firm and professional, and asked for my emergency. I heard the words come out of my mouth before I thought them: *My wife left me a suicide note and I can't find her.* The operator asked me where I was, how they could reach me, and I kept trying to explain, uncertain how to be specific with the location of the gardens, of no immediate address. *I can't find her, I need help,* I kept repeating in frustration when I couldn't seem to get it right, *please come and help me.* The operator reassured me the police were already on their way, someone would be there very soon. In the meantime, she stayed with me on the line there as I hurried forward through the trees to where the gardens reached their end amid a sort of bog, studded with thickets and obscured patches, brambles, shrubs, so many possible places to end up. Every time I called her name, it felt a little less like her; as if what those syllables had meant to me for so long no longer bore resemblance to itself, and in its place, a widening hole, larger than all else.

———

Reaching the end of the bog area, I turned and started back toward the street. Close to the entrance, along the patch of land where some local group had planted food, I saw two women coming down the slope toward me, one near my age, the other probably her mother. I could see at once they looked concerned, had come to the area for a reason. "Did you hear a gunshot?" I begged of them in a pinched voice, desperate to hear a different answer than what I thought. *Yes*, they said, they had, and I felt something deep within me break— ambient anguish so overwhelming I should have fallen to my knees but could no longer remember how. Like having the skin ripped off your head and being asked to run a marathon on live TV, the finish line of which ends in a lake of burning bile. It's not that time stands still in such a moment—it's that there's nothing you can do to make time stop, and every second lasts forever even as it's over, as if what you'd thought previously impossible has suddenly become the organizing principle of who you are. I asked how long ago they'd heard the gunshot. They said ten minutes. I asked in which direction, and they pointed in the direction from which I'd come. "Are you missing your dog?" the younger woman asked, as I turned back to hurry where she'd pointed. "My wife," I said, over my shoulder, and heard her groan like being struck, some broken bit of useless language: *Oh my god*.

———

I was completely frantic now, even more incensed with the task of finding as the world surrounding bent to blur; all locations interlacing in my periphery like abstract glyphs, behind one of which, somewhere, was Molly's body. Between my clearer memories of this transition in time's fabric, huge, wide blank patches, a jagged space in how I'd been that simply *no longer exists*. I remember moving away from those women as through a vortex, past cracks widening within my vision, the sound of my inhale like a black hole. As I hurried along the gardens' path again, expecting at any second to come stumbling onto blood, I noticed another form there with me parallel, a man hurrying along the massive drainage pipe that laced the property, trying to help. Back near the far end of the trees, he shouted at me for her phone number, so he could call, too, as if she'd answer him instead of me. The only numbers I knew by heart were mine and my mother's, I realized, stopping to stand there scrolling through my contacts till I found hers, then shouting it across the thickets for anyone to have. Right then, standing in the middle of a forest with my phone out, I felt as far as I have ever felt from salvation; like all of life's minutiae was nothing more than illness and detritus, empty gestures, worthless hope. What if I never found her, I imagined, already able to imagine countless variations of the desolation just ahead; what would life be, in this hole, where space-time seemed stretched far beyond the point of breaking, no longer even scrolling forward, but just flapping, tearing skin off, empty space? I could already imagine it just like that—the nature of reality, comprised in violence so innate you don't even need to find your loved one's body to realize, with every passing moment, that you can't go back, and that what's ahead is little more than an endless and excruciating blur. I could barely think to lift my feet, but I was moving, through somewhere so far beyond adrenaline it felt like the world had finally actually gone flat, my blood replaced with poison, being dragged. Somewhere above me, though, if something was watching, it would have appeared like I was strolling by now, taking care to admire the minor aspects of the terrain, laying my wide eyes on anywhere the weeds and branches might obscure the truth from being found, a secret place that so far only Molly knew the shape of.

———

Then I saw. There in the wild grass, just off the path obscured by saplings. Her body on her back facing the sky. Eyes closed. Completely motionless. A handgun clenched between her hands against her chest. Hair pulled up in a bun. Her favorite green coat. Her face blank of expression, already paling. A tiny, darkened wound punched in her chin, near to her throat. A single fly already circling the hole, lurking to feed. I knew at once that she was gone. Something else about me in my brain replaced the rest then, taking me over in that instant, clobbered blank. Like the atmosphere had been ripped off and all the air sucked out around us. Like the world was just a set that'd been abandoned long ago, and I was the only one still down here wandering around. I heard me tell the operator that I'd found her, that she wasn't breathing. My voice was steady, somehow, already cleaving onto *facts*. I heard me say that I was not allowed to touch her, right, because this was a crime scene. Because she was without a question dead. My wife was dead. Molly was dead. The operator told me yes. She told me they were having trouble placing my location, but someone would be there soon, so just hang on. I took a step back from Molly's body, standing over it for just a moment before putting my hands over my face, turning away. I didn't need to look any longer to see the way it was, now and forever—her image scraped into my brain, drained of all light. I tried to take a knee and instead fell on all fours, no longer screaming but just wailing, for her, for Mom, for God, but choking on it, out of breath, as meanwhile the white-hot silent sun above us burned, an open all-unseeing eye.

I have no idea how long I laid alone there in the dirt—forever, it would have felt like, but also no time at all, as time meant nothing now that there was nothing left to fear. Nothing left, either, to hide me from the blank above, all one long clear pale blue, the surrounding land flat and sandwiched in around me, as in a hole cut through a map. *This can't be real*, I kept insisting aloud to no one, simultaneously devastated and enraged, moaning for help and for erasure, anything that could intercede. I felt a sudden buzzing near my right eye, then, the hum of wings and then a landing, and a pinch. I slapped back at the place where I'd been stung, on my right eyelid, inadvertently hitting my own face in place of the bee, already moving on now, having delivered its weird joke. I'd never been stung before but as a child, too young to recall but by my mother's story of the memory— how I'd stepped on a dead yellowjacket and lost my mind, more scared than hurt. I think I howled then, almost like laughing, pawing at the expectation of a swelling while looking back at Molly's corpse, as if this was some strange punchline we might share—*something just stung me, what the fuck*—not yet having felt it sunken in yet that she could no longer respond. "A bee sticks the young king's hand for the first time," I'd realize later she'd written in a poem, like she'd known. "Alone on a slope where apples are rotting / under boughs in a sweet acid smell // and he'd like insects to cover him / for the effect it had on the other children. In rain / minnows feel the pond grow."

When the cops arrived, they found me on my stomach, talking to myself. There were two of them, a medic and an officer, and at first they maintained a distance, testing me out, as if I were a criminal or wild animal. Without needing to be asked, I aimed my arm at where

Molly's body was and the officer went to it, the other staying with me, not kneeling down but standing over, asking questions I can't remember to repeat. Something else was speaking for me now, a part of me that didn't need the real me to keep going. I heard myself call out after the officer to verify what I felt certain I had seen: that she was dead, right? Were they sure? Calmly, clearly, he said yes, simple as that, a legal fact. Was she pregnant? the medic asked, nodding just so when I said no. I could tell they could tell I wasn't in my right mind when I asked if they could tell where she got the gun from, and if so, would they be sure to let me know, please? As if there were anything I could do about it now, or that any second someone might come up and tap me on the shoulder, apologize for the confusion, and lead me back to my real life. Instead, other police had begun arriving, masses of them, so it seemed, coming from out of nowhere to take part in the production, right on cue. Someone put up the yellow CRIME SCENE tape around her body. Still, I couldn't bring myself to turn my head toward her one last time, to have to remember her there with all the cops huddled above her with their tools. Each incoming thought like this pressed in upon me, both in a rush and one by one, of a different ilk than I had ever imagined I would need to think before. Everybody else around me was all business, working around my open moaning, bawling, barking with eyes averted, if at once trying to give me space and do their job. I felt so helpless there in my detainment, sitting on my ass in the dirt like some dense mutant, never officially told to stick around but also knowing that I must. *These people are just at work,* I remember thinking, *they must feel so thankful they're not me.* What else was there to say? I knew they knew, as best they could, how there could be no real means of consolation, no reason to try to touch me, offer warmth. We were just here to take part today in what the day had produced all on its own—a kind of programmatic existential framework I imagined Molly finding sick satisfaction in, another brutal lesson from the void.

I wasn't sure who I could call—for years, my go-to would have been Molly or Mom. The absence of both options doubly underlined the absence of any place to call my own, right then and there. It felt insane, pathetic even, to call our therapist, and that's exactly what I did, unable to imagine any other person who'd be the one to force out of my mouth for the first time the awful truth. Against my ear, my phone felt like a wormhole, sucking my air out as it attached me to the world beyond my reach. Maybe if nobody heard the news, it would undo itself, go back to how it'd been just hours earlier. But our therapist picked up—only *my* therapist now, no longer *ours*, I understood, trapped in the midst of the ways words sometimes alter their intentions, right in stride with all the other shifting details of your life—and I heard the words I didn't want to have to say come flooding out: *Hello, it's me, Blake, I'm very sorry, but I didn't know who else to call; Molly shot herself today; Molly is gone.* I don't remember what she said, quite; only the texture of the saying, the sound of the voice there on the line held far away, someone who knew us both and understood what those words meant more than the other people all around me. I could see my body moving and hear the sounds that left my mouth, left with nothing else to do but play the role of my new self. I should call my sister, we concluded, after talking through it, like jumping forward through the hoops of future time arriving, point by point, like any day, though once I'd done that, sharing the news with someone hundreds of miles away, I feared it would become realer somehow, a final terrible seal forced popped. People would know soon, then it'd become old news, gossip, word of mouth. There'd no longer remain any way, then, that I could hold off reality from taking course, filling in around me where I was not.

I wasn't allowed to leave the scene. Instead, I was asked to tell and retell my story of what happened over and over, first to one detective, then another, then another, like infernal Matryoshka dolls with badges and guns. I could feel their eyes searching my eyes, reading me as I told the story as best I could. They asked if I'd had any sense that this could happen, which made me feel embarrassed to say yes, trying to explain in so many feeble words Molly's attitude, her personal history, her cryptic poetry. "I like poetry, too," one detective interrupted with a grin, somewhere between considerate and dense, like we weren't really talking about what we were talking about. They asked for Molly's suicide note, which I'd been clutching this whole time, messy with mud and crumpled up, now considered *evidence.* This letter was my last link to her mind, I felt, therefore to any frame that might be found to explicate her reasoning, and now I had to hand it over, following procedure like some suspect on TV. I begged them to be sure to return to me, to not let it end up missing, aware at the same time in my periphery of the handling of the body of my wife, the hunt for facts, none of which could ever change what had just happened, much less whatever might come next.

———

I was busy reiterating my story for another detective when across the mud I noticed Matt, one of my oldest friends, running toward me. The look on his face, the sound of his voice, the way he hugged me to him: now there was no mistaking what had occurred, no way to keep it separate from the whole rest of my life. I felt my limbs go limp to be embraced, as all of what had kept me upright no longer needed to hold on. At the same time, still in shock, I felt my body holding back there on the cusp, not letting me implode yet, as somehow the world continued on. I could touch my face and feel it there, part of my body, but who was I, and why, and how? Had what just happened actually happened, or was I living in a glitch world, an exact model of how it'd once been with just this one major detail brought to change? Like any second everybody would start laughing, including Molly, who'd get up and come to take me in her arms, without a need for explanation besides to say that she wasn't really gone. Then they'd roll the sky back, too, and show me everything else I hadn't known yet about my life, about existence. Instead, I listened in as Matt spoke up on my behalf, asserting that I should be allowed to leave as soon as possible and go home. Hearing him saying the word *home*, however, already clearly no longer meant the same as it last had, and in a way, that felt more frightening than standing out here in broad daylight at a crime scene, where at least there was a formal process underway. What choice did I have, though, but to keep going, which meant eventually going back to face the music of the future, unless I was ready, willing, and able to die, too? Yes, that made sense. Molly was my wife, my love—shouldn't I go with her, having failed her? Why should I be allowed to survive beyond this day? Already, in thinking back, I felt an undeniable desire that instead of doing the right thing calling the cops, I'd instead taken the gun from Molly's hands, laid down beside her, and somehow in her honor, doubled down. At my most dire, any other option outside of that, now and for some time, would bear the tint of a pitiful formality, tempered only by conditioning, as if all we really are is just the shadow of what we're not.

━━━

I didn't want to get mud all over the inside of Matt's car. I remained formal and polite even in zombie-mode, thankful to have something else to do, I guess, to see that I could still move even though I felt no longer in control of my own body—just following orders from the worm inside my brain that made me go. Back at our address, I trudged up the same set of concrete steps where I'd been standing when I discovered her suicide note taped to the door, a hanging haze there like the fumes after explosion. The front face of the house looked like a facsimile, designed to trick me into believing I existed—a secret shared between me and it alone, as to most anybody else, outside my mind, it was just another piece of property. I imagine that's how haunting works—only those who know, who'd been a part of it, can parse the signal linking the residue of history to how we are, what we're becoming amid our slow transition, step by step. I sat on the stoop with my head in my hands, trying to remember how to think, or not to think. I was focused, mostly, on her letter, getting it back, so I could read it over and over, search for its sense; as if, like Molly, only work could save me now. Matt volunteered to go back down and ask for information, if I'd be okay on my own, and I told him that was fine, that it might even be good for me to have some time alone now, so I could feel the way I felt beyond the reach of other eyes. I was well-accustomed to this aloneness, this want for independence having already accepted as natural law that no one could ever reach me but myself, the bells and whistles of attention that made most others seem to feel better for me more a distraction than a balm. As Matt drove off, I went inside and closed myself inside the bathroom, walking right past my reflection without looking, not wanting yet to have to see, and past the mostly pastel-colored painting Molly made in college and hung up there when we moved in, as if for forever, having planned this ending to our story all this time. I stripped my muddy running clothes off and turned the shower on hot and lay face down on the tile beneath the spray. I can't remember what words I made, only the thin, spent texture of my own voice, mumbling in monotone under my breath as if to anyone who still might hear me from Beyond, the same way that I had often as a child, trying to comfort myself mimicking Mom's lullabies.

▬

When Matt got back, he handed me a brown paper bag containing Molly's letter and her phone, along with the business card of the investigator for the Medical Examiner's Center and a second note by Molly found on her body, scrawled on the backside of a small envelope:

> *VOLUNTARY EXIT.*
> *I am an organ donor.*
> *My husband Blake Butler*
> (my phone number)

I took Molly's letter into my office, closed the glass doors. I knelt on the floor and read it from beginning to end once and then immediately again, trying to find some kernel of her voice there, something alive. These were Molly's final words, I realized, believing in them as some form of access to her brain—despite how out of sync they seemed, like a lost child trying to figure out how to explain her situation to herself while standing front and center in harm's way. Here was what she had left for me to hear. A widening terror within me renewed itself with every breathless word and hard return, underlined by an undeniable form of our failure, hers and mine. If only I had one more chance to hold her, I imagined, to tell her everything she meant to me no matter what. If only I could tear this paper up, as if it alone had been the cause and not the receipt. Any chance to contradict her logic, though, to reach beyond it and remind her she was loved, had been not only lopped off at the hilt, but imminently infected by the violent silence of the world—including the matted, jagged sunlight pouring in now through the windows, getting all over everything we'd ever had, nowhere to turn but toward the absence.

■

Blake,

I have decided to leave this world.

I want you to know first of all that I thought about what this would do to you and I know how painful it is going to be for you, and I'm very sorry. I don't want you to follow me. Please listen to me. Stay alive. I am very sorry for the pain.

But I simply do not want to live. I have no reason to endure this agony. I rooted around in the box of reasons to live for a long time and found there was nothing in there for me. I don't love people. I don't want to be a person. Helping other people stopped making sense to me since I don't think people should exist at all. It seemed to me, in my logic, that removing myself would be the best thing I could do.

I'm sorry to my mom and sister as well. I know it won't be easy for them to accept or understand.

And you, you have been a blessing to me and I thank you for that. You were the only one in the world, it seemed, who could make me happy. You gave me stability and you tried to tell me how you felt about me—I know you loved me. Your notes meant the world to me. Bringing me tea, sharing art with me, remembering our songs, caring for our birds together, and supporting all of my crazy dreams kept me going. The marriage we had was a place like I've never known. Safe and good. I am very grateful to you for the ways you tried to help me, and I will always love you.

I know you will understand why I did this more than anyone else. It might be too much to ask, but I hope your memory of me will not become bitter. I just came to the end of my life, that's all. Everyone's life ends, and mine is over now.

I tried so hard to do so many things, and it was not even the failure of their outcomes that one might imagine led me to such disappointment and heartbreak. It was that the straining itself, the work, couldn't save me. It solved nothing. Every future goal I set for myself passed through me like a ghost. I never even came close to accomplishing anything I wanted in my heart; I simply wasn't good enough. And there is nothing beyond this that I can find—no god in the sky, no love among humans, no revelations, no magic, nothing but a cold and dark universe in every direction. And I tried, I really did, for as long as I could. I even loved the cold universe for a while.

I wanted something I—in the end—couldn't do: to be a teacher, untenable in a cruel system, to help others, but unable to help while being flayed alive. I couldn't stand to be among writers, with their artificial grievances and their fraudulence—betraying what I cared about most, art itself. I failed to find what people call family or friendship, and I don't blame anyone but myself. I was deeply and incurably defective in every way.

Nothing could have stopped this. Your love, no one's love. The way I hate myself is simply so complete that nothing could change it, even as I hoped your love could. I really tried so hard for a while there to fix myself and be a normal person. But, I guess it's obvious now, I was not strong enough. I was not strong at all. I saw nothing, just an emptiness, in my future. I am sorry to have kept all of this planning from you—I wanted to have a normal time with you these last few weeks, just normal, nothing dramatic, and of course I didn't want to alarm you or anyone who might prevent my course of action. It was the most lonely time of my life, keeping my plans from you, and I know you'll be sad about it, and I'm sorry for that as well. I hope you will move away from here, to California or something, and start a press, and stay true to yourself. I do not want you to be alone.

I left my body in the nature area where we used to go walking so I could see the sky and trees and hear the birds one last time. Call the police and don't go down there to see it, please. I shot myself so it would be over instantly with certainty and no suffering whatsoever.

Please make art for me. I will read it all. I will always be with you.

I'm sorry. I love you,

Molly

▬

It feels strange to tell this story as if it's mine. I'm still here, after all, and Molly isn't. Tracing back over the way it went now, over and over, in a spiral, I keep coming back not to how it ended, but to all the other ways it could have gone. How I had sensed something was wrong and gone back in and still not seen. How there were so many points at which the possibility of tragedy appeared and yet remained held back, allayed just long enough to make me think that it could someday be okay. How she could have slipped up or said something at so many different points. How I could have taken so many different paths during my run that day and intersected with her, or otherwise somehow made it to her just in time. I'm not supposed to entertain these questions for too long, I've been compelled to understand; I'm supposed to be able to learn that no matter what I did or didn't do or see or say amidst so many tiny hiccups in the story it does not equate to bearing fault, or that it could have been even worse had I found a way to reach her, there in time only to see her pull the trigger, hear the bang. That even if I'd tried harder to comfort her, console her, most any moment, she would have only pushed me further off, or only delayed the inevitable a small while longer. As if the question of whose fault is the real prison here, and all that matters is what came after, what survives where she could not. As if Molly's death could be dissected and explained away through tragic math, in hopes of sparing any further bitter aftertaste for all of those of us who have survived her, much less those still here still suffering similarly, adrift without a rope for any reason to imagine what might change.

But trauma remains strange, rude in the face of such neat logic. Even as you learn to acclimate, as best you can, to what you've lived through, the floor of memory you've come to carry keeps on shifting, changing texture and direction, beyond anything like real control. You keep finding yourself standing next to some other version of who you were, trying both to listen and adjust to what you know, held in sync with how you feel. Knowing more always makes you know less again as the unseen circles of our deep being spin and blur, wearing out the rigging that holds it in there, at every point about to bust, so often void of any certain guide to show you how to change its course or make it stop. You either must learn to live within it, the mystery and the misery commingled, to carry on in spite of terror and of death, or you don't—and either way, with or without you, the formal story of time and human history carries on, both there and not there in every moment as it passes, like a ghost designed to haunt itself.

"Human misery would be intolerable if it were not diluted in time," wrote Simone Weil. "We have to prevent it from being diluted *in order that it should* be intolerable."[1]

———

I'm writing this, therefore, with what seems little choice: to shut my mouth and turn away, as might a stranger, or to force myself to look again, and then again, and then again. Stranded on its own inside my head, the fact of losing Molly, finding out who Molly really was after the fact, alongside trying to decipher any good reason I should carry on myself—at its best is but a blurry sleeve of rips and stutters, and at its worst it is the very maw of hell itself, hungry to bend me over and tear me open from inside out. Though there are times I identify completely with Molly's tragic logic—how hard it is to feel abandoned and alone; how so much of the mediated world reflects little more than further terror; how thin it feels at times to hold out hope—I find myself still hanging on here, in her absence, still furiously angry, suffused with what often feels like an otherworldly, almost ambient form of rage, but in another way awakened, forced to face myself there at the brink, in want of unutterable answers made only more elusive after having had to pay the highest cost. If I'm still here, as it would seem, I still must want to be, no matter how much the pain holds me in thrall, forever asking why. As I've tried to learn to navigate the lack of answers, the instant dissolution of everything I thought I knew, I can't stop hearing Molly's real voice trapped underneath that, somehow pushing back at once again being mistaken, reduced to decimals. "The facts" surrounding who she was, lined up on paper, to use her own words: "are easy to say; I say them all the time. They leave me out."[2]

1   Weil, Simone. *Gravity and Grace*. Translated by Arthur Wills, Bison Books, 1997, p. 60.
2   Brodak, Molly. *Bandit: A Daughter's Memoir*. Grove Atlantic, 2016, p. 5.

- Born in Rochester, Michigan on March 29, 1980.
- Parents divorced twice; father kept a secret family and
     went to prison twice for robbing banks.
- Received a BA in English from Oakland University.
- Received an MFA in Poetry from Virginia University.
- Married her first husband, Matthew Porter, May 17, 2008.
Later divorced.
- Won the 2010 Iowa Poetry Prize for her grad thesis, *A Little
Middle of the Night*.
- Taught comp and creative writing at colleges and
     universities in West Virginia and Georgia for more than
     a decade.
- Published poetry, essays, and interviews in hundreds
     of journals and magazines, including three chapbooks:
     Instructions for a Painting (2010), *The Flood* (2012), and
     Essay on Parts of Day (2013).
- Published *Bandit: A Daughter's Memoir* with Grove/Atlantic
     (2016).
- Married me May 11, 2017.
- Won a NEA grant for *Bandit*, which she used to write a
     second memoir, *Alone in Poland*, unpublished, tracing
     her family's origins through the Holocaust.
- Founded her own baking business, Kookie House Cakes
     and Treats.
- Won the Pleiades Press Editors Prize for Poetry for *The
     Cipher*, published posthumously.
- Took her own life in Atlanta, Georgia on March 8, 2020.

How can that last fact—*took her own life*—not automatically
restructure all the rest? What other details exist, hidden in fault
lines, that would possess a person most saw as wise, productive,
and accomplished to want to die? Her story, which for the most

part she kept locked so tight no one could ever really come to know it, has become, in death, inherently uncertain, out of reach. Vital information, it seems, remains missing from the picture, if also hidden within it, crushed among it. "This isn't about them," Molly insisted in her memoir about even the parts we think we do know. "This is about whatever is cut from the frame of narrative. The fat remnants, broke bones, gristle, untender bits." And cut from those? The parts that have no true name, that don't appear to fit where they appear; the parts left to be defined nowhere but in the absence of the subject, having failed to withstand them by herself, all of it suffused among the stunning silence that fills in over what can't be written, much less explained. Instead, it's my story *with* Molly that's mine to tell, I've come to think, even while beset on all sides with grief, as daily life as her survivor often feels: larger on the inside than on the surface, full of holes that lead to caverns, full both of darkness and of air; words that trace, if only as a shadow, how though we found a way, for a while at least, to bind together, to do the work of living side by side—the work of love; steadfast in the absence of certain meaning, any right name. My greatest struggle in peering headlong into the hole the void has torn in both our lives is less a product of my inability to narrate it, pull it open, than it is to step back and see the horror as from afar; to find nothing more than anguish, trauma, horror in a place I lived so long beside her in a sacred way, my only home. It would begin to feel like lucid dreaming more than living at times, in looking back on my old memories and finding them rewritten from within, made even more difficult to put in order or narrate meaning into without her here, not seeking answers as much as asking questions and trying better to interpret the texture of the silence left between. Want as I might to *understand*, or to find *justice*, the real project here is one of a certain kind of active faith—at once impossible, nearly intolerable, and at the same time, all I have. It is this faith, maybe, that I still understand about myself the least of all, more so than pain, or loss, or death; it fills the space where I've sought God, or something like God, despite His silence, providing shape, if not a guardrail, in the dark, where the only way I might ever come to know it more is less to act than to listen back; to seek a light shed on the secret, sacred parts of life we might too often prefer instead to cover over and let go. If anything could be said for certain about Molly, after all, no matter how much she might have tried to scorn herself about it, prove it futile, to me her spirit lives within her reverence for the search, and for the yearning after something more than merely human, the vast unknown behind our eyes. In that I refuse to pass this suffering on, let it consume me, so must I also, in the same breath, refuse to swallow it in silence or push it back, no matter how much some vicious part of me might wish I would, or how futile it might seem at our wits' end. Every end is a beginning, so they say, and every beginning another path. This is about that.

———

The first time I met Molly, I picked her up from jail. We hardly knew each other—I'd read her writing. From in the dark, she got into my car and closed the door. She had a funny story about the misunderstanding that had brought us here. We agreed to head on to the bar. At the bar, the main thing I remember is how she showed me the results of her recent MRI, which she was worried suggested the possibility that her brain tumor had returned. She slid the printout across the table like it was a panorama. She seemed so strong, and at the same time, so afraid. She told me that she loved me the next morning.

———

Love, a desire for love, always seemed to be on Molly's mind. After times together, she'd often leave me notes or poems, written in her exacting handwriting that I could feel like Braille inside my brain. Early on, as virtual strangers, I remember standing in a parking lot unspooling an accordion-shaped spiral covered with language, every syllable exact, as if cut from stained glass she'd carried with her all this way. She'd stood quietly beside me watching as I read it, hands at her sides, her deep-set eyes unlike anybody else's, hazel-flecked around the iris before darkening to pewter blue. Her Polish cheeks softened that intensity somehow, rosy and cherubic as if baiting her to smile, framed by her immaculately straight, nearly waist-length hair—bister brown when we first met, and later bleached blonde by her own hand since she didn't trust somebody else to get it right. "I couldn't walk anywhere with anyone / before you," her poem explained. "No, I could walk to some places with some people, like to the edge of a waving black sheet where I thought there'd be a grand hole. / I'd open my eyes and the hole never came. Just a cheer-up greeting card and a trove / of used moves / men faithfully learned. I wanted a hole. / I thought, / hole soon. // That was how it was before you knew me." Who *is* this person? I sometimes wondered, a bit taken aback by her intensity while also touched that she believed in me enough to let me see.

———

Molly was troubled—that was clear. She seemed to teeter at the edge of her emotions, unable to take lightly what darkness others often overlooked, and so I never quite knew what kind of mood she'd be in when we met up. Often she'd come over with a Tupperware full of treats she'd designed from scratch—root beer float cookies, pineapple cookies with orange glacé, banana fudge blondies, apricot custard hand pies, blood orange Oreos dipped in vanilla bean white choc. She'd insist I give her brutal feedback and didn't like it if I said, "They're all amazing, Molly," though they were easily the most unique sweets I'd ever had. Her recipes—the hundreds of them, handwritten in a brown notebook she'd been working with for half her life—were never done and could always be improved or given up on. An incorrigible perfectionist, she'd gladly admit, as if this were the only way someone should be. In her presence, I felt encouraged—no, *required*—to be frank in ways that others would have avoided at all costs. Underneath that outward confidence, however, I got the sense there was something pressing at the seam, starved for connection to the point I felt uncertain where to begin, what I could do to calm the tide. Throughout our early days, she kept me up to date with stressful stories of being stalked by a student who had been following her home, throwing rocks at her house, looking in through windows. On social media, she posted pictures of herself in an abandoned building, staring off into the distance, or sometimes head-on into the camera, like from the center of a bull's eye. Her seemingly ceaseless sense of circling doom, no matter how much I conceptually sympathized, made me wish for something I could say to let her loosen, take a real breath. When I held her, it felt like she might either meld into my body any second or turn to smoke and rise away. The more I held her, the more I wanted her to stay.

At the same time, in ways I hadn't learned to discern yet, I was also deeply wounded, full of rage. I spent most of my daylight hours at my parents' house, half an hour north of my apartment, the same place where I'd grown up, trying to get work done while helping my mom caretake for my father during the middle stage of his Alzheimer's. Dad was continuously restless too, due to the new restrictions on his freedom amidst the ambient confusion of everything around him gradually losing its familiarity. He'd spend all day pacing from one end of the house to the other, stopping only to try to pull the knob off the front door he could no longer remember how to unlock. He'd stand looking out our glass backdoor and punch his hand into his palm over and over, straining so hard his face appeared about to pop, aggressive if I tried to intercede, unable to remember who I was. Sometimes after I'd leave he'd end up falling, and I'd get a call from her asking me to come back and help her lift him. Mom was already overloaded from round the clock caregiving, so any spare second I had to share the load was at least some amount of freedom she could have amid losing her husband to the plaque claiming his mind. She refused, however, to put him in a home, especially after our terrible experience with dickhead doctors who'd drugged him up so heavily he couldn't do much of anything but drool. "You're going to have to face it, your husband is a vegetable now," the director of one of the most well-regarded facilities in Atlanta told my mom from behind his desk, eyes on his computer, looking up only to take the chewing gum out of his mouth and toss it in the trash—a scene I'd only narrowly avoided ending by jumping over the counter and assaulting him. My mom had always been my idol, my inspiration, and I felt indebted to her and Dad both, loyal to the point of putting blinders on to be there for them in their time of need, as they'd always done for me. *How had life gotten so far off track?* I often wondered when I took the time to try to think, otherwise manifesting as self-loathing, hitting myself, talking shit aloud to my reflection, irregularly seething pissed without exactly realizing why. No one had ever really loved me, I began to tell myself over and over, besides my mother, who day in and day out I watched give every ounce of strength she had to her husband, sacrificing her own mental health so he could live at home through his last years. It felt impossible to share, and impossible to want to; talking about it only made it bigger, I imagined, consuming time I could be spending on getting work done or having fun. When Mom died, I'd kill myself, became my plan—or so I began regularly repeating, as if to see how it felt to sound it out. In the meantime, I'd spend all my energy on writing. Fiction, at least, was a place where I could face myself, seek somewhere higher beyond the maddening tedium of the real, though even that, outside the work itself, often only led to further disillusion, still there in the background when I felt satisfied or proud. I decided that my next book should be my last, one so fucked up no one would ever want to read it, in some way intentionally sabotaging my fledgling semblance of a career before it started, both to spite myself and prove I could. This turned into *300,000,000*, a cryptic novel about a psychic viral illness that made every person in America want to kill and consume the flesh of every other person in America until there was no one left but one. "The only way for me to complete this book is to kill myself," the last sentence of the original draft had stated until years later when, inspired by Molly, I'd rewrite the whole last section of the book, finally able to imagine something more.

———

Besides my work, though, so as I saw it, I had little else to do or be. After posting up most of the day at Mom and Dad's, I'd come back home and start to drink—either on my own at home, or out at bars with friends or random dates, frequently blacking out by the night's end, which I thought was cool and normal, just having fun. I was too strong, I told myself, despite my aimless fury; too self-assured, with zero trouble I couldn't handle on my own. Either way, I felt no one really understood me, a fact I reinforced by the trajectory of my last two long-term relationships, spanning my 20s, each ending with my getting dumped. Sam had gotten sick of a still straight-edge version of me hounding her about her drinking even occasionally, fueled by my burgeoning anti-social tendencies that had yet to turn into substance abuse of my own. After she moved away to go to school and party, I'd hung around waiting for her to change her mind, which of course would never happen until I'd already picked up and moved on, cementing once and for all that no one really cared until too late. Not long after that I started drinking, deciding on a whim while away at grad school—in the presence of strangers who wouldn't judge me for the change—that I didn't need the brain cells

I'd spared through abstinence; that I rather enjoyed blacking out. Heather I'd driven nuts in a similar way, smothering her over any aspect of her admittedly evasive social behavior I didn't like, such as keeping male friends I was certain were only trying to fuck her, staying out all night without me while not responding to my texts, or smoking weed, which since embracing booze had claimed the irate throne of my new number one pet peeve. Back-to-back, then, my overarching will for too much control had outlasted my welcome, turning what had once seemed like intense loyalty into something scorned. Before all that, I'd been a fat kid, peaking at 270 lbs. in 9th grade, establishing a feeling of innate unwantedness that had continued to stay with me after losing a third of my weight in a single summer through hardcore anorexia—300 calories a day. Now, I was determined, therefore—having just turned thirty, rebelliously single with no lack of suitors—to remain unreachable beyond surface-level fun. As I'd taught myself to see it now, every person was just another chance at disappointment, arriving just in time to only let me down or tear me up. Couldn't I just be promiscuous for once and sleep around, not give a damn, the way so many other people did? Why should I always have to fall right back into monogamy, being "good"? What might I really desire, I wondered, if I stopped caring?

———

"Let no one in" had been my M.O. for half a year at least by the time I ran into Molly's Facebook profile in my feed, uncertain how or when we'd been tagged *friends*. Everything about her caught my eye—in particular, I'd tell her later, there was this one photo of her in a *Moby Dick* t-shirt while preparing a tray of candied bacon that made my imagination tick, not only because she was gorgeous, but a writer with rare style living in Georgia, just hours south. Her wall was full of funny quips and art she liked, links to publications of her poetry, which I found shrewd and dark and studied, just my type. Before, I'd thought I'd never want to date a writer, thinking that would mean they'd have to be at least as annoying as I could be about my process, hoarding time; now, in feeling scorched earth, I felt intrigued by the idea of someone understanding without a need for explanation why I was so often "lost in my head," "not fully here," as I'd been regularly described by both my exes, each admitting they felt excluded both by the wild abandon of my writing and the continually growing world of literary friendships I'd latched onto through the internet, people from all over who they didn't know anything about. Something about Molly cut through that superstition, intuitively akin right from the jump. I DM'd her to introduce myself and ask what she was up to in Augusta. "If you're ever in Atlanta," I suggested, "give a shout." By the next morning, she'd responded, mentioning that she'd been in the same room with me weeks before, at a reading I'd co-hosted, but she'd been too shy to approach. I remembered her presence that night, too, if just as fragment: how she'd slipped out without a gesture in the middle of someone reading, there by herself, hurrying off into the night. Coincidentally, she already had plans to come into Atlanta next weekend, "if my crazy roommate doesn't steal my car," and so we traded numbers, made plans to meet at a bar near my apartment, somewhere I knew my local friends would never be. That night, an hour into waiting without reply, I decided I'd been stood up and went back home, already halfway out the door again on the way to a birthday party when my phone rang, and for the first time I heard Molly's voice inside my head, strangely jolly about calling from the front seat of a cop car to ask if I could please come pick her up.

———

That first night, as it grew late, Molly acknowledged she had nowhere to go without a car. Her roommate's vehicle, which she'd been forced to borrow when he indeed did run off with hers, had been impounded for expired tags, right outside the parking lot where we'd been planning to connect. The roommate was going to have to come out in the morning to get the car out, she explained, and in the meantime, here she was, knowing mostly no one in the city except me. I didn't want to be too forward in suggesting she could stay at my place, really, as the context of our talk so far was mostly friendly, but I said that I'd be glad to take the couch, no problem, and she agreed. Even once we got back to my place, we were acting semi-formal, barely flirting beyond the clear lure that I felt and the unexpected situation. Molly seemed to like it, though, sidling beside me on the bizarre black leather furniture I'd acquired secondhand, my ex-roommate's excess hair stuffed into the cracks between the cushions. Later, Molly'd describe feeling relieved when I put my hand on her thigh during a laugh—finally, a signal of direct interest, and not long after, straight to bed. During sex, something felt off when she continuously screamed so loud it hurt my ears, shrill to the point I'd get a noise warning from my apartments' HOA any time that she stayed over. The screaming seemed out of sync to me somehow, exaggerated from what was really going on, as if the sex were a performance. If I asked her to bite a pillow or something, she'd just scream louder, laughing maniacally, perhaps inspired even more by being heard, or more so: getting us in trouble. "I've been telling myself to be careful to not fog that night with too many words before it starts to seem fake," she would email me later, after returning to Augusta, "so I've been just thinking in pictures and sensations. Like the way your apartment smelled when you opened the door, the way you drive, cop cars, your arms, your mouth. The shock of an actual experience makes me want to be quiet about it mostly and block the preciousness of remembering." By the end of our first year, the screaming would disappear, back towards silence, and eventually she'd claim to not remember it at all. "That must be your other girlfriend," she'd quip, cutting her eyes, a line that would become a regular refrain when any detail in our memories failed to align, as if one of us must be lying.

———

Molly hated long goodbyes. She preferred instead to turn away and not look back, not even waving, a habit she later noted as also true about her father. Each time she left my place, I'd wait and watch to see if this time she would break her rule, as an exception—she never did. She seemed even more annoyed when I'd call out after, as if I shouldn't have let her walk off in the first place, even if it was her who'd said she had to go. I read this coldness as a facet of her fortitude, some hard-earned independent edge that spared no small talk, which made me like her even more, though sometimes it left me wondering what she was really after, how I fit in. Our lifestyles were mostly very different, after all: I liked to stay out late and drink too much and act a fool, while she liked staying in, talking about philosophy and art, going to bed by 10 p.m. In her journals during this time—several dozens of them, spanning most of her adult life, which I wouldn't read until after she was gone—she describes me as someone she can't explain her attraction for, given how different I was from other guys she'd dated. Despite how normally she would have given up on me, she told herself, something else just underneath the way I was kept her close, hanging on tight, as if my better form was somewhere buried deep inside me, suspended behind some bruisy wall much like her own. Whatever her actual motivation, I could tell she wanted more of my attention, not just the fun parts, and though she'd play along with social graces for a while, it was very clear when there were others in the room besides us two she often wasn't fully there, but instead holding something in, anticipating exit.

———

Molly had little trouble, on the surface, sharing the central force of her heart's haunting, her clearest damage. She'd speak up quick, when asked, to share the story of her father and his crimes—how he'd robbed eleven banks one summer when Molly was 14, gotten arrested, pleaded innocent, gone to prison, served seven years, then after another seven years of freedom, robbed banks again, went back to prison. In the meantime, too, he'd kept a second family, a wife and kids, who remained secret until Molly's mother, Nora, went to the doctor, pregnant with Molly's older sister, Becca, only to be told she wasn't really Mrs. Brodak by the law. It'd been twenty years since then, and yet the emotions of the story followed close, hardened in her mind to something simple to explain but never share. She appeared surprised when I showed deeper interest, asking questions that didn't already so neatly fit. Over dinner, she'd recount strings of tragic memories, clearly moored there in obstruction of her otherwise quite steadfast cool: such as the vacation she'd taken solo with her father to a Cancun resort, during which he'd left her, as a preteen, alone at their hotel with $20 to feed herself while he went off all day and did things she wasn't allowed to know; she'd wandered on the beaches by herself that week, feeling stared at by kids in happy families, seeking out adventures of her own. The one time she'd name as evidence he'd ever loved her came from a day he'd left her and Becca alone at his apartments' public pool only to return and find them playing in the water with an older man—who Molly felt sure had earlier been watching them from his window and masturbating, she remembered—and chased him off in a barrage of violent threats, his defensive hysteria in her mind at least a sign he really cared. No big deal, she insisted when I said how sorry I felt, how much it hurt to imagine her being stranded like that as a child. She didn't seem to want my condolences, though I couldn't tell if it was because she didn't believe I actually felt anything or if she was so used to keeping tight she'd convinced herself she didn't either. "Friends I grew close to would learn the two heavy things: dad bank robber, such an interesting story; brain tumor, interesting story, how sad," she writes in *Bandit*. "I had a script for them now and I knew about how long it took to have these conversations…details managed thoughtfully, calm flat tone meant to deflect pity, the smiles, co-amazement, and bright gratitude to prove I did not pity myself."[3] She'd already long accepted, so she claimed, that this was simply how the world works, how people are, even if I felt I could read tight in her face the compensating strain, how much it wore on her whether she acknowledged it or not. There were obvious limits to her willingness to think it through, too, as if I asked too much, maybe the wrong thing, she'd pull away, say she didn't remember or had already said enough. High walls within her would shoot up suddenly from within the unspoken limits of the story turned opaque. I began encouraging her, instead, to write it

3   *Bandit*, p. 191.

down, perhaps a book; her story was fascinating, full of pain and power both, I hoped she knew, most of all for how she'd made it through. She laughed me off at first, insisting no one would ever care to hear about it but as a curiosity at best; and yet I could also read the way the idea lighted a fire underneath her, changed the grain of light behind her eyes. Three months later—motivated solely by wanting to impress me, she'd later claim—she'd have already finished a first full draft of what eventually became *Bandit*, seemingly embarrassed to find that once she'd started tracing out her story, she couldn't stop.

———

Molly began coming into Atlanta more regularly. Sometimes we'd make a date and she'd stay with me overnight, while other times she'd just hit me up out of the blue. I could tell she wanted to get together as often as we could, while I was more reserved, reluctant to let anybody get too close. Any resistance on my end—already busy with friends or work—would often only make her more aggressive, her messages shifting from courteous and curious to out of sorts. She'd text me late at night in broken language, asking me to drop what I was doing and come meet up. *If you're busy, just pull up and I'll come out to your car and fuck you and you can leave, no talking*, she'd suggest. Despite the allure, deep in my gut I often found her persistence in these moments more unnerving than enticing; they didn't seem to line up with who she was in person, half-unhinged and glad to deprecate herself for my unasked benefit. I didn't want to have to see her being willing to go to such extremes for my attention even if some darker part of me felt drawn toward the chaos of it, not knowing what would come next— so I'd comply, especially when already out of sorts myself, and we'd meet up at my place for the night. Molly when drunk, though rather rare, was more like me; rowdy and impulsive, in a fun way, if also one she seemed after the fact to prefer not to have become. I knew—or felt I knew—she preferred her studiousness, or at least serious talks about our feelings and ideas, which sometimes I felt game for and other times I just wanted to avoid at any cost. Most mornings after, still hungover, I'd find her already up early, sitting and waiting patiently for me to join her, irritated that I would sleep so late, as if it meant I didn't care. She seemed to loathe certain attributes about me in this way, so openly at times it made me wonder what she liked about me in the first place. She'd get super pissed when I'd say I didn't believe we landed on the moon, for instance, no matter how obviously I was only kidding. Conspiracy theories are for idiots who think they're smarter than everybody, she'd insist, glaring at me as if I were scum like all the rest and any second she might leave. It wasn't funny, she insisted, and all it did was grind her gears, as if the mere appearance of ignorance or negligence overrode all other faith. She refused to bend much to my attempts at levity or solace—I might be lying, covering my tracks—tending instead to what seemed an inordinate distrust, so splintered in her I couldn't help but wonder if she understood it as well as she seemed. Sometimes, after a night out, she'd ask one by one who I had slept with among the people we had seen, including my friends' wives, clucking her tongue when I scoffed it off. She didn't seem to like my friends, or at least didn't want to have to put on a good face and play along, as if there were somewhere else that we should be. She'd hint she'd like to have me back at her place in Augusta, though she never actually invited me to come, and if I could tell she wanted more from me, she didn't seem to know where to begin either. Our early months stayed scattershot like this, all stops and starts, somehow at once familiar and bizarre. I'd always been attracted to introverted, dour women, whose love could only be hard won, but paired with Molly's unpredictable intensity I wasn't sure quite how to act. Something's off, I kept telling myself, assuming it must be me, as if I could only ever get my head on straight and do the right thing, all the rest would fall in place.

After a while like this, putting more and more time between responses when she'd text, I decided to tell Molly directly I wasn't ready to be involved. I explained that I had no interest in another long, intense relationship, and I wondered if we weren't doing more harm than good by spending time together when it was clear she wanted and deserved more than I could give. I told her that I felt I wasn't really here, that I felt somehow missing from my body among people, and that when that first night she'd asked if I wanted to be alone in life and I said I didn't, I'd been lying. I hoped one day it might be different, but in the meantime, I didn't want to make her hate me by pretending, playing along. Molly said she appreciated my straightforwardness and that it made sense, given our homes' distance and how busy we both were. Being let down was no surprise, she also hinted, slighting herself as explanation for my reluctance, as though smiling through clenched teeth. "Even if you want to be dead inside," she wrote, "I would still kiss your dead eyes and it would be fine, I don't require pleasantness, I am not full of expectations like girls are… Just say a few words to me once in a while and I am completely fine. It doesn't matter what." She agreed it would be better to be friends for a while, at least; that she would take what she could get. In weeks ahead, she'd write long emails about her workday, how she filled the hours, what she loved—inviting me in, taking it slow. My own emails, in reply, seem paltry, dashed off, often too busy to write back, and this effect became reflected in her letters, trying to play cool while also still unable to stop pushing back, sometimes to the point of figurative violence. "I keep thinking of an image of a knife in a neck," she wrote one morning. "But I could never do that! I am so ready to do that. I have never told anyone that he could think of me as being in his pocket, but I feel like saying this to you…I think the feeling I am most comfortable in is longing. It's a bad word for it.

I think I secretly never want to get what I want." Closing the email, she writes, "I was in a carcrash the other day and have new bruises and a blackeye, it looks bad," including a photo of her posing in a slip, holding her hair over her head so I could see the massive purple swell around her eye. I felt her pain—could see clearly she was hurting, had been for some time—but I wasn't certain what to do; how to help or be a friend even without also tangling myself into the fire, when what I wanted more than anything was peace.

———

We began talking less and less. Eventually, we ceased almost completely, back to half-strangers, though we would sometimes still check in or run into one another at events. This phase feels blurry in my memory, like underwater, with only sudden flashes of congruence that hold up. At a bookfair in DC, for instance, I noticed her walking by herself from booth to booth, head down. I remember watching her move for a moment, in her own world of sorts, framed with a grace that made her stand out from the noisy conference ballroom like a deer. She seemed surprised to see me when I approached, sweet despite how disheveled I must have looked, having blacked out wasted and not slept at all the night before, far from my mind. I felt her looking up into me, grinning, warm and friendly, as if all we'd been through together thus far was just a dream. She offered me her room key if I needed somewhere to crash—which honestly still felt forward in a reaching way, like she would take whatever I might give—so I deferred, relieved at least that she didn't hate me. Instead, we walked around the conference ballroom, browsing the books and making jokes, more like old friends than messy lovers. In my memory of that day, I feel so much for her—her timid poise; her stunning laugh; how far away she seemed to loom inside herself there at my side, reconciled to some other version of her life than what was really yet to come.

I was out of town a few months on a reading tour when Molly emailed me—using the same thread I'd begun with my *we shouldn't see each other* letter—to let me know she was moving to Atlanta. She'd won a fellowship in poetry at Emory University and so would now be permanently in town, a prospect she seemed uncertain of, but also hopeful. "I am so happy in Augusta," she wrote, "but the future is crap here." I wasn't sure at first what I should think: partially aversion, in that I felt there'd be a pressure to link up, when very clearly that hadn't gone so well so far; and partially a deeper draw, given how receiving the very space that I had asked for in between us hadn't led to any deeper satisfaction elsewhere. If anything, I felt even more adrift than I already had been, underlined now with the deeper longing of wanting someone to be close to, understood by, which out of everyone I'd seen, Molly remained a beacon, surely unlike anybody else I'd ever known. My stupid wild streak had been fun, in theory, but failed to fill the void for very long, try as I might to convince myself that I could be something I was not, a stupid wild streak with no lasting effects. Molly continued to play it cool, too, knowing better than to push me, but also very clearly still involved, keeping up with me in bits and lurches, and soon living right there across town. Try as I might to remain evasive, as if already to see where I was headed from out of body, I knew already that our story hadn't yet reached its final end—that I couldn't help it, what I felt, and wouldn't want to.

The next time I saw Molly was at a poetry reading. My eyes moved straight to her the second I came alone into the room. She'd bleached her hair platinum blonde, was wearing a white dress that made the light surrounding her seem magnetic and alive. I remember moving past where she was sitting, feeling her presence but not quite looking yet, uncertain how she'd react after all that'd happened, and uncertain too what I should do next. Hours later, I found myself standing sidled up beside her at the back bar at Manuel's, singled off from the rest of the group. She felt familiar still, sweet in a way that unbound time had made more real, like there was a reason we were here again together—still at the virtual beginning of our lives. It didn't take long before she asked if I wanted to dip out, go back to my place, and we French exited. During the drive home, each in our own cars, I remember looking up at her in the rearview at a stoplight, studying her face, traced with the blank neutral expression she wore by default most of the time: lips clamped, unflinching glare aimed straight ahead, her mind on somewhere else. When I try to think about that image now, the glare of passing street lamps marring the windshield rushes in, obscuring any full semblance of a memory for very long, flung to the night.

■■■■

That summer, Molly rented an apartment in a semi-sketchy building next door to a sports bar in Midtown where they'd fill the nightly air with bad bar music and trivia q/a shared at high volume by PA. We joked about buying a megaphone and shouting the answers, playing black metal right back at them, prodded more by my discomfort with the noise than hers. Molly rarely seemed to mind the more unpleasant aspects of a space, easily able to ignore the little irritants, like how the enclosed common hallway leading to her door often smelled like a mix of sweat and mold, and sometimes sausage when her next-door neighbor would cook wieners out in the hall on game days so he "wouldn't have to smell it in his room." He'd slip heavily misspelled notes under her door apologizing for the odors, and he'd scream at her through the walls when the grinding noise caused by opening her silverware drawer disturbed his peace. Several times when coming over I saw him shitting with the door open, talking to himself and reading a newspaper, like some living, breathing Francis Bacon painting—the perfect nightmare of a neighbor, right there at the hard edge of her home. She seemed stuck there, somehow, and yet totally okay with it—no kind of prude, much less someone who took pleasure in complaining.

———

We started hanging out a couple times a week—mostly at her place, which felt much different than when we'd lived hours apart. I got to see her as she was, more in her element, how her days went. So much of what she owned seemed like relics recovered from some distant time: strange pairs of scissors; a bright-blue throw shaped like a face that you unzipped along its mouth; a knee-high metal owl with strange orange eyes; a closet full of vintage dresses, secondhand; archaic postcards tacked to the wall alongside clipped out cryptic quotes or science facts; bookshelves filled with mostly poetry, art books, and nonfiction, with occasional pages folded down at one corner to signify she'd found something there to admire, which made me want to slow down and see it, too. She had iconic taste, I felt, as stern with what she consumed as she was with people; in that way, she seemed to have lived twice her age at least, steely and refined where others, like me, were often frivolous, ridiculous. Nothing mattered more to her than good, hard work, much like my father, a principle leavened in her by a shadowy but magnetic sense of humor, able to shift back and forth between the serious and the absurd on a dime. She felt like kin to me in that way, of deep ambition, with high ideals delayed most of all by how much we could get in our own way. She made me want to be a better person immediately, to grow up fast and buckle down. I could tell she understood, at least to the extent that I would let her, the passion displaced in me by unseen pain; the alienation of having to pretend everything's fine when inside you feel beyond reach; the fury of watching the sad, weird world go on rewarding total bastards, worshipping bullshit. We talked a lot about our youthful conceits of literary meritocracy, and how that had turned to reserved bitterness over time; how far off we often felt from others, especially writers, though Molly took it twice to heart, unable as I was to don a mask in front of others and play along. I felt most like myself, at least, when I was around her, like I could breathe more freely, loosen my tongue, and I could tell she really meant it when she listened, in a way that made me want to learn to be more precise with what I thought. I loved her zero-bullshit sense of humor, the way she'd wisecrack where others stayed soft, laced with a torrid sense of independence, unafraid to go off on her own. Within that rubric, she carried high expectations of others and had no problem pointing out mistakes, levelling against any and everybody the same exacting eye for detail she expected of herself. I loved how thoroughly prepared she was, how I could count on her to show up when she said she would, which also made me that much more aware of my own drawbacks when I failed to meet her aim. Her presence carried authority in that manner, a mark of well-considered process, a certain taste that spanned throughout most everything she touched. It quickly became easy to see why many people found her intimidating, hard to know, despite the riches underneath. It shocked me how direct she'd be, moving past decorum to set the record straight or share the uncanny details of her day, like the odd expression of a person in a painting that she'd noticed, or the funny way the huge blow-up mascot at the car dealership had seemed to wave as she drove past; places where the world slipped out of line a bit, became unreal. *Cut out of time* is one way to maybe frame the way she felt to be around; of her own fabric, no one else. Like there were hardened scars in her that could not be diminished no matter how long passed or who grew close; quite the opposite, in fact, as her resistance to being hurt again compelled her to evade actual intimacy, instinctually certain nothing real and good could ever last. Occasionally, she made overtures toward our future—commenting over a steak dinner she'd prepared that she had many wifely skills—but also maintaining patience, avoiding pressure by playing her cards carefully, inviting trust. On our walks, I felt blessed to hear her recite from memory random facts about the local animals and fauna, just as her mother had done with her. I could point at almost anything, and she would know. She adored conifers the most and loved to stop and talk to them and touch them, same as she would for any cat, or if she could have reached them, any bird. Despite how heavy-handed she could be about her judgment, "just realistic," her passion drove her and imbued her darkest aspects with what to me embodied zest—for the mystery of the universe as much as for the simple pleasures, the things most people trampled over or left to rust. Some future spring, under the window in the house we'd spend our last five years in living together, she'd collect bits of moss each time we went out and built a bank of it where she would sit in bed and write. She could lay for hours like that, typing surrounded by books and snacks and pillows with the lights off. I never understood how she could write that way until after she was gone and I no longer had the will to sit up straight.

———

The more I opened myself to Molly, too, the more I found to love. In stark contrast to her dismay, her heart was undeniably full of dreams. She got up early every morning, ready to return directly to her most recent incarnation of the grind, with lists upon lists of things she planned to do next. Her daily calendar was organized down to the hour, often packed so full I'd feel the need to remind her to save some room for rest. Despite her outward wrath toward most people, she still kept heroes, idolized mostly for their singularity against the odds: the wit and depth of Herman Melville, her favorite writer, whom she'd lament for how misunderstood he'd been throughout his life; the rhapsodic detail of Paolo Uccello's paintings, which she described feeling unable to breathe in front of when she got to see one in person and up close; the cryptic acumen of Anne Carson, whom she idolized both for her bravery and brilliance, and whose *Float* she loved to teach to undergrads to show them the endless possibilities of form; the funny fractious gaze of Jean-Luc Godard, especially *Week-End*, the jubilant insanity of which put stars in her eyes; the mathematical meticulousness of Agnes Martin, whose lines reminded me of the peculiar, layered drawings Molly had filled her sketchbooks with in college, thinking someday she'd become an illustrator; the no-fucks-given of Lou Barlow, who she insisted as with a chip on her shoulder was the real genius, not J. Mascis; the artisan work ethic of Steve Albini, spurred by a six month period where Shellac became the only band she'd listen to, on endless loop, mournful for artists who recognized the value of good hard work; the magical logic of Wittgenstein, which when I asked her to get me a copy of a book of philosophy she loved for what would end up being our last Christmas, she chose *Philosophical Investigations*; the style of Sofia Coppola, particularly *Marie Antoinette*, which she would watch on mute, just for the colors and the costumes, though I think really she loved it all and didn't want to have to say, the way she'd sometimes get about the things she liked that she imagined other people thought were lame; the loner brooding of Cat Power, whose apparent madness she romanticized, solemnly relating a story of how Marshall once had played an entire show with her back to the audience; the highbrow lowbrow of Dada, and the exacting nuance of Dürer, and the symbol-structures of Klee, and on and on. She despised The Ramones and The Clash, enough to get angry if she heard them, anytime, though when she went for runs, she loved to blast The Dead Kennedys and Black Flag and Minor Threat— she wanted *passion*, something to *feel*. She knew all the words to *It*

Takes a Nation of Millions to Hold Us Back and would gladly bust into an impromptu a cappella performance of "Black Steel in the Hour of Chaos," gesticulating and enunciating every lyric like she'd been waiting all her life to grip the mic. Though many of her other favorite films were strange and dark—*The Saddest Music in the World, Picnic at Hanging Rock, There Will Be Blood,* Cocteau's *Beauty and the Beast*—she also loved the uncanny and absurd: *Tim and Eric, American Ninja Warrior, Dr. Pimple Popper, Dr. Phil.* She'd whip my ass at *Jeopardy!*, able to summon answers to most any subject before I'd heard the prompt. She'd cackle with delight over the exacting coldness of Angela on *The Office*, excited to see a hater of her ilk so well represented on TV. She loved to recite on cue her favorite joke, barely able to get the words out without cracking up—*A dog goes to send a telegram. He tells the teller he wants to sent the message, "Arf, arf, arf, arf, arf, arf, arf," to which the teller suggests he could add a few more arfs for the same price. "But that wouldn't make any sense!" the dog replies.* I felt her there, too, in a sweet, uncertain way, when she'd put on sentimental music just to make herself cry: belting every word to Celine Dion's "It's All Coming Back to Me Now" or frozen silent by Whitney Houston's rendition of the national anthem. We must have played a hundred times her favorite YouTube video of a cat being scolded for hiding in a Christmas tree, unflappable in being called out, half-asleep on high—an exactly perfect role model, as she saw it. She hated board games, unwilling to be competitive over something so arbitrary, though she did enjoy listening to me trying to explain the intricacies of poker or *Magic: The Gathering* strategy, as if trying to understand what made me tick. We loved to go to NBA games together, especially when Atlanta played Detroit. She'd get so into the game she'd jump up shouting at the top of her lungs into a lull, catcalling at Kyle Korver loud as she could above the crowd. Whereas I liked staying home, doing the same thing over and over, she loved scavenging from thrift stores, hunting for treasures others had abandoned, especially neophyte artwork, strange pairs of scissors, and figurines with tacky traits, part cartoon and part despair. Some nights we'd stay up late taking turns playing '90s music, reminiscing on DIY and how different life seemed before cell phones and the internet became widespread; how the era we'd grown up in felt more romantic and unbound than how it was now. Above all else, though, she adored nature: trees and rocks and weather and the sea—and especially animals: cats and owls and chickens, but really birds of any kind, which she would attract by stacking feeders outside the window where she wrote. She loved to hold our silkie hens tight to her chest and whisper secrets to them, make them feel precious. It moved my heart to get to watch her stand close to the protective glass between her and the tigers at the zoo, almost a girl again. She loved the rain, the way it drummed the house, its loosening smell, and loved to understand the innerworkings of the science that gave them cause, stacking up books I'd never heard of in every room, including her favorite of all time, *Rock, Time, and Landforms* by Jerome Wyckoff, a text in which almost no humans appear. The driving force behind her poetry and baking both, as she described them, came from her love of chemistry, a combination of discovery and formal process intertwined. One day she'd publish a cookbook all her own, she fantasized, testing and retesting her recipes in the inch-thick batter-splattered notebook she'd carried with her through the years, as if in hopes someday it'd all prove worth it.

Despite all this—or perhaps in light of it—most any ray of hope, no matter how vivid or hard-earned, would never shine inside Molly's mind for very long. There always had to be a bitter pill, a tarnish to the silver, already there or soon to come. The love she felt for nature could only eventually serve to fortify her disgust for people, whose very presence threatened the existence of all the rest. Humanity was nothing more than one big pathetic tragedy, so as she saw it, a viral blight that infected everything it touched. She'd spend hours curled up on the couch watching nature shows in tears, as attuned to her awareness of the destruction of beauty, by our hands, as she might the beauty on its own. The universe would be better off if we were gone, she concluded, and about this, there could be absolutely no debate despite its pith. How to respond, then, when someone you love looks straight into your eyes and says that neither of you should exist? What about if you agree with her, theoretically, and also would prefer she didn't die? Where does a moral value end and the complex nuances of actual reality fill back in? Despite our similar ambitions, we were in many other ways quite different after all, particular in having come from what seemed like wildly contrasting family backgrounds. While I'd lived in the same city my whole life, had more friends than I could count, Molly had picked up and started over so many times there were mostly only fragments and faded memories left in her wake. Her truest childhood friend, whom she'd loved more than she felt loved back by, as she explained, mostly ignored her now, or didn't seem to care—and yet she hadn't given up hope, twenty years later, that someday yet that friend would come around. This ongoing, lifelong conflict made me feel more tender for her, wanting to protect her, shield her from any further forms of pain, even if she often didn't seem to want to do the same for me. She didn't really seem to want to get to know my friends or family, for instance, as if despite her yearning for connection, there were hard limits and connotations she remained adhered to—*not like this.* Her resignation was no game, I felt I knew, but more so the evidence of how she'd made it on her own, as best she could, across a lifetime of feeling left out and alone.

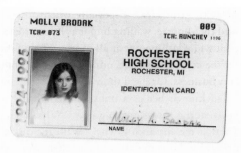

"Girls didn't seem to like me much," she wrote of sixth grade. "I was confused by their interest in craftsy friendship bracelets and gymnastics and stickers and Lisa Frank junk."[4] In her only senior yearbook picture, she refuses to make eye contact with the camera, head craned down, inside the listening lab at the library during lunch, the caption explains, playing tapes of native French speakers, the caption states, to improve her pronunciation. She loved to tell the story of how she'd once refused to read a Michael Crichton novel her English teacher assigned the class and negotiated instead to read Nietzsche on her own. As an adult she found these memories hilarious, if also concrete evidence of the benefits of isolation, as over time, the more she felt it, she'd decided that other people could only make her weaker. Time not spent on working or learning was time wasted, and no one else could try to change that tune without sounding like a fool. Closer to the end, she admitted that as long as she stayed busy with work, she wouldn't have to feel.

———

Much like love, death always seemed to be on Molly's mind. At times I sensed a part of her long locked up without a key, its entombed voice

4   *Bandit*, p. 63.

egging her on with grim ideas. Especially when upset, she'd turn head-on toward the rupture, wading into it as if toward some pulsing center of the pit while lashing out at all nearby. She'd refuse to wear her seatbelt in the car, for instance, admonishing me for pointing it out; none of my business. Or she'd show up chain-smoking Marlboro reds when I had known her as a nonsmoker, lighting up in front of me while pretending it was nothing new. "What does it matter?" she'd snarl back at me for asking why. "Who fucking cares?" Her serial shoplifting stood out the most of such behaviors, despite how casually she brought it up. She'd been doing it for years, paying her way through college selling stuff on eBay while getting to wear clothes she couldn't otherwise afford. She asked what kind of clothes I'd like to wear if money weren't an object, and when I came over next, she'd laid out piles of expensive brand name pants and sweaters in my size to try on. It felt bizarre, if only a bit, to hear her speak so easily of doing crimes, downplayed by her as pure routine despite the peculiar kit of tools she carried with her in her purse: rare earth magnets, a metal hook. She knew how to keep her cool, she'd explain, act like she was just shopping, and her white skin and pleasant features made her easy to overlook. The one time I was with her when she did it, it felt like nothing—she simply took the shirt I wanted and disappeared, later reemerging from the dressing rooms the same as ever, no big deal. Her acting out wasn't only all unconscious in this manner, as she saw it, mere bad behavior; it was a moral stricture, the only honest lens through which to read the world. Corporations deserved to be ripped off; money is bullshit; the game is rigged, so why not cheat—all these ideologies presented so frankly it would be hard to disagree without coming off as square. Any concern I might have felt about her recklessness felt mostly unnecessary; she seemed to have it all under control, and I liked the punk ass attitude she wielded alongside her highly polished posture, how she'd rail against things I'd never considered the other side of. Symmetry is ugly, she'd announce in that same mind, as a response to actions or artwork made too neat. Life just isn't like that, and true beauty had bumps and bruises, made a mess. "I like that you like making messes. Moi aussi!" she'd written to me in our earliest DMs, when for some reason I had included that detail in describing how I spent my time, though compared to her I was a stickler. I remember feeling shocked the first time I caught a glimpse of her MacBook desktop, covered up from edge to edge with countless thumbnails, files on files: screenshots of receipts and emails, scattered photos without order, old attachments never dragged into the trash—a stark contrast to her usual rigorous upkeep. She took my pointing it out as a jab, evidence of judgment, unwilling to listen to any explanation on my end. "Blake thinks I'm filthy," she'd tell others right in front of me, pretending to make a joke of it but clearly irked. I'd learn to be more careful about speaking up in general thereafter, keeping close tabs on what I knew might piss her off, what not to say, which in some ways felt like a good thing, given my penchant for being loud and reactionary. She'd take her own lengths, too, in making sure she didn't tip her hand if she could help it when I didn't immediately conform. In the heat of a moment, she might intimate she wanted more aggressive sex—helping my hands up to her neck to choke her or bringing out a strap-on I'd never seen, which only struck me strange given how out of the blue it was—then later, once agan, she'd insist I'd made it up, arguing me into a corner where I had to choose either to continue to defy her or agree, and either way thereafter I'd be labeled selfish, full of shit. She could go so cold from out of nowhere just like that—sweet one second, then dark, sarcastic, petty, mean—and even harder to reach her in those moments, bumping dark raw spots without realizing and getting boxed out thereafter as reprimand, a circuit burned. She could see herself so well, it seemed, until suddenly, flooded with fire, she couldn't at all.

"This conscious break with reality I am describing in the method of stealing, I know it is sociopathic," Molly explains in *Bandit*, comparing her shoplifting with her father's robberies. "I can explain what it feels like when it happens. Your plan numbs you. You focus on the plan. You know if the plan goes well, you'll be pleased afterward, but you are not pleased in the execution of it. There is no pleasure, no feeling at all. It *is*, Dad, a little like an out-of-body experience. Except that it's more of an out-of-morals experience. A purposefully-stepping-out of them. That's the difference, Dad. There's no helplessness involved, at all. You feel gross. But you choose to not stop. You have all the time in the world to stop! You have a million chances to not go through with it. But you do. It's like you're on the other side of yourself now."[5]

One morning, after leaving Molly's apartment, I received a Facebook

5   *Bandit*, p. 177.

message from a stranger: "Are you currently dating/seeing my wife—Molly Brodak?" I showed the note to Molly straight away; she hardly blinked. *Wife* was just a pet word that her ex-boyfriend used to try to claim her, she explained; really, he was just some guy she'd broken up with who wished she hadn't—constantly jealous, drunk and lazy, dismissive of her writing; someone from whom she'd surely and distinctly grown apart. This made me feel protective of her, of course, and brought us nearer. Men were like that, I understood—treating women like possessions to be hunted and kept, only regretful far too late. Molly could handle it herself, she reassured me; she knew how to put him in his place. I heard nothing else about it until weeks later, another message from him arrived in my inbox: an apology, sent with regrets, and a request: "If you are dating her, please be good to her. She's a really unbelievable woman as you probably know, and don't forget how lucky you are if she likes you, because she basically has a pick of whoever she wants and she knows it. I know she seems tough because she's so brilliant but she's really pretty frail. Be kind to her, she's been through more types of pain than you and I could ever imagine." *He doesn't seem to know you at all*, I remember announcing apologetically to Molly, unable to imagine how someone as stand-out and determined as I knew her to be could ever be called frail. This made me feel reassured and lucky to be the one who got to see her more correctly, thankful she'd moved on from him, gotten away, another ship long since sailed. Of course, there'd end up being much more to the story than she let on, most of which I wouldn't gather until she could no longer intercede.

Despite our rocky start and sticky differences, or perhaps in light of them, we grew together, bonded in a way I hadn't felt before. My prior dark desire to remain forever out of reach began to taper off, replaced with what felt like healing flesh over old wounds. It still wasn't clear where we were headed, what would come of it, but we knew at least we wished to try. We were officially in a relationship now, at least, and I had stopped seeing other people, which I made sure that Molly knew. I didn't feel I needed the same reassurance from her end, seeing as how she'd made it clear from early on that she wanted nobody but me. I'd already seen firsthand, too, the way that Molly handled guys who tried to pick her up at bars when in my presence, abrupt and cold, not even half-willing to flirt, much less even be polite. "In your dreams," she snarl straight-faced into their gaping, zero blink. "Drop dead." It seemed ridiculous not to trust her, especially given how my jealousy had all been a major drag on both my past relationships, always paranoid, if with good reason, about the parts of people's lives I couldn't know. Like Molly, I wanted to control my path so much I let it wreck me, creating hardship where there was none, or doubling down when something did happen, begging not to be left behind. By the end of my last long-term relationship, I'd found myself obsessively circling the streets outside my girlfriend's apartment when I couldn't find her, seeing red while wondering what it was about me that made her want to get away, and now I no longer wished to live that way. I'd already made up my mind, front and center, never to go to those extents with Molly—to end my snooping, overthinking, anticipating nothing but the worst. This was a new beginning for us both, and I would go forth in good faith, no matter what. I got the sense that reticence in this regard somehow annoyed her, as if my lack of envy and resentment meant she wasn't worth it or that I simply didn't care. She'd semi-regularly remind me there were other guys out there after her, such as the hipster dork at the laundromat who told her she had the most beautiful eyes; or the poet who'd sent her dick pics with a can of Coke next to it so she could see how big it was—incidentally, a person who I knew had been multiply accused of sexual misconduct, which didn't seem to bother Molly;

or Jonah Hill, who she said had come into the boutique sweets store she worked part-time at to supplement her fellowship stipend and asked her out, who she also claimed to reject a second time when he emailed her and told her he'd Googled her and read and loved her poetry. I believed these stories; they made sense—who wouldn't want her? I felt grateful for her forthcomingness about it, and her refusal to play along, which brought me closer, established safety in a way my previous relationship had worn down to a nub. When I did slip, every now and then unable to hold off my old suspicions given a chance, I'd sneak briefly though her phone's history, see who she'd been texting with, but all I would find there was her mother and sister mostly, friends I knew, or calls from work. She seemed more alone than anyone I'd ever met, I realized, despite her trying, and I felt lucky to be the one to get to change that; to let her in when no one else would, or so I thought.

<hr>

Another person in regular pursuit of Molly throughout this time kept coming up—a popular poet, whom Molly knew I clashed with, and who'd been emailing her regularly, regaling her with come-ons she itemized with me in kind, up front. She said she found him corny but at the same time kept responding to him and reporting on it when I asked. She clearly appreciated his attention, liked to describe it, to feel included in his version of the social world of poetry she claimed to totally disdain. I tried to trim the edges of suspicion in my mind, cutting her some slack where in years past I would have gotten testy, demanding to know every single detail of their interactions inside and out. Still, the presence of this other guy's attention made Molly act like someone else almost, or at least like someone who didn't line up with who she said she was. This became a point of minor tension for us, a pin in my pride when I'd see her comment on his status updates on Facebook in a clearly flirty way and posted pictures thanking him for sending her gifts. "I can see why that would irritate you," she'd admitted when I brought it up directly, trying to grow by expressing my feeling aloud instead of fuming, pleased when she agreed to cut it out. That same summer, that poet was announced as part of an upcoming event at the same reading series we'd recently reconnected at, now Molly's workplace, right down the street from where she lived. Molly didn't want to go, though, she made clear; instead, we'd do something else together that night, only further bonded in our mutual disdain. The night before the reading, we each stayed at our own places, as we would often, trading off days between doing our own thing and hanging out. Something struck me as strange, though, when she wasn't responding to my texts. After a while, I'd worked myself into an old familiar frenzy and drove at once across town to her place, trying to convince myself the whole way to turn around. To my surprise, though, despite the guilt I'd felt, I found a tour van with the poet's state's plates parked in her lot. Really seeing red now, I parked my car and stormed up to her door and firmly knocked, listening in for any commotion. A few moments later, Molly answered, speaking through the door first, then tipping it open just a crack, clearly distressed. She had her glasses on, a silky bed slip. "What's going on in there?" I demanded. "Aren't you going to let me in?" She undid the chain then, and I barged in, only to find the other guy there in her bed in his boxers and t-shirt, reading a book. Without a word, I rushed and threw myself at him, swinging my fists at his head, shouting insults. I told him I was about to kick his ass, no longer thinking what that meant, wrath coming out of me all blind. I'd never found myself in such a spot before, hungry for violence in a way that felt as if I could see me from above and couldn't stop. Molly stood there in the door behind us, crying with her hands over her face, clearly embarrassed but also desperate to have me hear her out. I demanded that she tell me what was really going on, and why; why, if she wanted us to be together, as she'd expressed over and over, was this dipshit here in her bed; why had she lied and acted like she didn't like him if this was what she really had in mind. She began to plead, said this was all a mix-up, that there was nothing going on; he'd twisted her arm into offering a place to crash and she was sleeping on the sofa, end of story. Already we were talking as if he wasn't in the room, the actual reality of what was going on there shifting over into semantics, shreds of fact. She knew she'd made a big mistake, she whined, and wished she could do anything to fix it, to be forgiven. *Please, don't give up on me, don't turn away.* I could see a certain terror in her eyes, activated by the possibility of something slipped through her fingers more than madness of the moment, so it seemed. She cleaved onto me as the other guy slunk off with his bag toward the door, looking back at us as he undid the clasp to let himself out. We seemed insane, I know, like two mad assholes in distress. "Yeah, go on and get the fuck out of here," I shouted at him, leering as I stood there in rampant fury with my future wife, beyond the pale.

■

I'm not that much embarrassed by my behavior, to be honest—I knew what he was doing, what he wanted, what would have taken place had I not shown up. Less so Molly, though; if anything, she appeared to like that I'd barged in, even found it reassuring somehow that I cared enough to go to blows. Over email, because I was too angry afterward to meet up, she tried to plea with me that this was all a big mistake, that she felt sick, and suicidal, over having messed up our relationship. "I can't believe I did this," she'd written in a cascade. "I can't believe I hurt you and now you are suspicious of me. It will be easy for you now to make up details or versions that suit your suspicions and I will have a hard time fighting against them, even though I have the truth and it is the real truth, the truth matters less now because I fucked with it. I am trying so hard because I love you. I am trying and fucking up. I am doing things right every day and sometimes I do a thing wrong. A huge wrong thing, I lie to you and it seems insane and impossible to myself I have done this wrong thing…I don't know what to do. I don't know if I have ever felt this way and I think I am bad off. I have never actually given myself a very good reason to hate myself before. I had just been doing it using small or unreal reasons. And now I have this reason. I feel like it would be so safe to die today, having been this horribly careless towards the only person I really care about, like what could be worse than that. How could I fail so thoroughly at something that is so important to me, this one thing that makes me even care about being alive." This implicit threat, the revolving door of woe behind it, made me uncertain how to reply. I felt immensely fearful of what awful things she might do to rebuke herself; she seemed capable of anything. Instead, because it felt less scary maybe, I let her tell me her version story over and over, filling in new details to cloud my doubt: how the poet had taken advantage of her, worked her down, wormed his way in. I believed her by the panic in her eyes she didn't want this to be the end of us, that she felt peril in having deceived me, and really wished to make it up. I'd been raised to tend toward forgiveness, understanding; that every person, no matter how flawed, was worthy of love; maybe more so those who hadn't ever had it. Maybe I wanted to see her as a victim of her own life in some way, sabotaged by the impulses and bad habits of the parts of her that didn't love herself, and I believed her when she swore she'd never make the same mistake again. In days ahead, though, when I would retell the story of that night aloud to friends, she'd join in laughing at my reactive madness, at once a little higher in her step and evasive about adding her own perspective to the scene, as if it was all just a tribute to her appeal. Ten years later, reading her emails in her absence, I'd realize she'd without question led him on; that if she hadn't already had sex with him that night, she surely meant to; that she'd talked dismissively about me to him in the same way as vice versa; and much like me, he hadn't blamed her for what happened, only wished she could have been straight with him, as it could have saved us all some pain.

———

Though I ultimately forgave Molly her deception, in the short-term things between us slowed back down. Whereas before we'd been growing closer, bit by bit, there was suddenly a different distance in the thread—a returned sense of resignation in my approach, and a mourning, loping cast just underneath Molly's determination to stay close. I knew she was struggling a lot during this time, too, if never quite being told why, to what degree—always uneasy, wringing her hands, a far-away look behind her eyes. I had no immediate idea of the intensity with which she'd left behind a whole life in Augusta and often still felt unsure if she'd made the right choice, as a lonely stranger in a new city, starting over. Perhaps as a corollary to her own hidden struggle, she rarely pressed me for details on where I'd gone after "heading home" from her place after she settled in early to go to bed. We continued hanging out regularly, but the times between felt less assured, spread out, peppered with nights I went out alone and drank to blackout, going wild. When really wasted, I'd often start referring to myself as Joey, a spastic side of me that loved to get rowdy, if all in fun, knocking the ceiling tiles out of the ceiling at the bar or throwing chairs over my head high as I could. I'd end up delirious at dance clubs, sopping wet from spazzing out all by myself, clearing the dance floor until they kicked me out, begging the door guy to give me a second chance: *I'll buy the whole bar drinks if you'll just let me dance.* Or I'd find myself alone at 4 a.m., eating Chinese food, texting old hookups in my phone, having left my car parked across three spaces outside, locked with a boot. I remember cursing out a SUV full of security staff in a blind rage after they stopped me from trying to drive with the wheel shaft still locked up. "You should get back in your car and go to sleep," one of them told me while taking my payment, to which I responded by screaming in his face. I know I felt surrounded and abandoned at the same time, uncertain who or how to tell how much I hurt, how far from who I wished to be I felt, and not sure why. No one ever seemed to wonder, much less ask, what was going on with me, and I was great at pretending everything was fine; that all my acting out was just for fun. Everybody has their problems, so who would ever want to hear of mine? Instead, I'd befriend a straggler on the street and invite them back to my car to finish off a bottle of Jim Beam, then drive us both to a diner and stuff my face, so I might sleep. My insomnia was out of control again, too—always much worse in times of stress—so I was exhausted most of the time, still spending most of each day's hours on my writing at my parents', nothing else. I began meeting back up with other women I'd been seeing before Molly came to town, and other women too, though this time I didn't always tell her what was going on, instead lying by omission, just as she had, like what you don't know can't hurt you. Often I could hardly remember for myself what I'd gotten into until the following morning, reading backwards through my texts like Jekyll learning about Hyde—and yet once the liquor got into my blood, another side of me took over, and I no longer really cared. If I'd been hurt, who cares what else hurt next, or who I offended? What did it even really matter what I did at all if in the end it all just felt a long, cruel, vapid game?

———

Either way, I tried to keep this vicious mindset separate from the daylight, honoring one path during waking hours and another buried deep within the black hole of my mind. The longer this went on, the less I liked it—it's not like I couldn't remember who I was when acting out; I just kept compensating with the idea that I was paying back on my misfortune, and soon enough I'd straighten up. I still wanted to straighten up, after all, someday quite soon; I didn't like the way it felt to play both sides, very much unlike any way I'd ever acted. If I'd never been a cheat, why was I cheating now? What else had changed? It went on like this a while, hung in a double bind, until one day, at last, I caught a snag: running into the other woman I was sleeping with out at a reading there with Molly on my arm. Molly had just asked me, a couple days before, out of the blue, if I'd be willing to come to Ohio with her to visit her father in federal prison, and then to continue on to Michigan, more to see where she grew up than meet her family, as she sold it—even still, a large ask, maybe, given our recent struggles, though also something I felt inclined, even compelled, to want to do. Since the fight, she'd been especially soft and understanding, going out of her way to show that she felt bad for lying to me, and wanted more than anything to make it up. I'd wanted that too, if in a way that had become split now, more back toward the abandon I'd been living before we met, using booze as an excuse to buck off anything that made me feel. Seeing Molly talking to the other woman, unable to parse the sultry look on the other woman's face as we made small talk, staring at me with a steely knowing I could feel all through my shoulders, between my teeth. This wasn't who I meant to be, I thought, but it's who I was being. Whose fault was that? How long could I go on acting out against the idea of who I claimed to be and still be me? Not very long, I knew, as much so from the tension of seeing a double life out in the open as from the certainty that the damage had already been done; that I couldn't take it back and couldn't change it. This was my life, and try as I might to pretend I wasn't living it, my gut knew otherwise. That night, after dropping Molly off, as if to reprove me, the woman texted and asked me to come over, and I said no. Time to give up on the bullshit and really try now, I decided. Didn't we deserve that, finally? Wasn't that really what I wanted—something real, and something close, and something true? What was I waiting for?

———

It feels hard to narrate this particular partition of our lives—to have to see myself making mistakes, even armed with the dim reasons that made me act the way I did while throwing caution to the wind, but also believing in some assured way that I knew what I was doing. Much easier to see from here how messed up I was in my own way, meshing with Molly's darkness in ways that remained most often out of screen. I'm not proud of having lied to her, broken her trust, even as backlash, and yet I also understand now, with larger context, how there were feelings and effects at work inside both of our lives I couldn't see, connected both to my own desire to drown my feelings out with alcohol and half-fused logic, as well as Molly's own deceptions, impossible to read beyond the way she spun the story, whether aware or unaware. The truth, if there is any, could be that it's both: that Molly really wanted love, faith, and forgiveness, and yet had already been so hurt she couldn't always keep them separate and wasn't sure which she could trust. She'd learned directly from her father, after all, to live with paradoxes intertwined, even if she'd seen up close how hard and fast he'd fallen when the facts of reality caught up with his deceptions—not superhuman after all, as she well knew, though still tinged on his end with an unwillingness to admit defeat even red-handed, with the cuffs around his wrists for all to see. All he had to do, he seemed to want to teach her, by example, is keep pretending everything is fine, and the rest of the world would follow suit. How much of him was right there in her, not even asking for forgiveness, but rather egging her on into his void? What would it take, were it even possible, to finally cut him loose?

The last time Molly had seen her father was during his visit to her bedside in the hospital after her brain surgery. He'd driven all the way from Michigan to Atlanta to bring her a cup of ice cream, stay an hour, then head immediately back home—a memory she shared the way one would a terrible punchline. She was extremely nervous to see him again now, especially in prison, which inspired me with a strength to want to be a man where he had failed her. We made our way slowly through security, past all the walls and wires designed to separate the criminals from the civilians. The central greeting room felt like a cafeteria, arranged into distinguished seating areas where other families awaited the doling out of precious time with those they loved. Molly didn't want to talk, already seeming to "get small," as she'd described the way she learned to act around her family growing up, making herself scarce amidst the chaos of never knowing what came next. She had no idea how much longer his second sentence was supposed to be and felt afraid to ask, as even under lock up, Joe was never forthcoming; she knew he still insisted he hadn't done what he had done. When he appeared through the prisoner's entrance into the area, I noted he was smaller than I'd have guessed, tight but also amiable, like a salesman trying to convince us we were in his living room, not a state pen. He shook my hand, eyes on the floor, then turned to offer Molly a brief hug, which made her bristle, flushing pink. First thing he wanted to know was if we'd brought the credit voucher he'd reminded her several times to please secure so he could use it to buy a personal microwave pizza from the vending machine. You couldn't get that good kind of food inside, he reported, only with company. He outlined exactly what items he wanted, the formal process of how to go about it, and I took over from there, leaving the two of them to catch up while I wandered off to fill the order. I couldn't help but notice that I was the only one of everybody there already tending to the vending. Across the room, I measured Molly's bearing: hands to herself, reserved, eyes big, seeking connection but afraid. I knew how badly she wanted to ask him about his life; to finally hear his story straight from him, in search of any indication of remorse, any thread that helped explain him. Instead, she watched him talk, frozen solid by the false front of his cheese, as if no one could read the shadows except him. I could feel the strain in her as I returned with the snacks, her holding back from cringing at his grin as he dug in, casually explaining between bites his ploy for joining the prison's religious program to gain credit for good behavior, until he realized this would offer zero discount on his time. She'd come all this way to see him, long after everybody else in her family had written him off, and here we were just mumbling about semantics, sticking to small talk, if occasionally veering into more directly pressing questions from him about the trajectory of her career, why she hadn't found the perfect job yet, what might be next. Molly continued to avoid my eye as she watched him eat and preen like some caged animal on display. I wished that I could hug her but sensed it inappropriate in front of him somehow. After a while, he said he'd arranged for a surprise, and we got up and walked to a sunset-colored backdrop where they had their photos taken as a pair shoulder to shoulder, each with a formal but blank smile. I tried to stay out of the way, to let Molly have the moment, following his lead, despite how inside I could see that she was screaming, still half a daughter searching for any reason to believe he cared while already knowing mostly that he didn't. She'd made it this far all on her own, I understood; this relationship was hers, damage and all, the only kin she'd ever had. If there could never be a hope for honesty, for healing, I imagined, maybe there'd come a point she might decide to let him go—a sensation reinforced when just as all the other visiting families seated around us had just begun to settle in, Joe jumped on a longer lull in conversation to wonder if we had somewhere else to be, as it was already getting late. That's all it took, turned on a hinge—we stood up at once, said our goodbyes, flat as the intros—then she and I were on our way out the way we'd come, leaving Joe there sitting by himself, as if awaiting someone else to come in next and fill our place.

———

The rest of Molly's family was another story. She still got on with them, she'd say, but struggled with it, and most of all with going back to Michigan, which she at once loved and hated with all her heart. She always felt she had to act a certain way, bending to others' wishes, never actually speaking up about herself, and even when doing so, not feeling heard—the normal family shit, but also very real and vivid in her, to the point that you could see the clouds form in her face and hear the tightness in her breath. Eventually, the long drives and darkened skies and heavy weather always got under her skin, a strong reminder that she could never live there again, despite the clear nostalgia and even pride she felt showing me around her hometown. "It's not as if I *like* damage exactly," she writes in *Bandit* of her conflicted mixture of nostalgia and despair for Detroit's ruins. "It's more that damaged things seem truer."[6] I'd steeled myself for anxious times going to visit, even more so after meeting her father, who despite his removal from the family's daily life seemed to hang over them like poison fog. I felt surprised right off the bat to find how kind and cheery Molly's older sister, Becca, was—full of warm welcome, bright-eyed and smiling, sincere hugs. Her house, set on a golf course, was large and warm and comfortable and clean— huge displays of rows and rows of DVDs, mostly big box office hits and comedies. Becca had adapted to the trauma of their childhood by filling up the void with creature comforts, Molly had told me, unwilling or uninterested in doting on the darkness, preferring

6   *Bandit*, p. 239.

instead to pretend it hadn't happened, or wasn't worth any further thought. Joe's arrest had been even worse for Becca, who had gone to live with him after the divorce while Molly stayed with her mother, Nora, which had resulted in him stealing money from her, and much more. It wasn't clear what "much more" meant within that context—again, unspeakable, understandably. Everyone just wanted a happy life now, to move on, and who could blame them? As sisters, after all they'd been through, Molly and Becca truly did seem distinctly opposite in many ways, and though I got the sense at times that Becca really didn't "get" Molly, I could tell she wanted to; she clearly loved her little sister even if she didn't exactly know how to connect, made only worse by Molly's deference in her presence, playing along, holding her tongue. Family time meant doing what *they* wanted, as Molly saw it, choosing instead to carry all this resignation deep in her heart, hardened to it in an almost religiously enforced sort of silence. Rather than speak up, I knew, she'd rather put her head down and barrel through and bear the wounds, pretending everything was just okay when clearly there was so much she had to say, overriding how small she felt inside in the name of treading water, waiting soon to go back to the safety of our real lives.

———

While I'd had a hard time reading Molly's tension with her sister, the line between Molly and her mother felt more distinct. Nora lived about an hour from Becca—on good terms but not as close as Nora and Molly—in a small house with her second husband, Jack, an ex-boxer and firefighter whom neither of her daughters too much liked, most clearly apparent in his headstrong manner, often needing to steer most any conversation back to himself. I knew Nora had been through hell with Joe, not to mention her own history with abuse and mental illness, and yet she handled herself with a bristly confidence welcoming us in. She seemed excited to have us there, overflowing with questions and anecdotes in a kind of manic energy that made Molly anxious, if in a way that felt more teenaged than the brittle silence she'd reserved for Joe. As she had at the prison, though, Molly mostly kept her eyes away from mine throughout the visit, leaving me to shoot the bull with Jack while she stood in the kitchen with her mom and watched her cook. I felt very aware of Molly's awareness of nearly every action Nora made, as if cataloguing it for review. Nora's decision-making process could be bizarre, she'd prepared me to expect; you never knew what she might do. She'd once substituted garlic salt for regular salt in a recipe, Molly still remembered from her last visit, somehow unable to tell the difference when it made the dish inedible—no big offense, sure, but one that Molly took as evidence that her Mom was from another world, forever teenaged in rapport. A lot though they might be, I liked meeting Molly's family, Jack and all; they seemed like well-meaning people, and clearly their predilections and idiosyncrasies were there in part in Molly, too, an unnecessary embarrassment she seemed at once aware and unaware of the extent of. Again, I wished I could pull her outside and hug her, tell her that I understood how she felt, and it was all going to be okay, though at the same time I felt uncertain of my place. For me, this was a window, temporary; for Molly, this was the backbone of her life. I'd heard her stories, knew their layers, and now I felt it in my gut like a black stone, hard to decipher from afar. Maybe it wasn't really all so bad, I thought, while understanding too how bizarre it felt to have a stranger experience your lifetime's loved ones up so close without a guard. I felt a bit unmoored in Molly's past life in this way, like a stranger trying to fit together pieces of a puzzle that didn't fit the way they meant to and didn't depict the same image as on the cover of the box. The next time we'd come back to visit, for Thanksgiving, I'd see this strain more clearly when Nora refused to invite her eldest brother to the dinner, which based on what Molly had told me—that Nora had been molested by him regularly for many years as a teen—I knew should never have been a question, much less an issue.[7] But if *he* wasn't invited, Nora's mother wouldn't come over either, apparently par for the course with how the situation had been handled throughout all of Nora's life: *Don't damage the family with your nasty claims.* Nobody even really seemed to want to be there anyway, so why Nora had to be demoralized in the meantime made little sense, a fact I felt reflected through Molly's silence at the table, refusing to comment, just absorbing.

———

"Thank you for loving my daughter!" I remember Molly's mother calling out as we left her place, being careful not to slip on the fresh snow, but more so how Molly moaned back, "Mom!", clearly embarrassed in the way she often got whenever her mother showed excitement or spoke up. I smiled and waved, wondering a little why I needed to be thanked for such a thing, though we hadn't said we were in love yet besides in the heat of certain moments, still uncertain what we were. For most of my life, I'd avoided official terminology or applied logic for my feelings, as if there were an unhinged power to putting language to it, something that once struck could not be turned. I'd convinced myself I had to know for certain, to the depths of it, to even use the word "love" at all, and in my mind had to take years to even begin to know a person. I'd learned this, I think, from my own family's comparative lack of expressing our feelings besides at specific moments, like during a birthday or after a fight, the texture of the love still clearly there but often taken as a baseline, an assumption. Unlike many of my friends' families, who said "I love you" coming and going, acts of affection were more occasional, spread out, which I'd never thought to see before until outside it. I

7   *Bandit*, p. 148-49.

felt a bit unmoored in Molly's past life in this way, like a stranger trying to fit together pieces of a puzzle that didn't fit the way they meant to and didn't depict the same image as on the cover of the box.

After dinner, while driving back to Becca's, Molly told me there was something that she needed to admit. She'd been divorced, she said with studied reservation—her ex-boyfriend who'd sent me messages was her ex-husband after all. She'd been terrified to tell me, uncertain how I'd take it, since most men saw divorced women as damaged junk, so she explained. I listened to her talk, gripping the wheel tight with both hands as she steered us through the icy Michigan night, her sight trained on the road. She seemed relieved, at least tentatively relieved, though, by my reaction: that it didn't bother me at all; that, in fact, the only thing that struck me odd about it was that she'd kept it hidden for so long, and she agreed, turning warm the more I talked, reassuring her from my repose. I remember feeling a mixture of relief and shame at the same time, strapped in her car seat, wondering how we'd ended up close, here with her family, and at the same time, so far away, layered in lies on both sides. I felt the urge to confess, too, right then and there—that I'd fucked up and wished I hadn't—at last to set the record straight completely for us both. What was I even doing here when so much else needed fixing first, and why hadn't I forced myself to confess already? Was I really as bad a person as I felt, sitting there smiling, acting the fool? Or was I more so something that I hadn't seen I was yet, needing others to push me toward it, almost in spite of me and in pursuit of me at once? What would it take to ever feel myself inside myself?

Because I didn't tell her right then, I wouldn't get the chance to in my own way. Two days later, after flying back to Atlanta while she stayed in Michigan a little longer, Molly called me crying to ask if I'd been having sex with someone else. She squealed when I said yes—too late to explain with any significance that I had cut it off for good. The other woman had already sent Molly threatening emails, including close-up photos of her vagina, bragging that she'd taken me for hers. Molly was driving while we spoke, letting me know that she was being reckless on purpose, speeding and changing lanes at random. She didn't care if she got hurt now, and yet she wanted to be told every detail of what I'd done, how it had happened and how often, sparing nothing. I understood how gross it was, I told her, how hurtful and insane. I answered every question that she had, down to the last detail of what I'd done, no matter how heavy-handed her want for information felt. I begged her not to do anything to hurt herself, to stay there with me on the line, and we went on for half an hour like that as she moaned and hissed at me, in simultaneous anguish and regret. Then she began threatening her life. She'd been driving to Lake Michigan, she explained, and planned to walk into the waters, not come back. *I know I'm worthless*, she kept repeating, *I deserve this.* For a while, she put the phone down where I could hear her struggling in the background, not quite sure what she'd do next, hanging onto her every breath. I tried to think of who I could call to go and find her from all these miles away. I considered hanging up and calling 911 but I had no idea where she would be, and slowly, as I stayed with her, she began to calm down, returning from mania to a more stolid wall of blank. Eventually she let me listen to her heading back to where she'd parked, promising she wasn't going to do anything rash, but that she'd need some time to think it through. She'd be in touch later, once she was back in town and had processed it some more, and then she'd let me know how we'd proceed. I felt relieved, most of all for that she'd come back down off the ledge I'd

Blake Butler 83

forced her out on, if also slightly skewered, like now the ball was in her court, with little recourse on my end but to make it up to her despite the other kinds of reservations that were still obviously in play. But, above all, I felt like shit and knew I was shit, shocked to find myself in such a spot after having remained faithful to every person I'd ever been with, until now. After hanging up, I drove straight to the bar and drank to black out, feeling afraid to look at my phone in anticipation of another incoming threat of self-harm, or something worse, and even more afraid of what would happen if I didn't keep trying.

———

Molly still wanted to be with me, she let me know up front, back in Atlanta, but now there were limits, ones she'd have to figure out how to assign. It would take her a long time to forgive me, but she could do it, and she really wanted to, even still. She understood I'd made a mistake and wasn't proud of what I'd done, a reconciliation that I felt grateful for, if also uncertain of the basis. In some ways, I'd only reconfirmed for her directly what she already felt deep down—that she was dirt—which in turn stung in an even worse way, having to accept that I'd just become continued proof of the self-loathing she'd been carrying around all her life. The effect of all of this against her already brittle confidence was palpable; going forward, at least for a while, she'd give up much more quickly when we argued, turning her back on any conversation that didn't seem to go her way. She jumped out of my car at a red light once in heavy rain and ran off when I refused to see something as she wished, allowing me to chase her down the block and beg her back. She liked when I demonstrated that I cared for her like that, a little drama-twisted in ways I felt I deserved, if with reserve of wonder why. Behind that, I thought a lot about her threat of suicide, how that was something that could happen, that she would wield it like that, whether she could help it quite or not. No matter what I copped to, there'd be a reason now she could return to as evidence that I would never love her, when she needed a weapon, to bring it all right back out, right back where we started any second, which made it hard to feel for certain that I knew what was really going on inside her head, much less my own. And yet there was a common drive that we would share now—of overcoming, of forgiving, even if at times I wondered what it was about me that made her think that I was worth it, why I hung on. Rather than obliterating our relationship, I'd ripped it open, in a way that guaranteed the road ahead would be uphill, but I owed it to her to make up for that, didn't I, to prove myself and be absolved in committing, finally, to something real. Couldn't this be love? Would it have gone this way if we'd met at any other time in my life, when I was less nuts? Could I be less nuts going forward? Coming clean, at least, for me, was a relief, and a turning point in my idea of how to be, centered mainly around the fact that Molly had seen the worst of me and still believed there was something worth hanging on for. All our bad blood would soon be in the past, which made me gracious for the chance at a clean go, if still unwilling to remove myself completely from thinking I had it all under control. I refused to go to couples' therapy with her, for instance, bullheadedly insisting that I didn't need a doctor to remind me I'd messed up. The path to our recovery was ours, not someone else's, as I saw it. All I had to do was make my mind up to be true, and that's exactly what I would do.

———

But still there's something missing from the picture: a haze over the areas of our life between our early struggles and how we ended up together for what, to me, felt like for good; perhaps a product of my looking at my own self back then and seeing through my habits and behaviors, knowing better only after having lived it, far too late. Even knowing what would happen to us, as I write now, there are still so many aspects of the timeline that don't add up, or at the least feel very different from the way I'd always framed them, to the point of no longer knowing what I should believe. Within that, there's sometimes a difference between what Molly believed was true, in direct practice, versus what she knows for certain is a lie. I'm only able to iterate this now, as I keep noting, without her here, having been forced to find so much of the evidence too late, as if none of this was ever as it seemed; that what I thought had been going on between us from day one comes out after the fact as bound from end to end with broken threads. One incident in particular during this period remains, from here, difficult to ascertain: a frantic phone call from Molly, out the blue one afternoon; her voice all tangled up and squealing, speaking too fast for me to parse. She was begging me to help her, it sounded like, though the line was muffled, full of commotion. Where are you? I kept asking. What's going on? I could hear her, but she couldn't hear me, causing her to panic even more. Blake, please, oh god, she wailed, in a voice that still stings me to be able to recall—truly afraid. I ran out into the parking lot of my apartment, flagged down a couple and begged them to let me use their phone while they stood there staring at me in a panic, made only worse when her phone went straight to voicemail, no response. Without other recourse, I sped across town to her apartment to find her front door left standing open, no one there. I found her cell phone left out on the hallway table, counting my missed calls. I felt my heart in my throat, then, thinking all the worst possible things. I ran along the hallways, around the building, shouting her name. I circled the lots around the building and then back up to her apartment, nothing there. I got back in my car and circled through the neighborhood scanning for any sign of where she was. I considered calling the cops but couldn't think of what to say was wrong, and instead started driving to nearby businesses we'd been to. After long enough later that I'd made it halfway back across town, my phone rang from Molly's number. Waves of relief to hear she sounded clearer now, a little calmer, as in bits and blurts, she got it out: someone had come knocking at her door, said the police were towing cars outside the building, said she should move hers if it was there. Like a fool—her words—she followed suit, rushed out the door, and she'd turned her back to turn the lock when she felt a concentrated point of pressure in the middle of the small of her back. "I have a gun," a man whispered from behind her, in her ear. "If you try to run or draw attention, I will shoot you in the spine." He had her walk silently along the hall, then, to the back entrance of the building, into the lot. She remained calm, she explained, thinking of all her options, what might happen, how it would feel, deciding she was better off becoming paralyzed forever than whatever else he meant to do to her. And so she'd bolted, anticipating the pending gunshot every footstep as she sprinted back toward the front street screaming, ready to buckle, but nothing came. She ended up ducking into the sports bar next door, realized she didn't know my number, so she'd waited there for some time on her own, until she felt like trying to go home. She'd already made it back to her apartment, locked the door, so she was safe now; but no need to come over, she insisted— she was too worked up, needed to lie down. Yes, she was definitely going to call the police, she promised in response to my concerns, soon as we hung up. She hadn't yet because she'd panicked, and now it was over and she didn't feel like it was necessary at this time, but she'd do it for me if I insisted, which I did. What I really wanted, though, was to come over, already worried about him coming back, kicking through her flimsy lock. I could wait there with her until the cops came and took her statement, just to be safe. Could I come over after they left instead? Molly replied, without much reason why besides the stress, which belonged to her, of course, and not to me. Hesitantly, trusting her judgment, I headed home and waited for her call on pins and needles, which didn't come till after dusk. The police had laughed her off, she said, hadn't bothered writing down her statement—no surprise. No one really cared what happened to her, or to women ever, she explained, and I agreed, feeling pure fury at the situation despite Molly's returning sense of cool. Anyway, she thought it'd be okay now; she felt better, and maybe it'd be good for her to think of something else. Here, at least, I drew the line: her apartment wasn't safe. She should pack a bag and come and stay with me a while—never mind that we'd been rocky lately. I could accept no other solution now that I'd felt what it would be like to lose her, if only by proxy, the pit of shock still raw and tingling in my guts. That made sense, she said, and she'd appreciate that. She stayed with me that night, and then on through the end of that week into the next—our first extended cohabitation, and simultaneously, the beginning of our transition from living mostly separate daily lives.

——

What struck me strange, in the time after, is how Molly wanted to keep the story of the gunman between us. I felt worried enough about recurrence that at the very least we should tell someone else, get their reaction, just in case. But Molly didn't want that, she insisted; she felt embarrassed to have been fooled, and it hurt to have to revisit the trauma in front of others. She stiffened when I told her I felt I at least needed to share the story with a trusted friend—for my anxiety if not her own. I was losing sleep again, imagining people bursting through her door during the night, tracing her paths, kidnapping her, and even worse. I started worrying about her while out at work or other public places too, anticipating at any time for the unforeseen to strike again, paranoid in a way I hadn't been since I was little, imagining ghosts out in the hall outside my room or in the yard. Even random wrong numbers and text messages suddenly felt like cryptic threats, misreading abstract signals darkly, and anxious when a message from Molly went too long without reply. Finally, despite her hesitation toward it, I brought up the story to two of my oldest friends one night over at their house, and Molly sat there stock-still, hardly blinking as I recounted the details, nodding when I tried to cue her to say more and adding tight-lipped to the story as my friends offered their thoughts. She saved her admonishment of me for the drive home, drunk in my car. This was *her* experience, not mine; and anyway, women put up with shit all the time, it's how the world is—so now you see. How could I argue against that? No matter what I meant, she knew how to remind of my place in the exchange, and all I really wanted was to know that she was safe. She'd be extra careful going forward, she reassured me, and would make sure to let me know where she was and how she felt. I took it as a good sign, at least, that she seemed able to pick right up and carry on. After a while, it was as if the incident had never happened, to be forgotten as just another fragment in the story of her struggle to survive, which we now shared.

———

So, had the story about the gunman been real or not? Had she been in actual danger or just manipulating me? It's impossible to ever know, much less to want to have the will to trace it out, despite the way my brain comes back over and again to moments like these, trying to make sense of who we were, how we had been. So many memories, almost all of them, feel altered or damaged in this way, after the fact; blurred out on both sides by features of forces Molly may or may not have been aware of, to some degree, at any time. To be clear: presenting this information in the context of it having any question of validity makes me feel ill. Despite whatever elements of Molly's projections and distortions I was aware of during her life, I never once thought of her as someone who might be so methodically controlling that I could ever come to second guess her presentation of the facts. At the same time, I find it hard to help it, given what happened, and what little of her I have left, and like any story, there's more to the story, even if without a complete picture, sometimes all we can do is try to guess.

———

"The cheater relies, fundamentally, on the honesty of everyone else," Molly wrote in *Bandit*, of her father.[8] Before I learned to see the way she worked her angles, I was aware of how she'd bend a story as she wished. This happened both in what seemed minor, mostly harmless ways and sometimes, especially in conflict or under stress, cruel distortions of our lives. Sometimes, standing right next to her in social settings, I'd hear her say things she and I both knew just weren't true—almost arbitrarily, without clear motivation. A lot of it was petty, normal nerves: she'd say she'd loved an album or a film I knew for sure she hadn't heard or seen; or she was a lock to be selected for a teaching job she'd just applied for and had great doubts of; or, more personally, that she'd loved a story I had written, but one there was no way she could have read, having not shared it— all "little white lies," really, in the long run, without any need to be called out; but still I noticed them. They added up, like little hiccups that didn't fit with how I would have thought she'd be. Happens to anybody, doesn't it? But I wanted to protect her from it somehow, avoid putting any further pressure on the part of her I knew already felt like an imposter, unable to more honestly relate. She didn't like when I even alluded to little quirks of hers like those, even in jest; would say I was mean or loved to make fun of her when asking up for clarification from confusion, when really I just wanted to understand

8   *Bandit*, p. 161.

her and feel close. Instead, I felt surprised how quickly she'd shut down from our regular playful banter, as on a mood swing I rarely could see coming, cold in a way that truly gave zero fucks for how I felt. When trouble brewed—I said something she saw as callous maybe, or I was running late, which meant I didn't respect her—she could go sarcastic, passive-aggressive, on a dime, prickly against any and all forms of recourse, including an apology, which to her also had parameters and rules. I would try to say I don't want to fight, can we please talk this out calmly together, listen to one another, and she would tell me to fuck off, then go and lock herself in the guest bedroom for the rest of the night. I learned quick that it was better to avoid pissing her off unless I was ready to have the hammer dropped, and I respected greatly what she thought, often more than I respected my own opinion. I'd been shocked when I suggested we watch Todd Solondz's *Happiness*, which she watched in total silence certain admittedly disturbing jokes I would have normally thought she'd understand. "Why the fuck did you just make me watch this?" she snapped, soon as the credits rolled after the film's controversial ending, a jocular, too-real critique of pedophilia, as I saw it. "What are you trying to tell me?" she wanted to know, all signs of her more reliable bleak sense of humor burned away in the wake of something that for once had gone too far, or too close to home. That same tone, too, in her reiterating the lyrics to Danny Brown's "Lie4" whenever it came up on shuffle in my car, "Yeah, Blake, what the fuck do you have to lie for?"—her eyes slitted at me like I'd put the song on to try to finally come clean to some big ruse behind it all. What made her turn against me like that, I wondered? What made her change as on a dime, suddenly unable to see herself, or changing the way she seemed to see me, based on assumptions? Strange for a person who otherwise seemed so shrewd and studied, having clearly put in a lot of thought on what she held true. What did it matter either way, these little bumps? Until it did matter, rapidly—as, other times, the snag in the story might be larger, impossible to overlook—how in a fight, thrown off her rails, she'd insist that I say all the time *how much I hate her, how I think she's trash*, that *I wish she was some other bitch*—words I would have never, ever uttered about her, no matter what. But once her walls went up, it didn't matter what I meant or wanted either way; the die was cast, the damage done. She'd felt the presence of *the terror* in her gut most all her life, a kind of blackened hold over the parts of her that registered logically the work of love, but couldn't trust it, or felt even greater fear in realizing it could once again be taken away. The cut in her was deep; so deep that sometimes it pushed her past the point of no return, and once it had, all bets were off.

I knew Molly had tried to kill herself before. She didn't like to speak about it much, except to describe how her first husband had found her lying with her wrists slit in the bathroom just in time; how the nurse who stitched her up had done so violently, to make her know she'd done wrong. I'm no longer certain if that's true, like so much else, or rather if it's how it felt to her, in how she refused to believe in finding help even while so clearly crying out for it. They say sometimes a failed attempt can inspire change, though if there were follow-ups thereafter, extended guidance, anything like ongoing support, it didn't seem to have compelled her. Instead, the story stood hacked off in the resigned silence of her sorrow—just another thing that'd happened, no big deal. She just hadn't really wanted to die that time, she'd flatly quip, because if you really want to kill yourself you don't do it by slitting wrists. Next time, she didn't quite say, she'd do it right. Well-aware of how much she'd lived through, I often interpreted her rigidness as fortitude, her resistance as experience, her morbid sense of humor as common sense. At the same time, though she never received a specific diagnosis—that I know of—in looking back after her death, it's hard not to read the DSM-5's description of the traits of borderline personality disorder and not find Molly there in every line:

1. Frantic efforts to avoid real or imagined abandonment.
2. A pattern of unstable and intense interpersonal relationships characterized by alternating between extremes of idealization and devaluation.
3. Identity disturbance: markedly and persistently unstable self-image or sense of self.
4. Impulsivity in at least two areas that are potentially self-damaging (e.g., spending, sex, substance abuse, reckless driving, binge eating).
5. Recurrent suicidal behavior, gestures, or threats, or self-mutilating behavior.
6. Affective instability due to a marked reactivity of mood (e.g., intense episodic dysphoria, irritability, or anxiety usually lasting a few hours and only rarely more than a few days).
7. Chronic feelings of emptiness.
8. Inappropriate, intense anger or difficulty controlling anger (e.g., frequent displays of temper, constant anger, recurrent physical fights).
9. Transient, stress-related paranoid ideation or severe dissociative symptoms.[9]

If any of this was at all on Molly's radar, it wasn't something that she shared. She'd been on anti-depressants at various phases in her life, though any discussion of that would quickly be silenced, wiped away as part of some other version of herself, at least to me. In the last year of her life, as she began in therapy to unpack the influence of

9 American Psychiatric Association. *Diagnostic and Statistical Manual of Mental Disorders*, 5th ed. American Psychiatic Publishing, 2013, p. 943.

her childhood on her mind, she'd wondered for a while, by her own assessment, if she might have bipolar like her mother. This would explain what seemed to be her mood swings, she imagined, her deep depressions, if in a way that only further filled her with regret; that, in the end, she was little more than a reflection of that damage, doomed to repeat her parents' programming, their multitudinous mistakes. No matter what she thought, however, none of it was enough to make her want to set the hammer down, accept a break—strong enough to lead herself to water, not strong enough to make herself drink.

When we first started dating, Molly hated drinking water unless it was scalding hot, for pleasure, insisting all the normal, cool kind would do is make her bloated. Only once we were married would she start drinking regular water, relegating the old way to a private joke we shared about how she could have ever been so stubborn.

When she would burn her arm on the oven while baking, Molly hardly flinched, nor did she care where the metal left a mark among the scratches from a pet. Harm to her body was a far cry to the pain already in her memory, I imagined; a way of playing with one's wounds that compared to darker options seemed just fine. She could kneel there staring endlessly into the oven, watching the process with all the patience of a stone. "Baking, for me, is not thinking," she'd tell the local paper. "It is a loss of self."[10]

10   Williams, Wyatt. "The Bandit's Daughter." *Atlanta Journal and Constitution*, 16 Oct. 2016, http://specials.myajc.com/molly-brodak/.

When Molly slept, she barely moved. She'd often wake up in the exact position she'd laid down in. Several times I had to check to make sure she was still breathing. When I told her, she repeated it back to me. "You had to make sure I was breathing," like it was something she'd return to later, alone, to see whether she wanted to interpret that in good faith—that I checked because I was worried, because I cared—or in bad—that no matter what anybody said, they'd be happier without her.

Molly relished eating junk. She'd show up with bags of snacks I'd never seen before, as if they'd been culled from some hidden world all hers. She loved indulging tacky brands with misspelled names and hokey copy and had sharp taste for which ones would be good. For our first Valentine's Day date, she'd insisted I take her to Golden Corral, partially a joke and partially because she liked to taste a little of a lot. "The first bite is the best bite," she'd say. "It's all downhill from there." Or as Agnes Martin put it, in one of few lines of *Writing*

marked up by Molly in the copy she'd kept out on her nightstand when we met: "The satisfaction of appetite is frustrating / So it's always better to be a little bit hungry."[11] She rarely finished a full plate, taking a disciplinarian offense when food got cold, a vital sign of lack of care. At group dinners, no matter who else was there, she'd sit down and dig right in, and I couldn't tell if she didn't realize this was conventionally bad manners, or if she simply didn't give a damn. Either way, I liked the punk in her, the part who couldn't help but ignore or spit back at any custom, though sometimes, in public, I'd steel myself for kickback when she snapped at people she perceived as being rude—at once unafraid to speak her mind, and at the same time, holding in so tight she'd barely breathe.

———

Not long after our worries about the gunman flattened out and Molly returned to her apartment, she called to let me know she'd missed her period. She'd just switched birth control meds and wondered if there'd been a fertile window in the crossing, as it'd already been a week, unprecedented for her. An over-the-counter test had come back positive, though she wanted to see a doctor to confirm. It might just be another effect from her brain tumor, she explained by email, caused by the "weird hormones" her body would manufacture in distress, though of course that sounded even worse. Either way, we'd already agreed we had no interest in being parents, Molly even more so than myself. What kind of fool would choose to bring life into this world where no one cares? Where God is nothing more than a cruel prank on all mankind? It was the most selfish thing in the whole world to make a baby, I'd seen her rant online, pissing off friends, and worse, to insist it had to have your DNA when there were already so many people starving and needing love, not to mention the massive

11   Martin, Agnes. *Writings*, edited by Dieter Schwarz, Hatje Cantz Publishers, 2005, p. 36.

carbon footprint of a person. Besides all that, she couldn't stand the idea of another life inside her. She was certain she would make a horrible mom. All this made logical sense to me, if clearly also rather affected in a way I felt I understood—why would someone who'd felt they'd never had a childhood want to force another through the same? Either way, I felt relieved to not be forced into parenthood without a choice. Almost blindly since sixteen, I'd made my mind up that writing was my life, and having children, especially at age 30, while working mostly freelance for a living, could only make life impossible, less my own. The last thing either of us needed right now, no matter how you sliced it, was a baby to look after; it'd ruin our lives, likewise the child's. Somewhere in the back of my mind, if I was being honest, I wondered what would happen if I fell in love with someone who really wanted kids, but Molly's choice, and therefore mine, was crystal clear. She didn't want me to go to see the doctor with her—not necessary—and after her check-up, when the official results confirmed our qualms, she headed straight on to fill her prescription for the pill. She wanted to take it that night by herself, too, no need for me there, and no further discussion. She said she'd text me when she took it, from in a bath where the blood would flood out from underneath her, as she described, filling the tub—a little sad, she said, but still the right thing. After that, we didn't talk about the abortion much at all. We agreed we felt relieved, if also shaken, ready more than anything to just move on. Our silences reinforced each other's in this way, matched on either end by jagged edges we hadn't quite figured out yet how to decipher as our own, which in turn became the standard for the ways we handled one another.

▬

The oldest of Molly's journals that I have is from the summer of 1992, when Molly is twelve. On the cover, a painting of a young girl in a white dress stands in a forest by herself. Inside, the text is wild, a collage of made-up song lyrics, formal poems, fragments of memory, transcribed dreams, strange doodles, and inside jokes. "My mother never loved me," she transcribes. "She lies to me. My father never knew me. He lies to me. I don't need a family. I have my tutors…" Her tutors, apparently, are boys, as on every page a different name appears, whole lists of names she prays will want her back, and maybe will be her "ticket outta here." Mostly, it seems, the guys are older, driving her around, taking her to concerts: Fugazi, NIN, Nirvana, Sunny Day Real Estate, Six Finger Satellite, Faith No More. She references dropping acid regularly, as well as dabbling in speed and pills and heroin, already describing drugs as one of the only reasons to live; the other: love, which often becomes violent, like when one of the guys burns her with a cigarette, it "reminded me of incense in the park…I want to live with him somewhere in a huge house with lots of plants and lots of pretty summer dresses. I want him to watch their comas with me. I feel his heart and I want to swim inside it. I want to be the only one he wants to be with and I want to kill his friends I know he cries and I want to kill his friends." Her handwriting becomes more manic, larger on certain pages: "Why won't you leave me alone please go away I don't want you anymore you scared me I can't tell anymore What did it go Where can I fall next Who else wants a shot at it And you never needed me why did it happen cleanse my mouth take it out If you really do leave I will be so empty Stay but go I will never know When I think about anyone else I start to cry get it out of my mouth stop it stop it stop it stop it stop it stop it." She mentions having a "disease" she can share with no one, "cause everyone's the same," and refers to her "dream of suicide" numerous times, often in lament of the death of her young idols, Kurt Cobain, Elliott Smith. She transcribes a story of her mother running away from home at age 15, walking 200 miles to a family cabin where Nora breaks in and slits her wrists, discovered at the edge of death by cops who take her to a mental hospital, where she remains for the next two years—the only story in the entire journal that contains a beginning, a middle, and an end. The rest remains as mostly fragments, colliding into one another, until by the end of the journal, there's language all over the place, written backwards or upside-down, crossed out and annotated like graffiti in a bathroom stall, or a page in a yearbook. "ASLEEP AWAKE ALIVE OR DEAD." "If EXPERIENCE is A JEWEL is INNOCENCE IGNORANCE?" "GOD WON'T LEAVE ME ALONE." "WOMEN SHOULD BE OBSCENE AND NOT HEARD." "DO YOU HEAR ME DAD?"

Molly, age 10, making a reading list:

Books I Hated:	Books I Liked:
Island of the Blue Dophlins	Hatchet
The Cay	The Secret Garden
The Littles	Golden Book of Fairy Tales
Indian in the Cupbard	Nature
Harriet the Spy	
Babysiters Clubs	
Box car Children	
Are You There God Its Me Margret	
American Girl Molly	
Across Five Aprils	
Sarah Plan and Tall	
Jacob Have I loved	
The BFG	
Diceys Song	
Charlots Web	

The Giver
Number the Stars
Sweet Valley Highs
A Wrinkle in Time
Girl with Silver Eyes
Where the Red Fern Grows
Bridge to Terabitha
Tuck Everlasting
Wicht of Blackbird Pond
The Great Brain

▬▬▬

"Childhood is work but underwater," Molly wrote in her poem "Post Glacier." "It means *without tools*." Her father was a ghoul, yes, the #1 disaster, or at least the easiest to explain using pure facts. Her mother's presence, however—especially given their attempts at continuing to maintain a healthy mother-daughter relationship—remained unmoored, spanning so much time so close up that Molly seemed unable to separate it from herself. In a certain way, she writes about it at length in *Bandit*, describing the strings of days she spent alone in her mom's apartment after her parents' divorce, left to find her own way to school and back, make her own meals, fill her own time. "I put food out for farries but it is still here today," she'd scribbled in her grade school notebook, alongside precious drawings of unicorns and butterflies, notes of hope for something good to happen someday soon. Hard not to compare this to my own experience of growing up: how every tooth I lost promised gold glitter and a silver dollar under my pillow; how my mother treasured my every whim. "I never cut myself," Molly writes as an adult, "but I did sometimes pound my skin really hard with a hammer until it bruised. I loved bruises, they seemed so romantic and beautiful. My room...had a walk-in closet and I dragged my small mattress into the closet and slept in there. I covered the walls of it with collaged pictures from magazines and things I drew, just abstract stuff, no people." Sometimes, when Nora did come home, according to Molly, she'd bring her social work clients along with her, or drunk guys she'd been picked up by at a bar—strange, creepy men that even preteen Molly understood were bad news. She'd witnessed her mother having violent sex numerous times, she let me know, out in the open in their living room, unable to do anything but sit and listen. Sometimes those men would still be there in the morning, too, hanging around after Nora left for work, no one there to oversee what went on. Nothing physical had ever happened to her, so as she told it, though there seemed to be a haze around the way the stories tapered off, clung to their limits of what could be said. It felt to me like there was an even greater violence just underneath them, pushed aside to try to overcome them or outrun them, despite how impossible this would seem to be for any rational person. "Probably you were abused when you were little and can't remember," she suggested several times when I got upset in a way I couldn't iterate, as if offering some sort of bridge between us, sight unseen. I didn't think so, but even the suggestion gave me pause, suddenly inspired to revisit certain junctures where my memory's vision harbored perplexity, long since gone blurred. What I remembered seemed to change sometimes depending on my mood, things I'd read recently, or with foresight gained through the discontinuous experience of inner life. Either way, it remained obvious that these experiences made an immense impression on how Molly understood her mother, which very often, also transposed directly onto herself. "I saw my mom in hospital beds so many times," *Bandit* explains, "pulled back from a death she thought she wanted over and over—I can't say how many times she attempted suicide while I was in high school. She used to joke about it, say at night she hoped maybe this time she'd 'wake up dead,' and I would laugh with her, a little... She felt awful about it, and about me and my sister seeing her, but she'd smile. Charcoal pumped into her stomach after an overdose attempt would catch in her teeth; I'd see it when she smiled and talked. Many times I saw this."[12] As an adult—one willing and able to share such intimacy with a reader, if not quite to integrate it into her own life—Molly said she wasn't sure why her mother had felt it necessary to always share her struggles so intensely, treating her most often like a friend more than a child, good for the gossip. This pattern had continued with the two of them into adulthood, including weekly phone calls that Molly would often come out of exasperated, feeling unheard but mostly unwilling to say so, leaving Nora in a sort of lurch that as a person who knew how Molly was, I felt both protective of her over, and also wishful that they could ever find a way to come to better terms. She wanted to love her mother, admired her fortitude and strength of will, and she cherished the happy memories they did have, but she also felt conflicted over her exposure and neglect, resigned to the mercy of Nora's whims. I understood why she didn't want to speak up, already assuming that it would at once beget no change, and rather instead create further disillusion, bending toward breaking the only straw of hope she had of ever feeling part of her own family. "In my mind I'd made her into a total naïve victim of dad and of circumstances," Molly writes of reading her mother's diary from Molly's toddler years, which Nora had sent her one day in the mail, out of the blue. "But really she was wild. Thrill-seeking. Building herself out on her precarious edges. Seems very pleased with her own recklessness, which surprised me. I probably would have written a different book if I had seen this diary sooner, which is maybe why she didn't give it to me sooner." Reading through the diary myself, it's hard to imagine what would have motivated Nora to share it with Molly—full of manic diatribes and desperation, including long lists of all the men in Nora's life,

12 *Bandit*, p. 141-142.

ranked and annotated by the amount of attention that they feed her, which one she might see next and when. The only mention of her daughters I could locate, before I had to force myself to put it down, is as a liability: who goes where when, including a brief confession of her inability to connect with baby Molly in particular, written in a tone that made it sound like this must be Molly's fault, flawed at her core. Within the context of any understanding I can glean of what it must have felt to grow up in Molly's shoes, it feels like a miracle she survived long as she did, and even more so, how rich her soul was, how hungry to shine.

———

In Molly's *New York Times Book Review* review of Leah Carroll's *Down City*, a memoir she'd been solicited to cover based on their biographical similarities growing up with troubled parents, she cites Alain de Botton: "It seems we cannot spontaneously feel important enough to ourselves, sufficiently worthy of carrying our absurd figure through the tangles of life, unless at some point…we were privileged enough to derive a sense of mattering limitlessly and inordinately to another person."[13] I remember feeling caught off guard by the review's tone once in print, having heard her talk flippantly about the book in a way that made me wonder if it hit too close to home. "Ultimately, Carroll untangles her identity from her parents'," Molly concludes, pointing out how the author's eventual ability to separate her own existence from her mother's "offers closure and inspires a pledge to ensure her mother's life—and her father's life—mattered deeply, and are redeemed by Carroll's compassionate reflection on their lives." The word my eye sticks on today, borrowed as a quote, is *privilege*; as in, the privilege of not having to survive what's forced upon you, spared of the work required of the abused in readjusting to their own

13   Brodak, Molly. "Home After Dark." *New York Times Book Review*, 2 April 2017.

life, especially the young, who've yet to begin to learn to think of larger faculties like justice, forgiveness, God. Anyone who didn't hate their childhood, as Molly saw it, as through clenched teeth, must either be a glutton or a fool, and therefore unable to relate to those unlike her, much less to love her, and maybe most of all those close enough to cause new harm. It really did feel like a privilege, in comparison, to not have had to grow up as she had, without a proper model to learn to cope. Comparing traumas bore little sense outside the actual experience, though it did seem to explain, at least in part, her endless rage, drawn like a veil over her head without a drawstring. Even if she never figured out how to forgive herself for who she was, I held out hope that her apparent awareness of it, her will to shine, might someday tip the balance back her way; that she might accept me standing steadfast at her side not as a brat who'd gotten lucky, but as an ally who wanted more than anything to pay it back.

No matter who and how much Molly scorned, there was one person who she recognized as worth it: her grandpa, Paul Brown, of whom she wrote, "He saved my life, he gave me books, he talked to me about the universe, he took care of my soul in a way no one else did." Paul had filled in for her father in that way, showing up in Molly's young life right when she needed him the most. Few things filled her with such clear reverence, tethered directly to something certain, like a home. I could see how much he loved her, too; how his face would light up when she came into the room, asking her questions about her work and life and feelings; how he'd hang on her every word, sometimes offering advice from his experience, other times just watching her, taking it in. He'd read *Bandit* many times, both as a book and as a manuscript; would call her up to talk about her choices in the prose, what it made him think of, what he hoped for her and her ambition, sometimes to the point that Molly began to wish he'd let it go. He seemed to like me, too, I thought, excited to turn most any conversation, after catching up, to philosophy and science. Was I subscribed to Kurtzweil's listserv? he wished to know, soon as we met. Had we seen *Ex-Machina* yet, and if not, would we take him? Very clearly, I could see Paul's vast impression on who Molly was; how, without him, she might not have even made it through the first half of her lif—a single human presence, among billions, lending another's life shape by making her too-short time on Earth feel *possible*, through an embodiment of *home*.

———

One afternoon, from what seemed out of nowhere, Molly offered me a gift—a tiny, battered pale blue on dark blue patterned Avon box with a gold bottom and two textured stickers of fluffy cats with long whiskers stuck to the lid. Inside, a tuft of stuffing on which sat two ivory dice small as the tip of a pinkie. She had carried this box around with her since a young girl—she wasn't sure why; she didn't keep a lot of stuff. Now, she wanted me to have it. It felt like being let into a dim gray room with many doors, behind most of which I still had no idea besides the smallest sounds that might leak through—a hum of bees, maybe; the silent glint of sunlight against some sea; the low, slow beating of a heart; a little signal sent from somewhere secret laced inside her, just a girl. Sometimes when I'm uncertain what to do, I take the dice out and roll them, read the numbers. Just now: 2, 1. I find I feel some simple comfort in the surprise of never quite knowing what it might mean, far beyond the limits of what I might imagine I do know.

Another day, she presented a watercolor she said she'd painted to represent the way she felt about me:

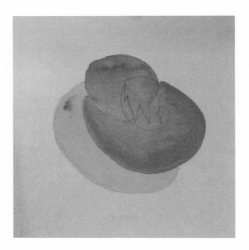

At once, this image hurt and warmed my soul. I felt her reaching out beyond her edges, uncertain how to open up but wanting to. I could see her in the blushing flush of orange, like a warm bruise breaking through the terrifying yellow of the parts of her she'd learned to hide behind, wishing for once for something more but uncertain how to act or what to say. Or maybe the yellow was holding up the blue from underneath it, too, I thought, at once a shield and a new mask, the lighter layers each at the mercy of the attention of the stone-shaped gray face, made of cancer, having latched on to feed, to take. It felt so helpless, a petri slide in stasis, some dark cartoon of human fear, somehow tender in its helplessness, its latent wanting amid being eaten half-alive. It all washed over me, an abstract image that seemed to mean as much from just its gesture as anything the image might describe. Either way, Molly had nothing else to say about it, shared with a glint touched in her eyes. I took the painting and placed it on the black shelf in my office with the many letters she'd already given me throughout the years, a swelling trove. When feeling lost or lonely, I might go and slip the picture out, stare into it, wondering what it might wish that I would know to do. Against my better intuition, I'd sometimes scour through her poetry in private in that same mind, trying to locate some solution to her cryptic lyrical code. "As a thief I wasn't wasted," concludes "Post Glacier." "As a cheat I wasn't wasted. As a liar I was wasted least of all." A thief, a cheat, a liar? Well, who isn't? Wasn't this just in part and parcel with all the rest of her extreme ideals? I loved her all the more for this—for peering deep, refusing easy answers, seeking mythos where few would will to go—certain that the only real solution to the poem is the poem.

———

"Love someone back," Molly wrote in "Hopes Up," which I read the first day I realized I already loved her and always would. "You just begin." So I began.

Love in return did not require much, Molly admitted. She called herself an easy sell, charmed by surprises—*anything to show I was on your mind*. I knew this didn't mean she didn't crave attention, but rather that she'd gotten so accustomed to disappointment that anything at all was at least a start. Small things really did go a long way with her—over the moon to just be held, to receive flowers, to hear her name soft in her ear. She'd light up so much when I'd leave her notes, a letter or poem on a slip of paper where she could find it in the morning when she woke. She'd keep them with her in her purse, or as a bookmark, before collecting them into a stack in her desk drawer, spanning the years, though if we had gotten in a fight the night before, I might find them in the trash. "Sometimes I start to think close friends or relatives are actually evil," she'd written to me in an email early on. "Everything they say and do I start to read with bad intentions and it gets horrible. It's like the instincts I have about people can be like amplified and distorted and confusing. I have always had this but it's getting worse." I took it as a challenge, maybe, a chance to prove she deserved more, though it also made me feel self-conscious, anxious about our tensions and our hopes both, wondering what she'd judge and wouldn't say. She'd known her prior marriage had been doomed while up on the altar at their wedding, she admitted, after he'd put her hand on her neck in a way she didn't like when he went to kiss her; that's all it took—a single simple misplaced gesture she'd never shared with him directly, held in silence. "I'm afraid I'm going to do something you don't like and never know it, too," I tried to tell her, but no need to worry, she reassured me—I was different; *we* were different.

━━━

To prove this dedication, Molly wanted us to get married right away. She'd poke at me for not already having asked, texting me her ring size just in case. "What's wrong with me?" she'd wonder aloud out on a date. "Am I not good enough?" She'd known what she wanted the very first time that she saw me, she admitted, at that reading, as a stranger in a crowd, across the room; could tell right then and there that if she could find a way in past my defenses, to my core, she'd be safe forever. She didn't like when I suggested I'd like us to live together for a while before a marriage. *I* was the one who might be a challenge for *her* to live with, I tried to tell her, too well-aware of all my tics and habits that'd worn down on us the last time I lived with someone: how I talk to myself throughout the day, singing and babbling both in good moods and in bad; how stolid I could be about my work time, hating to be spoken to when "in the zone"; how particular I could get about the arrangement of minute details of how a day went while also short-fused and seeing red when almost anything unexpectedly went wrong, shrieking at myself for knocking over a glass of water or any other such minor mistake. I felt immature compared to her and not quite ready to trade in my single-minded life for something larger, while simultaneously, I recognized I didn't want to make the same mistakes again and needed time to trust myself to do it right. Molly took what I said as "kicking her tires," trying to test her. My pragmatism was an affront, somehow, a dam against her drive to hurry forward into the next phase of our lives, wanting instead to be so overcome with love that we couldn't stand to be apart. She understood I wouldn't leave Atlanta, both with my dad sick and my mother struggling; not to mention the thirty years of friends I had from having stayed in the same area my whole life, unlike her, who'd moved so many times she hardly felt she had much of a past. Likewise, I understood that she was nervous about her fellowship at Emory reaching its end. She'd dreamed of being a poetry professor, having an office, a place she felt that she belonged, and though there were a handful of universities nearby, staying with me would set a limit on her path. I felt forced to be a letdown in that way, frozen in place between a past and future, unable to imagine starting over somewhere else. Life, by definition, had to hurt one way or another, its unforeseen shadow looming large over the whole field like a permanent eclipse, one you have no choice but to keep encroaching forward under, in the dark.

━━━

Amidst that dark, my father passed. Throughout the last weeks of his life, he'd been bedridden, sleeping in a cot at the foot of my parents' poster bed. In the late stages of Alzheimer's, he was no longer able to eat, and so I'd watched his body deteriorate in rapid fashion, slowly but surely losing his body's outline as a man. Behind his eyes, I felt I could detect the blinking pulse of that past person, as if stranded deep inside himself, mostly unable to make a word. Instead, he sucked at the wind, his breath so loud it felt like scraping. I thought a lot about smothering him, to put him out of his misery, and ours, forced to wonder what made a life worth living. Occasionally he'd break a smile, for just a second, as if there were something secret yet to be found; like how, before he'd lost his ability to speak during his last year, he'd asked my mother many times to marry him, all recognition of the 44 years they'd spent together disappeared behind a haze. I told myself I felt relieved that it was over, that his long struggle with his disease no longer held its reign over his soul; at the same time, I'd only just begun to feel like a man myself, mature enough to want to know him better, to learn, whereas throughout my teens and 20s, I'd mostly bucked his advice, refusing to let him show me how to shave. I'd just begun to comprehend him when he talked about his younger life, the two failed and very brief marriages he'd had before my mom, both of which had ended poorly, catching them cheating on him in their home; how he'd known when he met my mom she was the answer; how they'd gotten married after only knowing each other a couple weeks. I could have really used his advice, his direction; and now, instead, I'd had to watch him develop backwards, wholly helpless, no longer certain of my name. He'd gotten to meet Molly, at least, and in her seen my future, though by then he'd already lost the ability to remember who was who. Strange to think now of him grinning, shaking her hand, saying "nice to meet you" in the funny cartoon voice he'd use to introduce himself, a showman even then, just like myself. Molly seemed to know just what to do, too, there in my childhood kitchen, just after having watched his covered body carried out the back door on a stretcher—she baked us cookies, from her own recipe, by heart.

———

My mom told me she knew she loved Molly because of her laugh.

She said that you could tell when Molly laughed, she really meant it. It seemed to sparkle and refract, spilling up from some gem-studded center locked within her. I can hear it anytime I try. Making her laugh made me feel alive, like I'd really accomplished something. She still wanted to laugh, I think, despite a widening parcel in her telling her that laughter in a world like ours was for fools. When I think the sound of it now, it reminds me of a bird trapped in a ballroom, looking for anywhere to land.

———

Wanting company, Molly adopted a kitten. She'd never gotten over losing her previous cat, Beans, who been her best friend for many years. Despite my intense allergy, I loved watching them play, a true source of endless innocent joy for someone who allowed herself any. A few weeks later, she found the kitten curled up under her bed, dead of a heart arrhythmia, and of course she took it hard, calling it her fault. She'd probably never have another pet now, she insisted—too much pain to grow attached to something so fragile. I sensed she didn't really mean this, though; how could she? I decided for her birthday I'd buy her all new cat supplies and take her to pick out a friend, which she seemed over the moon for when the day came. She named the new cat Jupiter, a sleek, dark gray creature that immediately reminded me of her. Everything was wonderful until it turned out I was more allergic to this cat than others, barely able to breathe around her after a couple hours in the same room. This inadvertently led to tension, which led to arguments in which Molly called me cruel for having forced her hand. "You either (1) did not think we would ever live together, which sucks," she emailed early one morning, "or (2) did not care about my feelings when I'd be forced to get rid of it, which sucks… This is a perfect example of why I say you have little respect for me. Because this situation shows how you obviously think your feelings are more important than mine on every level." I took her point—I hadn't thought it through like that, had acted rashly, though I also hadn't foreseen how what I'd meant to be a sweet thing could blow up so completely in my face. I wondered why she had to pick the most aggressive way to set me straight, why we couldn't work together. What an asshole I must be, I began thinking even as I felt her wrath veered far too quickly out of bounds. "Honestly I try to help you because you seem like you need help most of the time, like you don't have a lot of strength to handle normal life," her email closes, "so I find myself often stepping back on what I want for your sake, but now we have another living creature involved and it's not fair." I'm sure I groused at that, certain I'd done nothing wrong despite her anger, as if no matter what I did the world was out to grind my guts and nothing else, all personal culpability denied as mere bad luck. In the end, we'd ended up with little choice but to return Jupiter to the shelter, a trying scene that Molly continued to hold against me for some time, to which the only response, having endlessly apologized and meant it, was deference.

___

Instead of rushing to get married, we got a loan and bought a house in Ormewood Park, one of the oldest neighborhoods in downtown Atlanta, just barely spared from Sherman's burning during the Civil War. Across from our porch sat the Georgia Department of Public Safety, its high-fenced and barbed wire grounds featuring archaic dead artillery left out aimed ceaselessly straight at the sky, a total eyesore, not that we minded, given how lucky we felt to find such a nice place we could afford. In the early 1900s the area had hosted an asylum, Molly discovered, a presence long since covered over by admin buildings for state police. What else might have gone on right there beneath our noses, she liked to wonder, long since forgotten?

There was enough ambient noise, though, to bring most any mind back to the present, given both the busy through road and local bus stop on the corner, leading to fevered bouts of shouting late at night, and sometimes gunshots. Our neighbors on both sides had big dogs, too, who barked and barked at almost anything, which made the backyard often feel tense, especially given Molly's longstanding fear of them after having been bitten as a child. The previous owners had left behind their chicken coop for us, along with two pet chickens, an unforeseen boon of pet-based compromise given that I was allergic to cats, Molly's true love. We named the Welsummer hen Sheed after her hometown Pistons hero, Rasheed Wallace, and the Polish hen Watermane, a joke that stuck, and quickly found ourselves enamored with the task of taking care of something other than ourselves. Our yard was large, though, in need of continuous upkeep, work neither of us wished too much to do. We planned to plant a garden, at least, already growing over; in time, the risen beds left by the prior owners would be nearly unrecognizable, so full of weeds grown high it was hard to tell them from real plants. Twice, I pulled up by the roots new saplings Molly had just installed, believing I was doing something right finally, tidying up, and though I expected Molly to blow up at me, she only shook her head and grinned. She knew me well enough already not to be surprised, and kind of happily resigned, too, that this was just another part of our shared life: that sometimes your big lug husband comes in behind you and rips up the pretty tree. To avoid this reoccurring, she'd plant the next one—a peach sapling she'd recovered while on a walk—square in the middle of our front yard, free and clear from all confusion. As spring arrived, she'd become incensed to find the squirrels would steal the budding fruit before it ripened, robbing her of victory—if not me, a man, then some dumb animal. To this, Molly responded by completely encasing the tiny tree with wire netting before it bloomed. "Those motherfuckers," she'd rant to herself with true animosity, adding on threats to set up with a BB gun, just as her father had when she was little, picking off pests in their backyard—the one time I remember her saying anything so violent about an animal of any kind, as if it were more like Joe there speaking through her.

As for the human neighbors, neither of us much were in the mood for making friends. We preferred instead to keep our heads down, stick to our work, busy moving in. One of Molly's first orders of business was to change the knobs on every door, replacing the dingy brass ones with hand-crafted crystal bulbs that fit more strangely in the hand. She had a vision of exactly the kind of place she'd wished to live, and I was thankful to get to help her make it come to life, with little idea of my own on how things should look or what was good. This gave Molly total freedom, as she preferred it, mostly, if also ready to accuse me of not doing my part when she felt stressed. Above our bed, she hung an arcane coat of arms bearing the inscription "Ex tenebris lux" ("From darkness, light"), and in the hallway to the kitchen her growing collection of "dark Garfield" cross-stitches, including a deformed Garfield with a syringe several times his size; in the kitchen, a pastel portrait of a folksy couple in the midst of flirting, which we would use for the invitations to our wedding; in the guest bathroom, she pinned a Robert Bly quote to the wall with one line circled, "Think in ways you've never thought before"; in the guest bedroom, above the bed where she would write, she hung a portrait she'd hand-painted of a pale blue sky obscured by diffuse clouds, inviting calmness. For the most part, I hesitated to hang up my own stuff, suddenly aware of how bachelor it all was, grateful for her better taste. We both had so many books there was hardly room to fit them all in, stacked up in shelves in every room. I loved to spend time picking through her collection—almost entirely poetry, nonfiction, and classics—getting a different kind of glimpse of her from seeing what rare pages she dog-eared, how she arranged them side by side. All in all, it felt like freedom to have our own space together, free of at least one strand of past uncertainty; a perfect landmark for the new horizon, all our own.

"If there were ever a gun in this house," Molly warned me sometime shortly moving in together, "I'd end up using it on myself." She said this flatly, knowing its fact the way another might know their age. I didn't like the way she said it, but also knew her sense of gallows humor—so natural it somehow felt more honest to admit it right up front. It was more so the unspoken and unknown that we should fear, the sort of monster that looms largest without reveal. Giving it a name, even phrased as an aside, provided grounds on which we could stand clear, learn to proceed, and I assumed that Molly felt similarly, given our shared proclivity for facing darkness through our art. Otherwise, there was often zero floor to Molly's loathing, aimed most of all straight at herself. "Imposter syndrome," she'd sometimes call it, when in a better mood, one step removed, and therefore able to turn the tables for just a second on her ire. This and other self-aware admissions like it, beyond the vortex that more often ran the show, would quickly become bitter logs laid into fire when her logic-based attributions fell apart and sent her right back to being stranded in her trauma-ridden baseline for "the truth": that she was irredeemable, a fraud; cut from the same cloth, some twisted part of her insisted, as her father, and at the same time, unworthy even of the grace she'd offered him. "I can't have imposter syndrome because I am aware that I'm an imposter," she writes in her journal, always ready to fire back at any logic of relief. "They just don't know me," she'd explain in response to any praise, admonishing herself after the fact for even wishing it were true. "If they actually knew me, they wouldn't say that." As for me, her partner, trying to offer a positive opinion would only serve to turn her trust against me too, yet another fool who doesn't know what they're talking about. No matter how well something might go, it always failed to resemble what it should've been, and therefore no one could label her anything she didn't know. She'd simply gotten lucky early on, she insisted, when her master's thesis, *A Little Middle of the Night*, won the Iowa Poetry Prize right out of school, on her first attempt at publication. Her husband, Matt, had found her out in their backyard that afternoon, fresh off the phone, hitting herself in the head with a hammer over and over, crying and shrieking at the sky. The fact they'd chosen *her* meant that the prize was worthless, the judges morons, one big sham. "No one is special," she'd remind me many times throughout the years, as if it weren't only her opinion, but hard truth. "No one *deserves* anything."

Sometimes Molly seemed to become someone else. The shape behind her face would change, as if the familiar part of who she really was evacuated, taking with it all possibility of compassion. The light behind her eyes would become glassy, boxing the both of us out from civil interaction, as in a fugue. "The Other Molly," I began referring to it, if only mostly in my mind, unable how else to frame her ruthlessness, unexpectedly extreme without clear cause. If I tried to point it out to her, to roll the tide back and calm down, it was like she couldn't hear me, stuck in neutral, the insults pouring out like black exhaust: *You're the most selfish person I've ever met. I wish you'd go away forever.* It hurt to hear her twist us up like that, and I knew she knew it hurt, too, at least in part. She knew I had a childhood fear of being punished for something I didn't do, connected directly to a memory of a day my Mom accused me of stealing a beer when I was young—*a friend and I were playing behind the bar in my father's den, and my friend had opened the fridge, playing around, which I realized made a sound like we were snooping, and then we went outside through the side door from there, a door we didn't usually use, and as we ran out, I remember thinking I hope Mom doesn't think we took a beer, because I was scared of what that meant—that I was bad—and then we went to hide around the corner of the house, my friend unaware of my concern until I heard my mom calling my name across the yard, wanting to know exactly what was going on.* For some reason, being asked, "Blake, did you take a beer?" terrified me more than anything I could imagine, like it meant that my mother wouldn't love me if I had, that I'd have been a letdown, ready for military school, which I'd overheard them talking about one night after they'd thought I'd gone to bed. Molly, of all people, understood what it meant to be haunted in this manner, and to feel accused, judged without a hearing, probably in far more intense ways than my own. She knew most of all what it felt like to have compassion withheld until she couldn't tell the fire from its roar, and yet unnecessary friction seemed to turn to fire out of nowhere just like that, unavoidable no matter how hard I tried to keep an even keel or what I did to try to bridge the gap. One day, she made up her mind to replace our dishwasher in sudden frustration, storming into my office to let me know she was heading to Lowe's immediately to open a new credit card and pick one out. She interpreted my suggestion that we do some research and make a concerted plan as obvious insult, meant to demean her, and drove off in a rage right after that, leaving me to stew in my own juices, unresponsive to calls or texts. Another time she came out screaming at me for using a hose to put out the fire in the yard where she'd been burning leaves, despite the wide piles of dead leaves and the nearby canister of kerosene attached to the grill. She said the fire would go out on its own, and I was a humongous asshole for assuming she didn't know what she was doing, furious when I laughed in incredulity, uncertain how I was supposed to be able to read her mind. Today, I think she was so used to not feeling seen that being seen hurt as much as not being; that my intervention served as a comment on the good times she'd had in going camping with her mother as a child, one of few such childhood memories that remained precious to her, actually real. Either way, once I'd set her off she'd make herself unreachable for hours after, without any hope of deeper discussion, which all but guaranteed I wouldn't sleep. Instead, I'd sit up in the living room and wait for her to come around, pissed at myself for having screwed things up again. In my dejection, I might try to offer peace by making her a cup of tea or apologizing through the locked guest bedroom door, which admittedly turned into banging on it, demanding that she let me in and hear me out. Rather than compromise, she'd get even more mad if she thought I was badgering her or pouting in a way that stole the spotlight. Sometimes she'd be gone, too, in the morning before I rose, as if to hammer home her point, spending the whole day away, or she might write me an extensive email about how intolerably selfish I'd been, unpacking vast networks of evidence she'd been archiving to explain precisely why and how I'd hurt her, both in the present and the past. After a while, I learned to give up pushing back and let her have her isolation, which might then linger as a grudge, each of us holding fast to stubborn predilections because we could. Given enough rope, I'd learn to convince myself that most of the time when we were disagreeing, Molly was right, and I was wrong—should have known the dishwasher was outdated and therefore taken care of it sooner; should have known she had the fire under control. In the meantime, she preferred to let me wrestle with her silence out of context and come to the correct conclusions on my own, explaining that it was labor for her to have to tell me how to act—I should just know. She didn't mind reminding me she thought she'd end up a cat lady someday; that she'd be just fine, so much more productive, living alone. I began to worry, unabated, that one day I'd return home and find her gone, having up and left without a warning, no last words. Up late on my own, I'd check the locks on the doors over and over before bed, paranoid for no good reason about home invasion, letting my worst imagination run amok as I had when very young. I'd inherited my knack for doting and fretting from my mother and her mother, so it seemed, and both had ended up sick with dementia by the end, an additionally potential hereditary fate made worse by my ongoing anxiety and insomnia. "Those things will never happen, BB," Molly would reassure me when I told her of my fears. "I wish you wouldn't worry." Were it me, though, trying to allay her by that same sense, she'd cut her eyes and pull away. "Don't say everything is going to be okay," she'd nearly snarl, "because it isn't."

——

But why couldn't it be? I often wondered, knowing very well how ruthlessly impossible life could feel, beyond control. I still had hope, somehow, or at least tried to, believing that no matter what bad things came about, we'd find a way to carry on. Why did Molly have to be so heavy-handed, so dismissive? What was I supposed to say or do so she'd believe me?

━━━

I proposed to Molly on our back porch. I lighted hundreds of candles that lined the yard and down the concrete stoop out front, put on a suit and sat out waiting for her to return home from class. I'd been planning this for several months now, having kept the ring hidden in anticipation for our dating anniversary to come around, the perfect day. Molly was late, stuck in bad traffic, and the wind kept blowing out random wicks, making me chase them with a flame to keep it perfect. In spite of this, I felt a long, deep calm pressed just behind that, like an unseen hand over the land, too heavy to know how to pet it right. The sky above like one wide plate, purple in my memory, and on the cusp of turning over into deep night. Molly said she knew something was up when, upon arriving home, she took my arm to follow me through the house and could feel my heartbeat through my chest, incredibly nervous despite that I had zero doubt she'd say yes, since she'd already told me exactly what ring she wanted and where to get it, long enough ago now I felt certain it would finally come as a surprise. On our back porch, within the low light, I got down on one knee and told her that she was the love of my life, my dearest friend, from whom I wished to never be apart. I could already read it in her face, the way she reeled and glowed there. Our bodies buzzed; we drank champagne, toasting to the future, then went to dinner, then, in celebration, of the new beginning of our lives. Afterwards, driving back home, we continued right on past our house, not finished yet listening to music we both loved, singing along, dancing in our seats, giddy, alive.

Our daily homelife as a couple—despite the hard times—was full of joy. We loved to jaunt around and make up dances, speaking in coded inside jokes that spanned the years. When in a light mood, Molly could be a super goofball, excited by extreme sarcasm and hearty camp, if often quickly underlined by her running baseline of feeling jaded, or as she might frame it: realistic. "The devil is in the details," announced a cross-stitch that she'd bought from a friend online and hung up in the breakfast nook where she sat alone, before I woke, and ate her frozen breakfast burrito with black coffee every morning. By the time I got up, she'd often already be gone, away to class or to run her errands, the hour's drive to Cake Art she made twice a month at least to buy supplies, or to the mall, where she loved to walk around and people-watch. We loved to go to the mall together, too, and wander for hours taking it all in, browsing through aisles without any motive to buy, more so looking forward to the comfort of the food court, where we'd both hung out sometimes as teens, or sitting out at the valet area eating ice cream and laughing at the rich bros handing off their sportscars, searching for famous athletes like the Hawks backup point guard Dennis Schröder, who we loved to tease from afar and always seemed to be there at the same time we were. We could find a good time almost anywhere, just wandering around, among the weather-beaten graves at Oakland Cemetery, or wandering through bookstores, where Molly always tended to the aisles of poetry and history and science while I chased fiction. Our tastes could be so different, which we agreed to be an asset, halves of a whole, and even more meaningful in the way we'd come together, often each uncanny in their own way, like the year we dressed up as the Insane Clown Posse for Halloween, taking turns painting our faces in the mirror together, cracking up, giddy as kids. Another year, we left the plastic skeleton Molly had brought home for decoration on the porch swing straight through the next summer, pleased when a delivery person would point it out. We must have watched *The Shining* a hundred times together, including the very first night we moved in together, thinking of it as a comfort movie, full of lines we worked into our own strange elaborations of rapport.

Primarily, however, during working hours, we each respected the other's time to work and shared a vision of devoting our lives to making art. While my pursuit was mostly always writing, glued to my desk, Molly had two modes: writing and baking, the latter of which she began focusing her attention onto more and more as frustrations with the former spurned her drive. It never failed to astound me, the hours upon hours she stood on her tiptoes in the kitchen, icing a cake higher than her head, the hours bent over the tiny table in our breakfast nook, hand painting details on cookie after cookie, like a machine. Anything you could come up with, she could find a way to summon, obsessively attending both to the appearance and the flavor profiles she'd tested and retested, every detail. Each year, for my birthday, she'd let me try to come up with something impossible to do. "Neon red outside, black inside, gooey, spherical." "The bathtub scene from *Scarface*." "Pentagram shaped, gray with black icing, ft. a portrait of 2 Chainz when he was Tity Boi." Orders from friends, which she started taking on spec more and more, spanned the works from 5-layer wedding cakes to heavily conceptual: cakes in the shape of a massive Diet Coke can, a tube of MAC-brand lipstick, an octopus eating flowers, or a life-sized, fully realistic roast pig; hand-crafted sugar flowers that looked so real you would be shocked they couldn't wilt, or a glass terrarium full of tiny plants, all of it sugar; cookies featuring meticulous portraits of famous female writers, the Atlanta Hawks, Killer Mike, our chickens; as well as classic cakes and treats of every stripe, each bearing Molly's inimitable style. Soon she was getting so much work from word of mouth she decided to open her own small business, for which she had a name in mind from childhood dreaming: Kookie House. She began accepting larger orders from corporate chains and local businesses, always insisting to do the bulk of work herself, up all night hunched over tiny details, always ready at the end to point out only the ones that she'd messed up. I'd be her driver for the cake deliveries, going half the speed limit the whole way there while Molly sat in the back with all the layers balanced out, reminding me sternly at every bump not to take turns so fast, to come to full stops slowly. Then, live on site, she'd build the cake on the fly, doctoring it up with the bag of tools she brought with her to smooth the hiccups, get it just right. The postal workers at the office near our house knew her well from coming in so often with huge fragile packages to mail across the country, then from how she also sometimes brought them cookies, too, as thanks. "She's so talented," one cashier always told me when I'd come in. "How does she do it?" "I don't know," I always told them. It really seemed like magic, after all; all this meticulously detailed work in a tiny kitchen with an oven whose temperature would vary, blasting somber dance music and death metal, or watching *The Twilight Zone* on loop, quiet as a mouse—though some days I might come in to find she'd thrown what she'd been working on so long already into the trash. She'd point to a dent or curl in the finishing fondant of a three-layer wedding cake and insist it ruined the whole thing, ready to start over from scratch no matter how tight the turnaround would have to be, how much new stress. I'd learned by now to stop trying to convince her otherwise, as her continuing negativity appeared at once to motivate her, to aspire to correct every detail in some exacting tribute to an impossible ideal, and to tear her down, to the point that any one perceived mistake wasn't the problem—the problem was *her*. She could never be a successful baker, she insisted, no matter who said what, because the real ones could see straight through her, most of all herself.

———

Still, she couldn't stop herself from trying, forever drawn back to the process no matter how much she sometimes wished she'd give it up. The strain of being strung out between writing, baking, and teaching, she'd decided, only made her unable in her mind to do either as she wished, and yet she'd bend over backwards to address something she might have allowed to slide a bit, for once—take on more orders, attend non-mandatory faculty meetings, almost as if to spite herself on every side. One night I came home to find her in a fetal position on the floor, facing the wall, inconsolable for hours over the fact that she'd mismarked a date and missed an order. It hurt to watch her struggle so much, though at times it would grow to irritate me, thinking I saw logically exactly what she could do to slow the tide. She mostly didn't want to talk about it either way, insisting that I didn't know anything, or that I was lazy, selfish, and entitled. Though at times she'd praise me for my work ethic, parallel to hers, the slew of hours I dedicated spending at my desk most every day, other times, when in a bad mood, she'd call it cruel, as if my coming in to say hello between tasks was passive-aggressive, dangling my availability in front of her. *Work hard, play hard*, I'd learned early from my father, deciding as a teen that owning my own time and will was more valuable than anything. Since then, I'd been cleaving together various freelance and part-time jobs—reviewing books and films and albums; writing about poker, porn, how-to, and Dos & Don'ts; teaching workshops and giving lectures; doing client work on manuscripts; editing for literary websites; and earning the occasional dollar on my books—to make enough of a living that I could do the work I really wished—writing fiction—with the main bulk of my time, seven days a week. To be fair it'd made me into a bit of a territorial beast in my own mind, forever holding myself to the fire when I didn't accomplish what I wished, often to the point that by the time I wrapped things up for the day, just before dinner, I was exhausted, half-underwater in my mind. Despite our common drive, I knew Molly held a bitter streak about my independence, offensive in comparison to how she felt pulled thin and uncertain where to turn. She'd been completely on her own for her whole life, even as a child, while I'd had a safety net, parents I could turn to, savings I'd accrued in being taught to stay prepared, no debt from school—all of it an easy target to strike up at when she felt down. She'd never had help and didn't want it now, she'd remind me if I tried to bring up talk of budgets, planning ahead. Even making more than I did most years, given her salary, she still had almost zero money in the bank at any time, always quickly spending whatever she had leftover on clothes and kitchenware, new packages delivered to our porch most every afternoon, somehow unable or unwilling to save up. She'd chewed me out after I'd convinced her to let me use some of my savings to pay off her student loans, openly weeping as I used her computer to transfer money to her account. Money, the wants and needs of money, the machinations of men for money, truly made her sick, part of some pretend shell game she refused to abide. Wedged into contributor copies of the lit mags she had work in, I'd find old royalty checks marked with her name, not compelling enough to need to bother cashing. Meanwhile, here I was betting on sports and playing poker, a long-running gambling hobby I'd gotten even deeper into after Dad got sick. Whereas before I'd never cared so much for sports, the adrenaline of putting up money on something out of my control helped me forget about my troubles, if only though another form of stress. I was aware, of course, of Molly's sensitivity around the topic, given how her father had ruined their family's life at the casino—and yet she seemed to trust me more given my natural transparency about the hobby, and how I knew my limits—when to slow down, when to stop. I knew my limits very well, could stand up and walk away after a loss, though after a big one I might rant and rave for hours or smash things in my office. Molly simultaneously seemed to respect my process in this manner and to scorn it, as if the very fact that I had brakes at all was a point of privilege. "Isn't this, me choosing to date a gambler," she wrote in an essay, 'Gambling Addiction Destroyed My Family…and Now I'm Engaged to a Gambler,' "isn't this just *that thing*, that thing people do to try to subconsciously fix their parents by dating a proxy and proving—once and for all—that the parent-ghost is ok, can be loved, *healed* even by healthy love? Or just some banal coincidence, some cosmic joke? Am I being naïve here? I don't know. I do know this for sure: Blake and I are fine, safe, and happy." A strange line there, then, in Molly's trust, one I trusted blindly maybe because it reminded me in some way of my parents— how my mom had been a high school art teacher from Owensboro, Kentucky, romanced by my father, a self-made entrepreneur raised on a farm, who loved Jack Daniels and fast cars—though simultaneously discouraging when she'd suddenly decide to hold it against me, knock me down. We seemed to dance around each other in this manner sometimes, never quite completely able to keep the ways that we were different from causing unclear tension, though eventually we always came back together in the end, if sometimes undergirded by a sense of suspension of disbelief, like there was so much she was thinking and wouldn't say. Over time, what had once been a thing we came together over—love of work—began to shift into a thorn stuck in her side, one I couldn't help extract because as Molly saw it, I already had everything I wished. However passive-aggressive she might be about the way I did things, including who and how and why I was, I tried to use them as a mirror to reassess myself, to learn to grow, if also in the back of my mind wondering why I couldn't just be me. Someday, I imagined, with a little practice, I might be exactly as she wished, the ideal man, or at least as close as any man could ever be.

———

"One day I'm going to write a book about what it's like to live with you," Molly came in to announce one afternoon—probably in response to me making weird noises or talking to myself in one of many voices I might use when I didn't realize anybody else could hear. It seemed like a nudge, partly a sweet thing and partly a threat, as if there was much to be said about me I didn't know. I was aware, at least in part, that I had abundant flaws like anybody—talking to myself, pounding on my desk, inattentive to the groceries, often sleepless, drinking too much, pessimistic and occasionally vindictive, obsessed with work. Molly admitted she often felt she had to tiptoe around me when in a bad mood or stressed out, which I already knew was quite more often than I wished. What fun and what a horror it would be to see our lives from her perspective, I imagined instead, all spelled out, bruises and all. After her death, I'd discover she'd already started working on a draft, just two brief pages, titled "My Novelist." "My novelist doesn't leave the house to work," the text begins. "When I leave in the cold dark mornings my novelist is sleeping, snoring sometimes, blabbering unconsciously sometimes. He'd stayed up till 2 or later most nights, reading the first 50 pages or so of novels publishers had sent him to review before abandoning them." The rest

goes on in similar fashion, ending in a list of fragmented comments—
It's a love story. It's a work story; Out of town, seeing photos of him—a
tight, cold mirror of me, I imagine, strange to try to read outside her
voice, from time gone missing. Stranger still to find myself instead
being the one writing out our life without her here—as if she'd
already known what she intended.

━━━

Some days, too, if mostly only near collapsing, Molly relaxed. She'd
spend all afternoon playing *Skyrim* on the Xbox she'd bought for
my birthday, in hopes I'd gain a hobby besides writing, which I'd
latched onto for a while and then let pass. *Skyrim*, however, for some
reason, really soothed her, establishing a virtual world where she
could avoid the open world game's assigned quests in favor of just
wandering around, having adventures, creating potions, minting
special armor, leveling up. As a child, her favorite game had been
Super Mario Bros. 3, until her father's arrest and national dubbing
as the Mario Brothers Bandit, turning what had once been a source
of play into an embarrassment. She felt embarrassed, too, when not
inside it, about the time she "wasted" on playing *Skyrim*, as if doing
anything but work was for the daft. When not aggressing, though,
the game gave her a place to go and forget about the world. She
played it over and over, on and off, for five straight years; if she got
bored, she'd select another hero, start from scratch. J'zargo, a feline-
like sidekick character that would follow her own character around,
doing her bidding, became her favorite part about the game. She
loved to dress him up in magic armor, give him the best weapons.
"J'zargo only has so much room to carry things," he'd repeat, when
she tried to load him up too much; a line I'd borrow from him as
a joke. If J'zargo died in combat, she'd wail and reset the game, go
back to the last saved file he was alive in. She'd align his stance so

he would stare out through the screen into her eyes. Her *husband*, she would call him, despite being formally married to another more man-like character in a hometown part of the game. He had a special ring that she'd picked out that he would wear no matter what else she equipped. It was sweet the way she loved him; how in the game's moments doing battle, making potions, she seemed to let her guard down. Just like all other respites, however, eventually her heart would waver, break its hold. One afternoon, she decided she'd played the game for the last time. She led J'zargo to a river, at digital twilight, and took back all the objects she'd equipped him with, one by one. Using the menu for dialogue between them, she told him she no longer required his services, so he should leave, and following the software, he complied. She stood at the river for a while then openly weeping, strangely touched, if also laughing at herself for getting so worked up. She asked me not to speak, and then to leave the room. She never played the game again from that day forth. No other game I bought in hopes of replicating *Skyrim* ever quite hit, and so soon the game, the machine itself, became another sore in Molly's arc—hard evidence of what a dork she was, a wasteful lump.

■

Our chickens, at least, never failed to soothe her. She loved to sit and watch them wander through the yard, pick them up and whisper to them, measure their health. No matter whatever else might be going on, our birds were there, eager every morning to come running down the ramp, enmeshed in a whole social economy independent of our reality. Those birds, as well as the dozens of others we'd raise together, procured in pairs, became a means through which we could find peace—Pyramid and Lindsey (the former beheaded after a half-survived hawk attack, the other named after Molly's teenage best friend, for whom she pined); Bing Bong and Crusher (the former ill from a rare disease that stunted her growth, the other snatched up by a hawk); Magic Johnson and Olex (the former actually rooster, impossible to distinguish until he'd grown up enough, at which point he'd attack my legs any time I tried to touch the girls, the other another hawk meal I witnessed firsthand); Olex 2 and Snacky (given away as a pair to a young family when we decided we no longer wanted bigger birds). We raised our last small flock—Woosh, Anne Carson, Hector, and $2 Bill—from live birth, shipped in a box to our house so that we'd be the first people they'd ever see. So many sweet memories derived from sitting for hours together to watch them hunt, narrating their habits and personalities like a family all our own. We'd learn only the hard way, over and over, how alongside that joy came hard times too, as soon our yard became a target for roaming predators, relentless in their multipronged pursuit through air and land. Several times, too, we'd have to put them down ourselves, either due to injury or illness. Molly had volunteered to be the one to wield the axe to behead Sheed after a hawk attack, taking over with rigid authority at the first signs of my uncertainty. We wrapped her in a towel and held her down, and I looked away as Molly heaved, then dropped the tool and hurried off into the house. "She had hid her wound under her wing," she'd reflect in a half-completed essay, "Sepsis," in which she also criticizes me for being in a hurry to dig the grave—probably too shallowly, she imagines, a shitty job. "She will always hide her wound under her wing," the essay concludes before it cuts out, "that's what 'she' means."

———

Before our wedding, Molly suggested I get a vasectomy. It would be better for her health than the pill, and we knew for sure we weren't going to reproduce. I saw two different doctors for assessments, each of whom immediately asked how many children I had. "Are you sure?" both asked with direct eye contact when I said *none.* Yes, I was sure, I said, without much need for reflection, certain as I was after so long. My only doubt came flooding in after the fact, sitting on the operating table with my pants off, feeling the finality of what I'd done. In a sudden something-like-remorse, I felt my mind racing forward through the future past fast versions of the aspects of my life I'd soldered off like no big deal. I thought about my mother asking how I could be so certain when I'd told her, wondering aloud what she'd done so wrong to shape my choice. She hadn't done any wrong, I'd reassured her; in fact, instead, she'd inspired me to want to be an artist first. Not to mention, I added on, borrowing from Molly, that our planet was already overpopulated, rife with misery and violence and the ongoing effects of climate change. The worst thing you can do for the world, when it really comes down to it, is have a kid, I let her know, parroting Molly, already fully armed with all the facts. "Oh," Mom had answered after a silence, clearly wistful, but polite. "Maybe someday you'll change your mind."

■■■

We were married in late spring on top of Arabia Mountain, half an hour from our house. Just the two of us and both our mothers, between the curving granite's makeshift moonscape and the wide, flat sky above, a threat of storm on the horizon in our minds but holding off. We picked a place to serve as an altar just underneath a single tree apart from the pack, dressed up amidst the rocks and dirt as occasional hikers wandered past. My mother stood close by beside us, parallel to Molly's, watching in a way I wasn't sure she understood, but still a blessing to have her there beside me for the beginning of the next phase of my life. Molly and I took turns reading the vows we'd written for each other, exchanging rings without realizing she'd placed mine—the same gold band my mom had given my dad—on the wrong hand. "Daily I am in awe of you," mine had begun. "Daily I am astonished to see the person you are. How much you put into everything you do. You live with a sense of care I'd been trying to force myself to forgo a search for in others. Whose vision, persistence, ambition, dedication, compassion, makes me see the reason for existence in." More than the words, though, I remember the rapt abandon in Molly's face as I pronounced each syllable, a holy moment we'd remember for the whole rest of our lives. It felt like a different sort of day, at long last, a loosening that would let light in; something finally true and finally ours. Our pasts were often opaque and elusive, yes, and the days ahead would bear their thorns, but we'd been made one, and in that moment on the mountaintop, at least for me, I felt renewed in something like faith. Our whole lives appeared to spread out underneath us from here ahead in a way we'd sworn to honor and protect. In conclusion, Nora read a poem to commemorate the moment, one of Molly's favorites:

"Love" by Czeslaw Milosz

Love means to learn to look at yourself
The way one looks at distant things
For you are only one thing among many.
And whoever sees that way heals his heart,
Without knowing it, from various ills—
A bird and a tree say to him: Friend.

Then he wants to use himself and things
So that they stand in the glow of ripeness.
It doesn't matter whether he know what he serves:
Who serves best doesn't always understand.

We really made it, I kept thinking coming back down the slope as wife and husband, hand in hand—free in a way I hadn't felt in long time, braced by a new strength we'd gained from all we'd been through each on our own and would carry forward with as one, together. Everything—for real this time—might really be okay.

■

Just short of three years later, I'd return alone to that same mountain to scatter her ashes.

It'd be a while, too, before many other issues present that day came to light—secrets Molly kept that might have split the story down the middle then and there, or maybe not. Would I still have married her had I really known what she was up to behind my back? Is it worth looking back and wondering, or only really bait for further pain? I suppose the answer, as with most things, all depends on who and when and how you ask. From the beginning, I've insisted that I'd do it all over again given the choice, trauma and all, though lately I've come to wonder if the only reason we got married as we did was because our mothers were the only people she could bear lying through her teeth in front of so distinctly. Either way there's no real way of knowing, which doesn't mean truth doesn't matter, then or now. It only means it matters even more how we respond.

To celebrate our bond, we threw a party. We rented space at the Carlos Museum on Emory's campus, site of the source of what had brought us together in Atlanta from the start. Amidst ancient relics from extinct civilizations installed as décor on all the walls, we hired friends to decorate with flowers and to DJ. Molly made our cake, of course, having already imagined exactly every detail of it as only she could bring to form. At the event, beloved faces from both our lives filled the room. Molly's grandpa gave a toast, looking straight at Molly as he told the story of his own seventy years of marriage, proclaiming how he was proudly passing the baton now on to her, which made her weep. We danced our first dance to Metallica's "Nothing Else Matters"—Molly's suggestion, in honor of our shared teenage recognition with that band, the funny tenderness of their lone love ballad somehow a perfect fit. Her original choice had been "Midnight, The Stars and You," the outro music to *The Shining*, originally played over the static image of Jack Torrance trapped in time among the dead. I danced with my mother, feeling her trust me as I led, lit up from inside in a way I hadn't seen since Dad passed: a rare clarity there in knowing I had found in Molly's arms what I'd been looking for so long. In departure, all our loved ones lined up side by side to form a tunnel, raising burning sparklers along the path where we would walk together, two in one, never more aware of all we had, truly grateful for the day.

On our honeymoon at Jekyll Island, we rode horses on a beach. I rode behind her, and she would turn back to look at me, aglow from half a minute of a gallop, total freedom. We both agreed how perfect the time was, how beautiful the sky fit to the land, and how lucky we were. From here, those precious days, even more than others, feel encased behind wide walls of glass, shifting like a scene in *Last Year at Marienbad*. I can see us walking down the halls of the old hotel where we slept and ate and swam and laughed, just for a while, before we had to pack up and head home to actual reality and our shared future yet to come. Later, in "Horse and Cart," one of the last poems Molly wrote: "I can't even imagine a horse / anymore. / That we *sat* on their spines / and yanked their mouths around."

Time moves strangely passing in retrospect between the clearer phases of one's life. From here and now, I can hardly tell the difference any longer between how it felt to know Molly in the beginning, when we lived more than a hundred miles apart, and how we were there at the end; how Molly went from someone I only knew from online, to my wife; the sprawl of life comprised in passing, past the moment, already gone. All I see now, having already reached the end of her part of our story, is the direct, descending path between who Molly thought she was and who she wished to be, spread thin between the belief, shared in them both, that nothing good could ever last, could not be real. She'd already seen the soul-deep cracks in all our human models of how to be, those same cracks finally breaking open into craters, full of death, just like how sometimes now all I can think of is all the ways I could have tried to reach her in our time, had I somehow only been allowed to know the future. You always think you have all the time in the world before it's too late. You always think you'll come around.

<hr />

Throughout much of our first year married, my mother's mental illness cast its shadow over all. She'd been officially diagnosed with dementia, including the uncertain presumption that, like with my father, it would turn into full-blown Alzheimer's given due time. It was worst for her at night, when the effects of her sundowning would make the house she'd lived in my whole life seem somewhere else. She'd call me scared, having locked herself in her closet, wondering why I'd left her at the church, or why there were so many women in her kitchen, making fun of her. Why had I left her here like this, she'd demand, and could I please come back and pick her up? I'd often spend an hour on the phone talking to her to calm her down, convince her this was all just a bad dream, and in the morning she'd feel better, which very often she really would. I was the only one around to take her for groceries, to make sure she remembered how to feed herself and wouldn't leave the house and wander off, much less whether she was happy, had any other human contact besides me. I wanted more than anything to avoid having to send her to a memory care facility—another nightmare akin to death, I knew from dad's stints—already aware it would be next to impossible to have her come and live with us; I could see the distance writhing behind Molly's eyes as I opened up to her about it, a lack of tolerance that would certainly not translate to opening our home to Mom's disease. I didn't blame her for this, really, already knowing well how hard a life would be in implementing full-time care. Instead, I drove up to see Mom as often as I could, which meant sacrificing both my ability to work and be with Molly. I felt stranded in my ability to split time across locations, both in my body and my mind, much less my heart, my will to live. I strung together makeshift solutions in the meantime, hiring nurses from nursing websites, organizing visits from her friends during the time I couldn't be there on my own. I felt abandoned in that way, too, seeing how some of the people she had known through her whole life stopped coming around, calling me up to offer warnings that something was wrong with Mom, as if I didn't know it, as if my mother hadn't been my biggest hero. She's still in there, asshole, I held myself back from screaming at them, feeling judged and up a creek at once. Even my godmother, a friend of Mom's since college, harassed me blindly, sending aggressive messages and showing up to snoop around her house as if for evidence of abuse. One day, out of nowhere, I received a call from Social Services with word that they'd received an anonymous report of possible neglect, which would be quickly wrapped up after an official visit, no harm done but to my heart. Why the fuck were all these fucking pieces of shit turning their back on us like this, my soul screamed, right in our time of deepest need? Why would my sister choose now to move an hour north, further from both of us? Who could I ever ask for help and actually get it? No matter what I thought or said or did, responsibility solely fell right back onto me, struggling to keep Mom happy and safe without adding pressure by losing my cool or telling her directly what was really going on—that bit by bit, just like my dad had, she was losing the threading of her mind, and any day now she wouldn't know the difference between her face and my face. All of this is just how life works, I'd remind myself, reinforcing my position by deciding there was no one else who could care for her the way I would—par for the course. If it had to be me and me alone against the world when the rubber hit the road, so be it.

———

"The last ten days have been a mess, so much I don't know how to really even process," I wrote in my caregiving journal during the spring of '17. "Mom had an extreme reaction to a new brain med her neurologist prescribed to slow dementia as a result of her testing. It began with her having an intense stomachache that she then began to describe as 'filling my chest with acid.' By the fourth day of the med she was so ill she couldn't walk and was throwing up all food, including water. I spent the night there on a Thursday to make sure she didn't dehydrate and around 2 a.m., I heard her in her bedroom talking to herself, saying, 'I miss my sister,' the sort of nostalgia my dad began to have in early stages. She didn't seem to know where she was and kept referring to 'the screen at the far end of the house,' which she said wasn't the TV or my laptop, but a glowing light that had happened to her before. She said it was me who was making it happen. She kept insisting she had to get the acid out and was trying to make herself throw up. Her speech was also intensely slurred, speaking in fragments, to the point I thought she might have had a stroke, though she passed the verbal tests I found online to see if she had any other symptoms of it. She was chewing the crackers I tried to feed her very slowly, sucking on them and describing 'trying to connect them with the acid to make it better.' While using the bathroom, which she could no longer walk to or find, she threw up on the floor and in the trashcan, all water. Finally she calmed down and went to sleep and in the morning we went to the doctor, who barely seemed to listen to her but said she should stop taking Aricept and eat only liquids until her stomach settled. I got the sense the doctor gave zero fucks about what was really happening; she disappeared before I could ask certain questions about what should be done. Nothing got better over the next twenty-four hours and when my sister heard her slurring on the phone we decided to take her to the emergency room to see if she'd had a stroke, not knowing what else to do. The admitting nurse in the lobby of the ER asked her the same set of questions all the other nurses would ask relentlessly throughout the coming days: what's your name, what's your birthdate, what year is it, who is this with you. Some of it she could answer but she often had no idea what year it was, sometimes saying 1999 or 1984. After Morgan left, I spent 8 hours in the ER that night waiting to be admitted after they decided she hadn't had a stroke but that her sodium was so low she might have gone into a coma. She kept doing this thing where she would fixate on one thing she needed and keep asking about it over and over until it was completed, such as wanting a pillow, which I could not find anywhere and the nurses kept forgetting to bring. A guy in the stall beside us came in and was cursing in raps until the police came and told him if he wanted help he had to shut up. The machines were beeping over and over and no one would come, which also made it impossible for Mom to rest. She refused to sleep anyway, not knowing what was going on. By the time they admitted her, she seemed completely gone, unsure of where she was or why we were there; she kept wanting to get up and go home, confused as to the tubes in her arms, not quite sure what I was doing there to help. It was clear the nurses thought she was fully into dementia; they kept asking me if she really lived by herself, to which I had to keep insisting that she'd never been this way before. This would get worse over the next three days, to the point that by the fourth day she was talking in complete run-on gibberish, synthesizing parts of the past, distortions of the present, and some circular logic that never found an end into a running monologue of total disorientation and dementia. She also couldn't use the toilet without help, struggling to stand, and not seeing where to sit down, though she was able to brush her teeth when led to the sink. It started to become clear that she might not only not be able to go home alone, but that she might need to go to a rest home, which I began to research from a list the hospital provided. The reviews of these places are all three stars and below on any site you visit, with horror stories of treatment and despair much like what I remember from the first two places Dad went. Meanwhile Mom would call from the nurses' station every few hours if I went home, in total disarray, asking me to come get her. Heartbreaking to not be able to say I could help, but that we had to wait to see what would come and that the nurses were doing what they could. Everything seemed to be spiraling in on top of me, needing to make decisions fast while seeing the person my mother had so recently been pressed out of her, gone as if a switch had been flipped. I prayed aloud to myself in the bathroom for what must have been the first time in forever, begging for help for my mother, to find a way out of this, what had been done to her, what was being done. I remember being so tired from all the back and forth and stress that I wasn't sure who I was myself anymore, which made sense as to why caregivers eventually become dementia patients themselves; the logic begins to infiltrate you, roll you over. It is relentless and fills in in your exhaustion, not letting up even when you are on the cusp of breaking. No relief... This morning the floor of the shower appeared somehow both lower than it felt to be in standing on it, and higher than it appeared in my perception, as if I were trapped in two phases of myself standing in the same place, some crux of touching eras. I found myself thinking again about suicide."

━━━

As usual, I took my rage out on myself. I was back to drinking heavily, now more than ever maybe, and mostly on my own at home, hating myself and how life was. I found it hard to ever get out of my own way most of the time, affected by so much high stress to the point of an unwillingness to slow down enough to feel. I stopped listening to most any kind of music except metal and rap and noise, startling the hell out of myself when I'd get back in the car after a late night of heavy drinking to find I'd left the volume at ear-bleed status blasting Three 6 Mafia, wrappers from 2 a.m. Taco Bell drive-through under the seat and nacho cheese smeared on the steering wheel. That I'd been lucky not to kill myself or someone else in blackout mode, unable to remember how I'd gotten home, barely gave me pause except to laugh, insisting that being wasted made me a better driver, more vigilant to the rules of the road. Such reckless confidence could just as quickly switch back into loathing or frustration any time, making a hair-trigger of most any moment, ready to blow up even more so when something I expected to go one way went off-course. "How am I still alive at 38?" I wrote in my journal one afternoon after not being able to get our lawnmower to start. "How have I ever accomplished anything, including bathing? I don't understand myself at all, so often it's like there's someone else inside me, though that someone is the better part of me, a strange companion who has been observing my activities and thoughts for as long as I have without control, waiting for me to finally do something so idiotic there's no coming back." Meanwhile, whereas before my tics had been random lyrics and gibberish syllables, I got in the habit of screeching "like a gorgon" by sucking air in through my teeth, a terrible sound that Molly hated. She felt like she was walking on eggshells around me all the time lately, she admitted, made worse when I would bang my fists on my desk or the wall when something minor knocked me off my kilter, such as bumping my shoulder on a doorframe or biting my tongue while chewing. One bump could spiral into many just like that, whole afternoons erased by tiny details that unsettled everything, adding wound on top of wound on top of wound. When I tried to talk about my problems with Molly, she could offer fantastic consolation when in the mood. She was concerned, of course, though also busy in her own way, and uncertain how to help except by encouraging me to rest. She volunteered to take Mom out for dinner after her classes once a week, and this alone meant the world to me, despite how at the same time I could read her deeper reservations through her face; that she didn't like family, and her sympathy could only go so far—a blinding there she didn't seem to mean to use to hurt me, but which very much hurt in ways I hadn't yet identified beyond the roar. Instead, I'd pretend I had it all under control when I knew I didn't, and there was no one else but me to shoulder the load. Hiding my screech, I'd stand and punch myself in the head in the mirror instead, talking trash under my breath. *Please kill me*, I'd repeat into my reflection, over and over, like a refrain I only partly didn't mean. *Life is shit*, I'd say, with no one listening but the other versions of myself, *a string of trash and hell so long and relentless there might never be an end till I implode.* The drinking, at least, I thought, gave me a means by which I could remove myself from my own life, drowning out the bitter silence with redoubled anger at anything that didn't go the way I wished, which felt like absolutely everything, all the time. Who or what was offering any better, if not reality, and certainly not God, whose silence in response to my prayers—the first I'd spoken since my early teens, during confirmation—felt like a wall marking a world to which I hadn't been invited.

It went on this way for I don't know how long until finally, after coming home blacked out at 4 a.m. and falling down face first in our driveway, denting a gash into my head, Molly came to sit beside me on the bed, immobilized, and told me something had to change. She couldn't stand to see me in so much pain, she said, and it was wearing on our marriage, to the point that it was time to draw a line. She'd written up a list of local therapists and wanted me to pick one, try it out. *Isn't it nice to see a doctor when you're in pain? Therapy is like seeing a doctor for your mind* is how she described it, trying to find the right kind of words that I'd accept, submitting that for her it was one of the few times in a week she actually sat down and thought about herself. If I refused to comply, she said, she might have to consider other options on her own, and so against my reservations, I agreed, if for no other reason than my fear of what she'd implied; I'd give it a chance, *for her*, is how I put it, still not believing for myself. Really, the last thing I needed to do was spend more time ruminating on my troubles, as if talking about it could ever solve anything on its own. Also, I needed all that pain, I thought deep down, as many do, to fund my writing—working it out, finding relief, could only make me weak, as if the act of seeking counsel for my pain was something craven, not in the essence of a man. Despite my misgivings, I made the calls and left messages with every doctor on her list, and in a week still had no lead, much less replies. I called our insurance provider and asked for help finding a contact in my network, finding myself admitting only to this anonymous operator that I was having regular suicidal thoughts, if not a plan. This fact, at least, got me an answer: someone could see me in three months, the soonest opening available. That was fine, I said, relieved to have fulfilled Molly's demand, though also shocked by how long I'd have to wait—what if this was an actual emergency? I wondered, while also reaffirming it was not. But maybe I really did need help, I began thinking in the meantime, warming up to how it loomed just out of reach, and rather than accepting that, heeding my ego, I began to rely on a much more palatable idea: that if I closed my eyes and held my breath and waited, someday a better path would simply materialize out of thin air. Wasn't that what faith meant, after all? Remaining steadfast to something unseen; believing whether you had clear reason to or not? What purpose was feeling so fucked up all the time really serving? What was my time worth if all it led to was another darkened mirror?

———

Three months later, by the time my appointment came around, the doctor welcomed me into her office without looking up. "What kind of pills are you interested in?" she asked, finishing up paperwork from the last patient. I said I wasn't there for pills; that I was there to speak with someone. "Sorry," she replied, "I'm not that kind of doctor." I drove home speeding and cursing the whole way. I would refuse to try another therapist until after my mom died.

———

Alongside my own frustrations, Molly's teaching career was in distress. The small tech school she'd been employed by for several years now had just been absorbed by a larger university, shifting the entire texture of the campus where she'd only just begun to feel at home. Her new boss was a train wreck, too, inexperienced with either leadership or teaching, Molly explained, and meanwhile wreaking havoc among the department by pushing off her work on underlings, bullying longstanding faculty into quitting. Of course, Molly refused to stand by and wait out each new injustice as it appeared, forever putting herself in the line of fire by speaking out at meetings and in emails, despite knowing that it brought her even more into the line of fire. She'd come back home from school crying or despondent almost every afternoon, on the phone with peers for hours consoling and discussing what they should do. At one point, when a scandal arose after someone anonymously sent her chair a bizarre letter, quoting Shakespeare in what the boss had decided to interpret as a threat against her life, it was Molly who became the central suspect, which she denied. "Was it you, though?" I remember asking, partly laughing at my own inability to rule her out. To be fair, the situation did seem terrible, and it drove me nuts to have to see her struggle with treading water through red tape, never quite able to land tenure, much less a position where she felt free from the axe. Throughout her adult life, teaching had been the rugged bright spot in her self-image, the only good thing that she could say she'd ever done. Every year at the end of the semester she'd break down crying while reading her student feedback, truly grateful: "Prof. Brodak was honestly the best teacher I have ever had." "Do not take anyone else but her." "Makes literature interesting and inspiring if you're not really into it." "If you ever need help, she's there for you."[14] Why couldn't these bureaucrat academic motherfuckers just let her do her job? Why did absolutely everything have to become a catastrophe? I tried to encourage her to focus on her teaching in the meantime, wait for the system to sort things out, but Molly didn't really want me to respond to her complaints; she seemed annoyed to have to underline that for me, expecting instead that I simply listen and not react while she continued to run herself into the ground. *Please, God, let there for once be something good*, I prayed so many nights inside my head so she couldn't hear me and shoot it down with all the rest.

---

14   https://www.ratemyprofessors.com/ShowRatings.jsp?tid=1923257

As if to escape her damned employment, Molly decided to audition for reality TV. *The Great American Baking Show* was coming to Atlanta and had an open call for local bakers. She knew she'd never make it, but it'd be fun to try, a direct relief from real world troubles, if one that also required even more work. If she did well, however, she dared admit, maybe she could parlay that into a business and leave academia behind for good—and so she threw herself into her whim with classic Molly style, setting aside all else in the name of perfecting her approach. She drew up recipes from scratch in response to the audition's prompts and practiced and perfected them with every spare second that she had, including teaching herself to bake bread. Later she'd be shocked when the judges singled out her first attempt at sourdough as the best of anybody's—maybe she could really do this after all, I saw her learn, slowly but surely gaining momentum as she proved her own doubts wrong. Several callbacks later, no surprise: Molly had been chosen as one of ten from among thousands to do the show, the only fully self-trained "hobby" baker they selected. She'd spend the whole next summer in London for the filming, which she'd have to find a way to balance with her classes. Molly was ecstatic, of course, newly enlivened by having seen her mark and hit it, just like that. All her free hours at once became diverted into the planning and preparing, as she'd have to submit her recipes for every challenge on every episode ahead of time, with only a few weeks to work them out. A little hope, though, would go a long way—as evidenced with the diligence she put into testing and retesting every tiny detail of her plans, her favorite of which was a gingerbread house designed to model our chicken coop and all the chickens in the snow. In the first and only episode that would end up airing, you could really see the determination in her eyes, hungry to shine more so in having glimpsed a window all her own. Hard to remember any other time I saw her beaming so completely while gathered around the big screen in our living room with our close friends, proudly sharing her behind-the-scenes experience like pouring water onto arid sand, a real insider, live onscreen. Just wait until they saw her make it all the way to the finale, one of three—undeniable proof, finally, of her great talents. Even her employers appeared to appreciate her new success, featuring her media appearance on their website amidst the wash of media attention the show brought both to her and to the school—kind of depressing to come from here after all this time teaching, Molly admitted, but at the same time, now that things were looking up, who really cared?

▄▄▄

Such elation would be short-lived, though. On charges of sexual misconduct against one of the show's male judges, the show was cancelled, never to be aired beyond its premiere broadcast. The network didn't appear to care that canning the show would only hurt the all-female finalists the most, and Molly struggled with the balance of sympathizing with the accuser, while also very clearly crushed, sick to her stomach for having dedicated so much time and energy, her mental health, only to have it once again struck down and erased. What a fool she'd been to waste her life on such an idiotic lark, this reconfirmed, as not only was she a leech for having wished to be on TV, all her efforts had been thrown out, like proper trash. She hated herself for having wanted it at all, only to end up even lower than she started, all evidence of her accomplishment to be buried in a vault; and whereas before she'd been exhausted but determined, now the wind really fell out of her sails. She had even more reason now to loathe herself, more of a failure now than ever, so craven, lame. She didn't want to talk about it, she kept insisting; she'd already wasted enough time. She made a sour face when I ordered flowers and they arrived bearing my name instead of hers, as if this simple mix-up reconfirmed her dim reflection in the world. Suddenly, I seemed to represent part of the chorus of those who'd seen her exposed, no matter how much I tried to tell her that what I'd witnessed of her work had filled my heart; that she was my star baker forever, no matter what. Bullshit, bullshit, bullshit, I felt her thinking most any time I opened my mouth, filling in over my voice with one she already believed in, sinking right back even deeper into old wounds, now open wide.

—

"I really don't know who I am most of the time, like I am unthinkingly just there, not anywhere, nowhere," her journal states. "Or I see myself, as I did today, staring into the oven watching the cookies bake, and see myself as fundamentally bad, a bad poet, dumb, unexamined. Pathetic and unattractive, a real waste. I wonder if everyone feels this way. Is this an old habit now, this line of thinking, which produces no useful action or inspiration for change, just more encumbering feelings of self-hatred? This could be ameliorated, I know, with discussion, with therapy, or deliberate re-choosing in thoughts. I indulge, indulge. I have no reason not to. I have no children looking up to me, no moral imperatives, no sense of spiritual responsibility in my soul." In another life, she might have been a geologist or chemist, she sometimes thought; *but it's too late now, I'm already old*, at 37. At the same time, she was sick to death with writing, claiming to be too fed up with the surrounding social scene to concentrate. She'd had a rough time publishing *Bandit*, struggling both with the editorial process of having to explain herself and with the guilt she felt in sharing her family's story for all to see. At the same time, she was sick to death with poetry even more so, embarrassed by her passion for it in the face of what so often felt like a mob scene, run by philistines. Most poets only ever had something to say about pop culture or themselves, she loved to rant, especially in response to success she perceived as unearned, the product of intellectually lazy swine desperate to hide behind their accolades and social preening. The whole scene was just a bunch of half-wit jokes and ambient ass-kissing, obviously. Acknowledging these observations out loud didn't help much either, no matter how frank it meant to be in looking back, and any consolation I might offer, reminding her that what appears on the page is all that matters, not the fanfare, she'd twist her face and look away, as if saying, *I know that, motherfucker, but I also have to live.* She simply no longer fit anywhere, she'd come to believe, having failed to find a publisher for any of her last three book-length manuscripts—*Comedie* (2012-2013), *Hologram* (2013-2015), and *Kin* (2015-2016)—each rejected numerous times over, to the point that Molly's early confidence after her first book's publication had all but disappeared. No one liked her, she imagined, and even those who did must just be dumb—including me, whose opinion didn't count because I *had to say that*, like it's my job; a double-edged sword there, designed to cut up most any source of potential traction it might touch. Suddenly, the years she'd spent publishing hundreds of poems, essays, reviews, and interviews in national magazines to the handmade DIY zines alike could hold no water. Between 2011 and 2013, she'd written 170 poems; in 2014, only 14. In 2015, she'd even tried and failed, by her opinion, to write a novel—titled, *Occupation*, inspired by Thomas Carlyle, about a maid who comes home to find God has made himself her houseguest and will not leave—despite for the most part hating novels, she loved to claim, "because there's already enough of the world." Her life in the arts was over, she concluded, as like the true mother in the Judgment of Solomon, she'd rather give it up than see it bleed. "I couldn't stand to be among writers," she'd later write in her last letter, "with their artificial grievances and their fraudulence—betraying what I cared about most, art itself. I failed to find what people call family or friendship, and I don't blame anyone but myself."

In direct contradiction to her own assessment, on the strength of *Bandit*, Molly won a 2018 NEA grant for prose. This was ridiculous, she insisted—forever a poet in her heart, even still—and it had only happened because she'd taken the easy way out and written about her life. Grudges aside, now that she'd been given all this money— more than she'd ever had at once—what could she do with it? She'd love to be like Rebecca Solnit or Anne Carson, she admitted, publishing timely, scholarly works of social anthropology that spoke back directly to the world. Maybe nonfiction had something for her after all? Uncertain where to begin, she began to itemize her interests, spending weeks brainstorming into a six-page "Master List of Things I Like and Might Write About," which in due time, much like her childhood reading list, would be redacted:

~~Moss~~	Cakes
~~Ferns~~	~~Candy~~
~~Conifers~~	~~Pastels~~
~~(Basically all "prehistoric plants")~~	~~Melville~~
~~Cats~~	~~Blue~~
~~Sugar~~	Green
Dessert	~~Gems and Crystals~~
~~Peonies~~	~~Smoking weed occasionally~~
~~Clean sheets, beds~~	~~Pleasant piano sounds~~
~~Aarvo Part~~	~~A woman singing~~
~~The Flamingos~~	~~Owassa Turner~~
~~Motown~~	~~Durer~~
Detroit	~~Michelangelo~~
~~Public Parks~~	~~Klee~~
Ponds	~~Kelly~~
~~Basically all birds~~	Martin

~~Owls in particular~~
~~Tea~~
~~Blankets~~
~~Skyrim~~
~~Makeup~~
~~Nigerian Market Literature~~
Geology
Interesting rocks
What's under the ground
~~Fine tipped pens~~
~~Popcorn~~
~~Snake Grass~~
~~A cool white room in summer~~
~~with ceiling fan~~
~~Brass and gold~~
Fossils
The ocean
~~Almond butter with a banana~~
~~Toasted pecans~~
~~Making gumpaste flowers~~
~~Ethereal things~~
Old buildings
~~Boarded up houses~~
~~Old books about plants, trees,~~
~~animals, or food~~
~~Nature shows~~
~~Japanese gardens~~
~~Japanese prints and design~~
~~Sad old poems~~
~~Identification books for animals~~
~~or plants~~
~~Laying down and reading with~~

~~The Dadaists~~
~~Kilgallen~~
Cookies
~~Cherries~~
~~Honeydew melon~~
~~Minimalism~~
~~Rug patterns~~
~~Cats~~
~~Seaweed~~
~~Teardrop shape~~
~~Canoes~~
~~Nice hands~~
~~The sound of a room full of~~
~~people typing~~
Hard work
~~Philosophy~~
~~Conceptual Art~~
~~Mild weather~~
~~Cherries~~
~~Michigan~~
The Great Lakes
Lake Superior specifically
Glaciers and glaciated land
~~Lowlands and swamps~~
~~Waterbirds~~
~~Steve Albini~~
~~Grant Park~~
Historical Sites
~~Very early American history~~
~~Native American history~~
~~Spooky things~~
~~PT Anderson~~

snacks nearby
~~Going for walks, looking at~~
~~plants and animals~~
Listening
~~Teaching Lit~~
~~Fixing something~~
~~Maple trees~~
~~Birch trees~~
Windows
~~Grilled cheese~~
~~Very large trees and very~~
~~small trees~~
~~Skirts and dresses~~
~~Being in water~~
~~Mushrooms~~
~~Lichen~~
Cells and how they work
~~Atoms and molecules~~
~~BB~~
~~Our Chickens~~
~~Basketball~~
The Moon
Clouds
Landscape
~~Driving up Woodward~~
~~Tigers at the zoo~~
~~Thinking about how big the~~
~~universe is~~
~~Ancient Greece and Rome~~
~~Harper's magazine~~
~~Massages~~
~~Clover~~

~~Sophia Coppola~~
~~Goddard~~
~~Antiques, Old Basements full~~
~~of dusty junk~~
~~Early seasons of the Twilight~~
~~Zone~~
~~Tofu~~
~~Emerald Green color~~
Museums
~~Dark rooms~~
~~Nice theaters~~
~~Things that make me cry~~
~~Iridescent things~~
~~Fresh laundry smell~~
~~Toolboxes~~
~~Watercolor painting~~
~~Sunny winter days~~
~~Shadows on snow~~
Writing in Journals
~~Reading other people's~~
~~journals~~
~~Heartfelt notes~~
~~Jokes~~
~~Details about daily life~~
~~Patient and good drivers~~
~~Dusk~~
~~Birdsong~~
~~Brass things~~
~~Happy houseplants~~
~~Petit fours~~
~~Donkeys~~
~~Swans~~

~~Small plants~~
~~Honey~~
~~Augusta~~
~~March~~
~~Spring~~
~~Caves~~
~~Small Streams~~
~~The Paint Creek Trail~~
~~Old train tracks~~
~~Apples~~
~~Going to Target~~
~~The mall~~
~~Small dishes and plates~~
~~Nice pots for plants~~
~~Jadeite~~
~~Nice wallpaper~~
~~Wood floors~~
~~Libraries~~
School
~~School supplies~~
~~Ancient artifacts~~

~~Myths~~
~~Heroines~~
~~Nordic things~~
~~Lullabys~~
~~Quiet, observant people~~
~~Sturdy backpacks~~
~~Mint gum~~
~~Pencil sharpeners~~
~~Chapbooks~~
~~Glasses~~
~~Garlands and buntings~~
~~Swags and ribbons~~
~~Large leaves~~
~~Long soft grass~~
~~Deer~~
~~Gravy~~
~~Butter~~
~~Salt~~
~~Cream~~
~~Muted colors~~
~~Interesting dreams~~

From this, she'd narrowed down her list to two main subjects: Geology and Landscape. "Related—sense of 'underness'—under water, under the ground, digging for treasure, new worlds, the past, layers, truth, secrets." Following another whim, one summer afternoon she marched into our kitchen to announce she was going to dig a hole in our backyard deep as she could. She made a face when I suggested she do it closer to the back fence, maybe, more out of view; instead, she resignedly agreed to shift it back a few feet from dead center. She'd already gotten started, she explained, sifting through the surface soil while taking extensive notes about the layers.

Any reservations I might have about the damage to our property felt quickly pale in that I admired her abandon and felt happy that she seemed excited about writing for the first time in a while. The idea that she could find a purpose right there in our backyard, one that clearly lit her up from the inside, far outweighed any eyesore; all I hoped was that it'd work, that she'd find whatever she was looking for.

—

Over the next few weeks, Molly scheduled meetings with local authorities from a variety of backgrounds and beliefs to advise her on her dig, including a psychic with whom she seemed to become somehow fast friends. I remember them sitting on our porch swing, talking about a woman who supposedly haunted the house and didn't like the new colors of the walls, picked out by Molly: deep gray, emerald green—dark in the daytime. "Your partner needs to get out more," Molly said the psychic had informed her after meeting me briefly in passing. "His energy is clogged." She wasn't wrong—in addition to my own workaholic mode, we were both going out less, preferring in most cases to stay home no matter what was going on. While I was more spontaneous, Molly required several days' notice to prepare herself, she let me know, especially if there was going to be a crowd. Even then, she'd often bail at the last minute, unwilling to play along when happier at home doing her own thing, no matter what kind of plans we'd made, how long ahead—she had too much work, or she was tired from too much work, or she just wasn't in the mood. Anyway, no one would miss her, she insisted—your friends, not mine, so I should just go ahead on my own. This got old fast, always getting bailed on, even as I tried to understand; she simply wasn't willing to play along, make up a good time, and so instead of wasting time, she'd rather do her own thing. Clearly, she was lonely, though, and how could she ever expect people to get to know if she never came around or opened up? Most people I knew really liked her, when she let them, even if at the same time I knew she could be intimidating by her aura, quick to judge, a bit on edge. Likewise, didn't she want to go spend time with me, at least, if not the others? Couldn't she see that I was struggling to keep my head up, could use a break? But once Molly's made her mind up, that was it—your problem now. Everybody is an asshole anyway, she'd add on, when in a worse mood, able to pick apart most any person who came up for why they sucked—stupid, petty, boring, vapid, annoying, fake. Her criticisms often made sense, if heavy-handedly, and gradually I began acclimating to staying home more often, too, making no plans until stir-crazy, just to get out for a while. It was likely time for my social life to change anyway, I told myself, trying to justify the way I chose to react to her dismissals and resistance; all my friends were getting married, having kids. Going out less meant I had more time for work, too, just like Molly, which was good, and I really liked our quiet lives held up in backdrop to the messy madness of past years. We didn't need anybody but ourselves, I started thinking, as we made distant plans to someday sell our house and move away into the woods, far from all else, never speak to anybody else again, with nothing left to do with all our time but all the work we'd always wanted.

———

At the same time, having failed to find a proper therapist, I began instead to wean myself off alcohol by smoking weed. I'd never experimented with drugs before besides drinking, but long gone was the straight-edge teenage version of me who couldn't see why people turned to substances in times of need. In the depths of my worst drunkenness, I'd still imagined I had it all down pat, able to jump through burning hoops forever, stronger and better able to see myself than those around me. The way Molly put it, though—that alcohol is mind control, celebrated by the state because it makes you stupid, sick, and weak—made certain sense, and if I was being honest, it'd become clear that for the most part drinking did little more than stoke my rage and make me nuts. Marijuana worked much better, I realized after impulsively binge-eating brownies at a party: it blissed me out and calmed me down, relieved anxiety with increased hunger, freer laughter, better sleep. Even the drawbacks—paranoia, lethargy, snacking—felt a far cry from how I'd end up when blackout wasted, the only way I liked to drink. Altering my habit gave Molly and me more room to bond, too, suddenly on the same page in a place we'd differed, given her longstanding but mostly amorphously described lifetime of experience with drugs of every stripe. Not so long ago I'd gotten mad when she asked me to get her weed—too dangerous to drive around with, I'd insisted—and now I couldn't get enough. We began spending our free evenings getting stoned while watching movies and queueing favorite songs or going out to dinner at nice restaurants completely blitzed, turning heads when my loud voice broke through the room joking about Jeffrey Dahmer or how sad the women on dates at adjacent tables looked—at least somewhat more lighthearted in our coping than simply throwing caution to the wind. It felt contagious—both my ability to self-medicate more cleanly, and, like Molly, to chase that impulse with a turning inward, as if my only source of strength could come from deep within, as all else would surely fail us in due time—including friends, including family, including art, including all. Suddenly I couldn't remember why I'd ever drank at all, much less why I'd ever choose to leave the house.

—

Several weeks later, almost as impulsively as she'd begun, Molly gave up on the hole. *Stupid idea*, she'd insist if I asked what happened. *What was I thinking?* She abandoned the several inches of digging she'd already done just as it was, to be healed back over by the weather, and I knew better by now than to rationalize with her about it. She didn't need me to stick my head in, certain that I could never comprehend despite the fact I'd been revising the same novel for the last five years, with zero certainty at all what I'd do with it when I finished, a different sort of a struggle, sure, but one we might have shared. She'd figure it out in time, I told myself—she always did. It almost felt like part of her process was this ongoing sense of self-attrition, burning through most everything to see what stuck. Even if she hated everything she'd ever done, it still existed. We were, the both of us, alive.

—

The following summer, in another manic burst of inspiration, Molly used her NEA money to fund a trip to find her father's birthplace, a concentration camp near the border of Poland and Ukraine that had since been wiped off the map. Her renewed interest in this biographical anthropology immediately struck me as promising, just the sort of project she'd been seeking all along—perfectly timed, too, within the wake of Trump's burgeoning presidential campaign, as now the concept of national identity and social politics consumed the forefront of the American mass mind. The ongoing mental strain the dumbass salesman evoked with every word he uttered had put the whole country on its edge, splintered from inside in a more immersive way than we had ever felt before. In years past, I'd never felt too interested in politics, having decided early on that the whole thing was a rigged game, but now Molly insisted I take it all more seriously, going so far as to announce in front of friends that she felt embarrassed by my thickheadedness. She needed a partner who gave a shit, she shouted at me, so irate she couldn't stand to look at me. Her passion was convincing, if unnervingly delivered, and quickly easy to relate to, given how more and more extreme things seemed most every day, and more so when what had once appeared impossible came true. "If I could give my life to take Trump out, I'd do it in a heartbeat," Molly announced following his inauguration, turning from the nightly news to look me dead into the eyes. "Give me one shot." Instead, putting her money where her mouth was, she planned and scheduled a three-month trip abroad in rapid fashion, with little guidance but the burning in her gut. Among her goals was to get better at speaking to strangers, to break her lifelong shyness in the pursuit of truth, and that she did. She rented a car and drove slowly in the Ukrainian countryside as locals tore past "with abandon," shaking their fists, only to find a small forest village risen in the place where the death camp once had been. She visited churches and lit candles, saw children singing, searched her mind for reasons to pray. She visited

Dachau, where her grandfather had been interrogated and beaten, and Auschwitz, the latter with an entirely French-speaking group, where at the end of the tour, she asked the guide, in French, "Why is no one crying? But me?" Most of all, she watched and listened, thought about what it meant to be Polish, a country whose identity was made amorphous by its sad history and blurry borders, the butt of jokes. "And nobody loved Polish jokes more than my dad, who drummed their singular, recurring lesson into my head: Polish people are stupid and backwards. 'Polack' (which simply means a Polish man) was an insult. Now, the Polish joke felt like a ghost: the spirit of the Nazi myth of the *Untermensch*, the subhuman, lingering on as joke, a trace of evil sustained by laughter."[15] Despite the intensity of the trip, Molly thrived in pushing through it, having found a counterpart for the violent unrest in her soul. There was a greater purpose for her now, at least, at last; a brimming confidence drawn up within her as she saw herself drawn like a moth into the flames. She felt exhausted, sick, and lonely on the road away from home, but also able to taste the blood-soaked bit of her own history in a direct way. It made sense, once immersed in her family's origins, that her imagination felt so entwined with rage and suffering, a part of her she felt haunted by but never knew. "Every day I thought about the dead," she wrote. "I carried them with me everywhere, my own personal grandparents and the anonymous dead, situating them across the landscapes I was seeing, to try to find out something about the past and what it's done to us all. The living, to me, became the mythical ones, the hope-shapes, hurrying around, ignoring everything but their private lives. They seemed to hold everything, everything, the past and the future, all of the truths there are, everything that could ever be, with such unthinking looseness … And yet everyone seemed to indicate they thought of themselves as mere passengers in the vehicle of history."[16]

15   Brodak, Molly. *Alone in Poland*, unpublished, 2019, p. 14.
16   Ibid.

I spent most of that summer on my own. The house was quiet, and I used my hours working, writing, reading, watching films, and getting stoned. Besides keeping up after my mother, who by now had part-time care coming by every few hours to check in, I wasn't sure where I belonged or what I wanted out of life. Having seen my parents' minds ruined by dementia, I'd become more aware of how fast the days flew past, becoming years and decades, lost to the blind. How long until I fell a victim too and no longer remembered how to wipe my ass? Would I be able to see it coming, unlike them, or would I go down swinging just the same, thinking I had it all under control? Either way, the days were wasting, my indefatigable inner taskmaster loved to make sure I kept in mind. As if to combat this, burning at both ends, I began writing two books at the same time—*Aannex* and *Aabyss*, one during the day, sober, and one at night, wasted—as if the work itself alone could somehow save me. Little else had ever seemed to keep me sane, though I also hadn't given much space for contemplation beyond my foremost urges as the present fed forever into the past. A strange elasticity to time there, in that you think you understand how it might feel to look back and wish you had another chance to do what you'd have done could you have known, as if all we're ever waiting for is any sign of an intentional design, the kind that grabs you by the throat, says, *Now or never.* Too often, though, it's only in a crisis that we come to this, as if what we really wish to do is like a phantom limb, unable to be lifted but by the mind. If we could only always get it right the first time, without such struggle, right? But then what would it mean to have lived? If there's a God who created, or just allows us to create each for ourselves, the work of boredom, suffering, silence, what should we expect in return without seeking change within ourselves? Could it be that though life is hard, wet with confusion, dislocation, constant strain, without the struggle there'd be even less to want to live for? Sounds like bullshit, on the one hand, as grief and pain leave no certain legible receipts; and on the other, there's the awareness that sometimes you have to survive something to know why you even should. Some gifts take your whole life to figure out a map for, while maybe others weren't ever meant to have a given use, but rather to be a plank in a bridge, a plant in a landscape; or like a painting of a landscape, only for those who somehow end up in its presence, looking back; or like a memory of a painting of a landscape, which is yours and yours alone unless you learn another way to share it.

———

Upon returning home from Poland, Molly dove head-on back into work. She seemed to have been humbled somewhat, and clearer-purposed, if also newly ignited by a more incorrigible mode of inner rage. She'd gone to stand on hallowed ground, looked baldly back into the pit of Holocaust from which she'd come, and now returned to endless updates of our own country in its own crisis, debating borders, human rights, state-sponsored murder, and even the very nature of information, its manufacture. It felt like living under psychic siege, even on "normal" days, hidden in spin, pulled up at the roots, with little remaining clear consensus on what was true, what might be true tomorrow, but the need to froth more, to get online and run your mouth. Meanwhile, people were saying it was *the golden age of television*, backed by corporations so well armed with data-driven branding that there seemed less and less a choice to stand apart. Molly, as usual, couldn't help but want to turn it on herself, in stark contrast to the ongoing spectacle of social media's spastic version of social justice, where everybody just seemed to want to blame everybody else. She knew as well as anybody, at least theoretically, what happens to repressed trauma—how it ends up getting passed on further down the line, multiplying, taking new form—and yet her experience simultaneously didn't seem to serve her but as renewed desire to hold her own hand to the flames. "It made me sick," she wrote of coming home. "I could see my family's story of being rescued by America, the story of the American Dream, truly as a farce, a dark and pain-filled comedy against the context of the past and everyone else who did not make it. We did nothing to deserve our rescue."[17] I find myself thinking here of Holocaust novelist Imre Kertész's response to *Schindler's List*, a sentiment Molly and I had shared an awe for: "I regard as kitsch any representation of the Holocaust that is incapable of understanding or unwilling to understand the organic connection between our own deformed mode of life (whether in the private sphere or on the level of 'civilization' as such) and the very possibility of the Holocaust."[18] Isn't that what had driven her to want to write about her father, from whom she clearly learned more than she thought, with such compassion, when the whole rest of her family refused to give him the time of day? Wasn't that what she had gone in search for, back to the primal scene of her family's origin, smack in the middle of the most massive atrocity of all time? "We are mostly bad," Molly ends up concluding. "The world is mostly cold and tough, and those who come to any genuine understanding of it tend to be the same. It is in this context that kindness has meaning."[19]

A few months after her return, Molly's grandpa, Paul, fell deathly ill, no longer able to summon strength to stand, or then to speak.

17 *Alone in Poland*, p. 78.
18 Kertész, Imre, "Who Owns Auschwitz?" Translated by John MacKay, *The Yale Journal of Criticism*, 14, The Johns Hopkins University Press, 2001, p. 270.
19 *Alone in Poland*, p. 79.

She'd known that this was coming for a long time, Molly could say rationally, and yet she didn't want to have to think about what a world without him could even mean. She'd never experienced death of a close loved one, and even just the mention of his name, near to the end there, filled her eyes with tears, her mouth tight-clenched, holding it in. Molly wanted to fly to Michigan to see him immediately, as soon as she finished up the one large baking order in her way, feeling stranded between the commitment to her client, and the worry that she wouldn't work it there to see him one last time. This moment's hesitation, as Molly saw it, would provide no end of future guilt, when just days later, before she even realized how dire it had been, Paul passed away. She appeared to take it more discreetly than I'd expected, on the surface, shaken up but sober. She didn't even seem to want to hug me, insisting even more on digging in on painting cookies while I sat beside her, trying to console her, to be near. I understood her terseness; how hard it is to push beyond the walls of grief and let another person in where it hurts most. "He was the only one in front of whom I'd be embarrassed to die," she finally admitted, turning to me suddenly, glaring. "There's nothing holding me back now." *Including you*, she let the icy silence loom to imply, another wall there where we might have found commiseration, if not consolation.

Paul's memorial was held at his home, the same place he'd lived throughout most of Molly's life. Before the rest of the family arrived, we wandered around the rooms as she reminisced about her years there growing up. It hadn't been so long since we were last there with him, listening to him narrate memories while Molly browsed for mementos to take home, most excited by a package of old letters between Paul and Molly's grandma Barbara, his wife of more than sixty years. She seemed most intrigued by how the letters made her wonder if there were secrets between them no one knew, as Paul had been a traveling salesman for many years, and men who traveled for work most likely had affairs, didn't they? How else to explain the peculiar scorn her grandmother had shown him? Either way, it was too late now to ask, leaving the mystery alive like a little blemish on his perfection, as if somehow that made it easier to comprehend. Upstairs, we looked in on the guest bedroom where, when she was little, Molly had often slept when staying over, long since out of use but still the same—in particular, the flat beige carpet and grated air vent by the window, underneath which a preadolescent Molly had hidden folded slips of paper scrawled with secret notes, a memory I thought sweet but shared by her without a smile. Downstairs, the house was bustling and full of kin, including dozens of Molly's aunts, uncles, and cousins, most of whom she rarely saw outside of holidays. I stayed close by, holding her hand when she felt like it, and especially when she spoke up to honor him among a few who also offered words. I could tell she felt uncomfortable, irritated by the noise of speech and laughter during a wake, but also intent on honoring him, already knowing this would be the last time she saw the house. Afterwards, we went back to our hotel room, which Molly had suggested renting rather than staying with family, knowing she wouldn't want to be around them, not like this. How appropriate, she quipped, parting the curtains from our room's window to reveal a massive metal dumpster occluding the entire view.

━━━

Every sentence that I write here, I imagine Molly rolling her eyes. I hear her in my head, interpreting the way I write about her life and our relationship as further confirmation of the fact that no one can hear or understand her, and worse, how even her suicide was not enough. *At least she's no longer in pain*, bystanders often try to submit as consolation, as if death at least can be expected to assuage the mentally ill. I know they mean well, while also wanting to believe in an awaiting future respite for themselves. *To live is to suffer*, yes, and in death, we imagine, at the very least, we should no longer have to be beholden to our pain. Other times, all of time, and all existence, here within the wake of ambient tragedy and fear, feels like one long hour of one day covered in flames, from which the only reprieve could ever be God or the void. It's easy from here to see the points where Molly hid herself, concealed her suffering, in the name of trying to carry on, continuously shuffling, on the surface, within the gulf created in between how others saw her and how she really felt she was. Pessimistic isn't quite the right word—more like semi-consciously determined to interpret every aspect of existence through her pain. "Someday you'll really love me," she'd say sometimes out of nowhere, grinning as she said it, like she'd come up with some great grim joke. Responding with "I will always love you, Molly, including now," just seemed to reinforce for her the fact that how she felt, even within that love, across the board—fully defeated, all alone—would never change, could not be helped. The other response: "Why would you say that?" might only underline the gap between the two, like a red flag before a bull. If I tried to ask her what she meant, she'd look away, allow the moment to dissolve, or she'd snap and tell me to stop staring at her if I looked on too long, trying to coax back any sign of how she really felt beneath those words. No matter how else I might have responded in these moments, therapy tells me, from far beyond the point of no return, there's little reason to believe it would have changed her story's end. *Chaos felt more like home to her than happiness*, I've tried to hear and slowly, fundamentally, accept about her time, seeing how her higher highs could only fund the lower lows, continuously preserving her grim worldview with the idea that anything not rotten to its core must be a lie. But how about you go ahead try and get that through your head about your partner, the central pinion your life? You be the one who must accept, front and center in the greatest of all your fears, *I did everything I could*, and within the failing of that, still imagine: *There's something left to live for*. Too little, too late, of course, no matter how well we think we know that some things can't be seen for what they are until they're over, and for the most part, not even then.

▬▬

Not long after the funeral, I flew to Paris for the launch of a French translation of *300,000,000*. Molly would be fine, she said, despite her heartache; if anything, it'd give her more time to catch up on her work, as she was hell-bent now more than ever to get a draft done of her new manuscript amidst all else. We'd each gotten used to traveling without the other, taking turns fulfilling our writing-related obligations while the other stayed home with the chickens, but I noticed Molly remained mostly tight-lipped once I was overseas, quite unlike the normal way we texted. Any time I asked what she was doing, how she felt, she gave straight, simple answers before turning the conversation back to me, clearly busy and exhausted, I imagined, in her weaving between tasks. Most of my week passed in a rush, too—events, museums, press—until, two days before my return, Molly asked me to give her a call soon as I could. She'd written a suicide note, she explained, calmly and clearly, once on the line. She'd realized immediately afterwards that it was just a poem, though, so no big deal—she'd written poems like that before, plenty of times. It'd scared her enough, though, that she decided to tell her therapist, who encouraged her to tell me, too. She'd waited until the end of my trip because she didn't want to make me worry, mess up my fun; and it was already all okay, she swore, just a byproduct of stress from work and all the rest, a feeling she was very used to.

I couldn't read the poem, though, nor could she remember much of what it'd said; she'd already deleted it, and she felt better having found a way to get the feelings out; better, too, in being honest telling me and knowing I was flying home the next day. Her therapist had been checking in with her each afternoon to follow up; a relief in that, at least, having help, despite Molly's admonition that it was only because she was paid to do so. All while she spoke, opening up now from seven thousand miles away, I felt an empty itching in my face all and through the line, simultaneously terrified and helpless to come to realize she'd been able to keep this information to herself throughout the week, allowing me to leave the country without a warning. Sick to my stomach in imagining her left alone at home, all the other ways it could have gone; though grateful, too, for her having been able to come clean, even if it'd taken such an extreme to make her realize that she should. It felt like progress to her, too, she explained, that she'd been able to share, and so I shouldn't worry in the meantime— she had plenty of work to fill the time till my return. She promised to keep her phone close and let me know if at any moment her urge changed; to be transparent with how and where she was, no matter what—a thankful if uncertain state to have no choice but to rely on, and little else to do but lay on the bed with my phone on my chest and wait for a plane.

━━━

Molly was relieved to have me home, she said, even as her work continued to keep her glued to the dining room table, tracing and icing cookies for several large orders she'd piled up. The horror that'd driven her to write the suicidal poem had led to a breakthrough in her therapy, at least, making new strides unpacking the recent pain of the *Great American Baking Show*'s cancellation, which she'd only just begun accepting was okay to be upset about. The show had been a chance to put her talent on display, to be seen, she admitted sheepishly, embarrassed that a TV program could mean as much as that. Having had that chance snatched out from under her again was more than just bad luck; it bent her in a way that words couldn't capture, only more so for how she'd trick herself into writing it off. Not how she wished to see herself, sure, but better to address it than to ignore the cavalcade of broken feelings underneath, memories she could hardly begin to want to name in trying to imagine how to confront and unpack them. She'd been neglected as a child, she could admit finally, and neglect all on its own is child abuse and not her fault. She'd already felt this, at least in part, about her father, still in prison, but having to apply it to her mother also felt much more intense, given how they remained under the appearance of good terms. Was even Nora aware of what she'd done? If so, would she able to imagine how Molly felt now, after all these years, or would she not be able to see it and understand? Molly had already written a bit about these problems in her memoir, and yet there was clearly more there underneath, perhaps made even more unwieldy in having spelled it out and still never found a way to broach the actual experience behind the writing with her family in a more conclusive way. What other horrors had she kept hidden even then, unable or unwilling to narrate them into her consciousness, much less a language? At the very least, after years of therapy, she'd finally begun to want to face it, trace it out, even if she couldn't quite yet wrap her head around the flooding feelings so close up. The more we began to talk about it, front and center, the more the Molly I knew best—fierce, independent—came back to life, learning slowly how to walk, in recognition. Her coming forward early on had saved her life, we both agreed, and though the road ahead would be uncertain, we'd find a way.

My mother's doctor referred her to see a specialist for cancer. She'd been having terrible stomach pains, and there was reason for concern, but it was hard to say exactly what the trouble was. Her mental health had gotten a lot worse and rather quickly, no longer able to remember when to eat or bathe on her own, much less reliably report on how she felt. She couldn't tell one end of the ranch house she'd lived in for nearly fifty years now either, instead referring to it as *upstairs* and *downstairs*, or *her house* and *her other house*. I'd hired full-time, live-in caregiving, lucky to have found good local help instead of a rest home. Adapting to letting someone else take care of Mom was both a blessing and a blur, like I was slowly losing control over my ability to keep her close. Losing her had been my greatest fear since I was old enough to know what death was, and now I was being forced to watch it happen very slowly, bit by bit, just as I had with my father years before. The whole last decade had been one long hell ride through what felt like a procedural dismantling of everything I'd ever felt I could rely on, turning all my life's baselines into mush. The specialist appointment was supposed to be exploratory, though when the doctor came into the waiting room with her results, I could feel the narrow air there sticking to me, filling my mouth up like a bit. Ovarian cancer, she reported, plain and simple. Mom had about two weeks left to live. Mom kept talking to herself over the diagnosis, beyond delirious, and certainly unable to recognize why I was crying, clinging to her. We took her home and set up a hospice cot in the middle of the living room where I'd been raised, with hand-painted portraits of us from our childhood hung up on either side right where they'd been for our whole lives. I spent a final Sunday there beside her by myself, feeding her water, telling her stories, kissing her head. She had no idea what was going on, but for certain moments would catch my eye, mumbling gibberish. The large plate windows on either side of the space filled the room with open light, a texture there I already knew I would remember for forever.

The following afternoon, three days after her diagnosis, her caregiver called to say that she was shaking so much I should come over immediately, as he wasn't sure how long she'd last. Molly wanted to wait a bit, even then, to finish decorating another tray of cookies first, frustrated by the interruption. I told her I couldn't wait; I was leaving right now, with or without her, and diffidently, she came along. We made it there in time to sit together at Mom's bedside as I held her hand and watched her struggling to breathe on a respirator, her head loose on her neck, spasming around. The cancer had spread up into her chest, and there was nothing in her face beyond the strain, the choking on black bile that'd filled her up. I agreed she should be given morphine, a final dose of droplets under her tongue, without much other choice. Side by side, Molly and I watched her breathing become a gulping, then go flat, the color quickly draining from her face as she went still over the sound of the last strokes of the respirator, pumping and sighing, trying to force breath. I clasped her hand, feeling her grip it back from in the blind until she couldn't. Then it was over, just like that—my greatest fear now made definitive reality, already in the rearview, a day to age but never fade.

Later, Molly told me that experiencing death so close had made her remember how precious life was, how she should be more grateful for her own. I could tell she felt sorry for me, if also reluctant to commiserate too much between her busy schedule and her ongoing and unspoken contempt of my dedication to my mom. She couldn't relate to why I spent hours on our sofa reading back through the thirty-something years of Mom's journals, which I'd been bringing home in bunches for some time, already long aware of how much they'd rip me up once she was gone, and what a gift. "I'd never do that for my mom," Molly pointed out, underlining our hidden wall. Nora had called to wish me well, though, and mentioned she wanted to come down for the funeral so she could be around and help us out, if also clearly wanting to commiserate, having just lost her own parent months before. But the last thing I needed now was houseguests, I insisted; there was already too much going on, and it just really wasn't a good time. Reporting our wishes back to Nora didn't register, however—she'd get a hotel room nearby and do her own thing, whether we wanted her to or not. There wasn't time to argue anyway, given how much I had to do now in preparation for the memorial—spreading the word, planning the service, picking an urn, writing a eulogy, completing paperwork, closing accounts— much less focusing on mourning, with hardly enough bandwidth to separate the present moment from the past or future. Time seemed to be moving far too fast on every side, like melting glass. Death required a professionalism of the mourner in this manner, forced with little choice but to negotiate the entourage of minor details of the rites that come along with each life's end, legally and procedurally as much as emotionally and existentially. With what seemed little choice, I put my head down and felt the ground beneath me pass, as if no matter what I did or wanted I'd continue being pulled into the blank.

▬

When the day arrived, I drove myself, Molly, and Nora to the same funeral home we'd hired for my father five years prior. Due to a mix up in the arrangements—having made a point up front that we didn't want an outwardly religious service like the one they'd provided for Dad—I was given no choice but to the host the services myself, with zero preparation besides the eulogy I'd written. They messed the slideshow music up, too, playing the same song over and over as a result of having failed to rehearse beforehand, not that there was anything left to be done about it now; the funeral was underway, and I had no idea what part of me was up there in front of all my family and friends, speaking as if from through the hole cut through where my mother's voice once lived inside me, already in the midst of shifting from actual to virtual and growing only more disorienting the longer I tried to convince myself to comport myself with grace. I'd imagined I might explode on site at mother's death, but here I was somehow, playing along, maintaining obligations, wearing a face that looked like mine but felt like someone else's. After I finished, the floor was opened, and despite having said beforehand she didn't have anything to say, Molly stood up and came to front. She reminded the congregation to make sure they took time to see and touch my mother's quilts, spread out on display throughout the space; to take time to admire the composition, the textile's textures; how they were meant to be examined from up close, handled and felt. I felt surprised and grateful for her veneration, the kind of tribute she would have never offered elsewhere, if only under the light of the one thing she continuously revered: *work*.

—

Back at home, right after the funeral, Molly immediately returned to decorating cookies, and Nora stuck around, too, putting herself to work by doing random chores around the house to try to help, while I went into our bedroom to lie down. After a while, Molly came in and said Nora wanted me to come into the living room and let her do a guided meditation for spiritual healing, just the two of us, though I'd already explained multiple times how all I wanted to do was be in bed. Maybe I'd change my mind, Nora told Molly to tell me, and she'd be right here if I did, refusing to take no for an answer, much less a hint. Feeling the pressure, and with zero tact on Molly's end to intercede but as a messenger, I snapped and told Molly I wasn't going to do it, that I had no will. Wasn't it obvious that I wouldn't want to meditate right now? How many ways would I have to say it before it stuck? Fine, Molly said, cold as a stone, and went out to inform Nora and take her back to her hotel. For a while, the house went silent, far away, hot pools of acid in my body buzzing and unfurling underneath the numbness. I wished that I could be held, hugged, allowed to cry, but instead time kept passing on, as on a treadmill, with little room to mourn, much less be solaced. Once she got back, I approached Molly at her worktable in the kitchen, already intently refocused on her icing. You're such a selfish piece of shit, she screamed back soon as I spoke, back turned, tool in hand, refusing to hear anything I had to say—that it wasn't that I didn't like her mother, but that I missed mine; that we were both on the same side, or were supposed to be; that if I couldn't take care of myself today of all days, when would I ever? In return, Molly took my fire and fed it sarcastically right back, saying she knew my mom was a saint and hers was trash, okay? Nora had been like this her whole life, unable or unwilling to think of how others felt in times of need, and that was her problem, not mine—isn't that right? Right, you motherfucker? Having said her piece, beyond retort, she said she had to work now, and I should fuck off and go away. A line in the sand, of sorts, I realized, standing there in shock over how this day of all days had become twisted. I felt maybe as small as Molly had herself once, quite long ago, having grown up immersed in this irrational, unbending form of love, or whatever else filled in where love might have, where it didn't matter what you felt, and all you had left to soothe yourself was your own arms.

Like the abortion, we didn't talk too much about our mothers after that. Instead, we let the blow-up fade, chalked up in my mind as caused by stress, if also clearly shattered into shards across the backdrop of my mind. Eventually Molly apologized in passing, admitting that she'd wanted to avoid her mother that day, too, and hadn't figured out how to speak up for herself against the manic mono-focus she was used to her mother bringing into most all their interactions, refusing to take no for an answer when she wanted something. Instead, she put her head down and tried to wait it out, find her own clearing without the need of Nora knowing how she felt, often the same way she handled me. Even having calmed down, conceded her affect, she still bore what felt like negligible remorse over the scene, much less the devastated state losing my mother had left me in. After finishing her cookie work, she sat beside me on the couch and worked on her laptop while I listened to old cassette tapes from my childhood, recordings my mom had made of us together making up stories from before I was old enough to remember how it'd happened on my own. "Such a little brat," Molly observed wryly, listening to a three-year-old version of me play pretend, over-excited and unrestrained. The brief gleam she'd shown up with at the funeral, along with any other shred of compassion, had been displaced, underlined with a gritty, tragic realism that, while likely factually accurate, refused to harbor any ardor, hard and fast. "If you don't write about your mom's quilts," she'd pointed out while staring straight into my eyes, "no one will remember. They'll be forgotten."

———

Not long after Mom's passing, I left my body for the first time. Layers of gray on gray formed to appear there in my mind just at the cusp of touching sleep, worn out and far away within myself, through rolling folds and tufts of mist like walls in time. I found that I could scroll my mind-state forward from on the far side there, like open falling without the boundaries of physics or intent, a space I recognized from years of a recurring dream depicting the vast backstage of the world of human drama: vertices and walls and troughs and valleys that connected all the levels of the world together in one network, its entrances and exits hidden in plain sight. Among these folds, I met a presence, itself in midst of transit—some opaque shadow, without clear form, who knew at once I didn't quite belong. I could hear it speak inside my mind like dragging gravel. It wasn't God, it said, but it did know God: an entity heavily misunderstood; non-aligned with the mechanisms of righteous judgments that had beset Him; of a form of reason that once immersed in became innate, obvious without the need of recognition or relation. But there was much more to where I'd was now than just God's notion, the presence explained, and now I had a choice how to proceed—I could leave my body for good and continue deeper, or I could return to my life and live it out. It didn't really matter in the long run either way, the voice explained. A human lifetime was hardly any time at all, would be over before I knew it, and I'd be back there soon enough. It could tell I wasn't ready yet, it said, and reminded me that if I was scared, all I had to do was use my mind to move my arm; then I'd be able to remember my body, and my wife's, right there beside me, and I'd see that I was fine, that I could return back to the vessel of my flesh and enjoy the gift of human life while I still could; then it was gone, the flooding layers all surrounding, spilling out around me, until eventually I chose to wake up, and I awoke. Only later would I remember to relate my uncanny experience, no matter what it was, with my mother's description of her own near experience of death—how she'd found herself floating above her body while giving birth to me, after two prior miscarriages, looking down and seeing the doctors working on her in the white room; how she'd begun to feel a passage of ascension toward light, and there within that, pure understanding, as if the universe and all existence had been unfurled in an omniscience, which itself had been the guiding force that let her know she needed to go back to mortal time. Upon reappearing in her body, on the table, she heard the doctors saying that I, her child, might not survive; that I'd been taken to the ICU in critical condition, barely pulled back into the world from infant death, 1 out of 10 by Apgar's score. This was obviously a miracle, my mother knew; a sign insuring she'd do anything for me, forever, if at the same time a fuel for paranoia, more aware than ever of all the ways I could get hurt, wiping my hands clean if a stranger looked at me, overtly worried about anything she couldn't control. No wonder, then, about my own longstanding anxieties, passed on despite best efforts like anybody, whether we're aware of it or not.

———

Feeling lost enough inside my mourning to want help, I agreed to an appointment with Molly's therapist. Should we really see the same person? I wondered aloud, which for some reason pissed Molly off, as if there was something I was hiding and didn't want her to find out, or maybe that what was good enough for her wasn't good enough for me. Really, though, I didn't get what therapy could be, expecting to be corrected in my assumptions and mistakes, told why I was the way I was, and given exercises I'd have to do to improve myself. I went in with my game face on, ready to supply all the proper answers on demand, fill in the gaps between my action and my feeling with lines of logic. We'd figure this all out, I thought—maybe a couple of weeks and I'd be better, problem solved. All we did, though, when I got there, to my surprise, was sit and talk. I explained my situation, how stressed I was with Mom and Molly, uncertain where to turn for help, angry at myself most all the time without clear reason, overwhelmed with blind angst and loathing, up a creek. After spilling my guts for 45 minutes, I asked what my homework was, and the therapist responded simply, "See you next week." I didn't get it—what the need of telling someone all my troubles could ever be. Every second that

I spent there running my mouth felt like less time I had left to do the work I needed or wished, and the deeper I got in, recounting memories, itemizing troubles, the more there seemed to come back flooding out. It felt like steam pouring off the top of my head, released from feelings I didn't know I had, able to see myself a bit more clearly in the wake of simply hearing what I had to say aloud given the chance, without the crosstalk of anybody else I knew needed to hear. Every few sessions, as I got used to this rapport, I'd come in and announce how I felt much better now, that everything had clicked, and I could do this on my own. I was still counting in the back of my mind the time and money spent on what felt like workshopping my life, ready to name a limit as soon as I imagined I got the gist. Slowly, though, I began to become more aware of how I acted out of bias and old habits, realizing how to cut off at the pass the parts of me that no longer served me quite so well—the seething parts, the bitter fire, the violence I'd taught myself to aim at my own heart in my depression. Opening myself up, analyzing my life directly, didn't diminish me, nor did it make my dark parts go away, as I'd feared therapy would; rather, it made me more able to see the factors of influence underneath, the connections between my feelings and my reason, and why when I got hot, nothing ever seemed to work. This wasn't a concession, a weakling's fix-all, I started thinking; this was a source of recognition I'd long sought, a practice that allowed me to move past longstanding instincts that had only ever gotten me in trouble, and to be able to speak back, or at least be aware where I might snap. The fact that I was paying a professional to listen to me, which I'd once thought lame, bridged the gap I felt in keeping to myself despite being sick of my longstanding hateful habits and kneejerk thought. My efforts appeared to affect Molly, too, relieved to no longer be the only person I relied on to come to with my troubles. Instead of dreading therapy, I began looking forward to it, hungry to hear what else might come out of me as I let my guard down and looked in.

Now that I was willing, too, we decided to try couple's therapy "as a preventative measure" meant to help us know each other better, improve our communication—much easier with someone else there making sure we did it right, with proper care—one foot in front of the other, one step at a time.

———

News arrived that Molly's father had been released from prison again. He was an old man now, and he had a girlfriend who'd stayed with him throughout his second sentence, financially supporting him despite the fact he hadn't told her about his felonious past till behind bars. Given their interaction during his stint, Molly was worried he'd expect her to be part of his new life, or that he'd show up at our door sometime unannounced—totally in his range of possible behaviors. In therapy, she'd been reminded many times that a sociopath will never change, does not know love or remorse, only wants to use others for their gain. "The difference is, I don't care," Molly insisted. "He can't hurt me. I already know." Clearly, however, this wasn't true, given the degree to which his influence continued to haunt her, kept her wondering what he really thought. *"Aren't we together on this, Dad, together on missing our dads, and what it has done to you and me?"* the only italicized section in *Bandit* reads, like some sort of sacred tribute, held in thrall. *"You left an unknowable self behind, with us, your cover story, your dupes, and I kept following. And I'm still following, somehow more than ever, in love with this trouble, this difficult family, in love with my troubled mom and sister and you too, maybe most of all you, the unknowable one."*[20] I felt I understood her hanging on about him, at least a little, trying to imagine how it would feel to have a father so defunct. He'd forever remained a mystery at least, while so much of all the rest of her interpretation

20 *Bandit*, p. 25.

of the world stung bitter-clear. "Do you think my dad loves me?" Molly asked me suddenly, as if to catch me off guard, read my real feelings. I must have not been able to hide my ire, though, given how quickly she clammed up when I said no. She deserved so much more than his half-assed badgering and dodging, I tried to explain, and she'd already given him more good faith than he deserved. Just because he was too fucked up to treat her right that didn't mean she wasn't worthy. I took it as my job, I said as she studied my face, to be the difference, to make up for what he'd taken from her with my own love, so one day she could see herself through other eyes, to fill the void that no one else could. This was my privilege, after all, why I'd been put here. Molly said nothing, just staring back at me from somewhere between resignation and pure rage. He'd already reached out, she said, wanting to drive down from Ohio and have dinner with us, and despite her better judgement, it was clear she felt compelled to give him one more chance. Maybe all that time locked up had done him good, she thought; maybe, just maybe, despite what everybody else thought, he might be ready to open up. We went to meet him and his girlfriend down the street from our house, at a crappy pizza place we'd never been before, so he couldn't ruin it. He looked a lot older than the last time I had seen him, all smiles and salutations, insisting on springing for the food. He and I stood around in line waiting to order, staring up at the menu overhead with nothing to say to one another, while Molly sat and spoke with the girlfriend back at our table, as if that was who she'd really come to see. While waiting for our order, Joe and Molly talked about the weather, traffic, the neighborhood, and Molly's work, without a word about anything substantial, like how strange it felt to be there, how he felt in being freed, much less all the years of anguish he'd inflicted on his family. Molly mostly blushed, uncertain what to say without his lead, gripping my hand hard under the table, gritting her teeth. After twenty minutes, we'd finished eating, and her father went out to the car to bring her back a birthday present: a neon-colored cake made of silky fabric, inedible and garish. He asked to take a picture of us, just she and I—then they excused themselves and began the long drive back to Ohio, an exact tone-match for his short visit when she was in the hospital after brain surgery. On our own way home, we agreed how it seemed he'd only wanted the photo so he could have to show people, to prove once and for all he was a father. Underneath that, I understood now more than ever, all Molly had really wanted in return was any signal of his love, even just his pathetic, hasty, brutalizing brand; to know that she was worthy of it, as his daughter, as *a person*; that he might not actually be as remorseless as he seemed. Instead, he'd let her leave, behind his false front, full of his own ego's piss and wind, as if nobody could see him but himself. Back home, soon as we pulled into the driveway, Molly jumped out of the car and slammed the fake cake in our trash bin, tore to shreds his store-bought card, signed with nothing but his name. She said she didn't want to talk about it any further, didn't want a hug or such—really it had gone exactly as she thought, she swore, no big deal—then she put on a nature show about the destruction of the ice caps and wept silently for a while before going to bed two hours early.

———

"This memoir is full of lies," writes a Books-a-Million customer named, "Joe," from an "undisclosed location," in his 1-star review of Molly's memoir, titled, *The Real BANDIT!* "The author was deeply loved by her father who never consciously hurt his daughter. I am the man pictured on the book's cover." Prior to this, discovered only shortly after their last meeting, Molly had no idea whether her father knew the book was in print, much less if he'd read it—it certainly hadn't come up at dinner. She sat there staring at the comment on her laptop, laughing at it incredulously but also very, very mad. She'd already felt conflicted and embarrassed for having spilled the beans on family secrets, despite having gone to great lengths to give her father a fair shake, and now here he was, indirectly calling her out in the comments section of random website. "I know what it's like to make the wrong choice, over and over," she'd written of him, "as if taunting the consequences, practically asking them to come straighten you up. And to act secretly, build a whole small, bad world in private, like an invisible dimension running just under the one everyone else lives in." This was something they both shared, she thought, if in a way that felt to me like collateral damage, a way of blaming herself for what he'd done, and at the same time, a way of forgiving herself too, if only by proxy, behind the blind. Hadn't she'd learned directly from him, after all, to live with paradoxes intertwined, unwilling to admit defeat even red-handed, as if all survival might require is pretending everything is fine? How much of him was right there in her even still, gripping the wheel through muscle memory, egging her on?

▬

Not long after that last meeting with her father, Molly started describing an experience of waking up no longer sure of where she was. She'd wander around our house at the cusp of dawn, frightened and listless, trying to remember where her memories began. "This morning when I walked into the kitchen I saw the timer was moving," she writes on March 4, four days before she decides to take her life. "It was at 95:58 and climbing. How was it set off? How was it possible it ran all night—what, starting over again and again? I'm not sure how I even noticed it was running. Seems to be a sign." As the fog cleared, over maybe fifteen minutes, she would come back into her own, the familiar landscape of our home's contents reassembling into meaning, and yet not quite a full relief: she was still herself, still here, if just a failure in her own eyes. Recounting the experience, she seemed afraid, like she wanted to share the space of dislocation, but also didn't want to have to hear what I would say—that she should see a doctor soon if it kept on, and in the meantime, speak with our therapist about it. For a while, we worried if it could be her brain tumor coming back, though Molly remained skeptical and light, certain that if it were the tumor, she'd start lactating out of nowhere, as she had the time before. Her body would show signs, like crying out; in the meantime, she'd assume everything was fine.

Molly's nonchalance about her troubles feels much different to me now than it did then. Her tumor in particular—how could it not have been on her mind, screaming in the background like a revolt against cognition whether it ever actually returned or not? And yet this pain was never something she'd much shared with me beyond her anecdotes, in passing glimpses, playing it down as if uncertain how to trust me with it, terrified of what still might prove yet to come. I understand this sort of hidden worry very well, having my own ongoing fears about dementia I'd prefer not to have to iterate aloud, as if that'd make them more real somehow, or I deserve the worry. It doesn't seem like a coincidence Molly would choose eventually to put a hole in her head herself, a friend points out, aimed at where the tumor once had been, using a gun just like her father had while robbing banks, as if attempting to reclaim power from her past. "To lie habitually, as a way of life, is to lose contact with the unconscious," writes Adrienne Rich in her essay "Women and Honor," in which she underlines the long history of women lying to survive—to please their lying husbands by modifying the body, faking orgasms, hiding abuse to prevent further abuse. "It is like taking sleeping pills, which confer sleep but blot out dreaming. The unconscious wants truth. It ceases to speak to those who want something else more than truth."[21] Rich goes on to describe the maddening feeling of being lied to in a

21   Rich, Adrienne, "Women and Honor: Some Notes on Lying." *On Lies, Secrets, and Silence: Selected Prose 1966-1978*. W.W. Norton & Co., 1995, p. 414.

relationship in particular; how deceit there changes the way we see the universe; how honor "has to be created between people," which in turn extends "the possibility of life between us." But: "I am not good at the truth," Molly writes in her poem "Good At It." "It doesn't / elate me // like it does / good people." Could that be true? Or is that more so just how Molly feels from comparing herself to her own impossible ideals, betrayed by right and wrong alike? *Methinks the lady doth protest too much*, I might have thought reading her poem and trying to compare the person I knew best against the person she clearly felt she had to be, as if we aren't all of us many people, both in each moment as it passes and all throughout our lives and others' lives. Really, though, the inability to ever truly understand the way she felt, to feel it too, suspends the math of *true* or *false* behind an even thicker, higher wall, one that mere companionship can never topple. In the end, maybe that's what makes the work of wanting to understand her feel so impossible—like a bit in the mouth that leads you nowhere, gripped by a hand you cannot access, much less tame.

Seeing no better end in sight to her boss drama, Molly quit her job at KSU. She'd decided it was in her mental health's best interest to move on from there as soon as possible, as had several of her peers, and in the meantime, she could bake and write until something better came along. The sudden glut of open time seemed to inspire her to only take on even more though, filling up her calendar so completely every day's column was crammed with notes. The lack of larger structure to her timeline increased her sensitivity tenfold, ashamed for having "no career" in her late 30s, despite having worked full time her entire life and having just launched her own small business. She already had her hopes up, too, about the possibility of a tenure track job at a nearby university, her lifelong dream, and her new memoir, *Alone in Poland*, was mostly done and about to make the rounds to publishers—fingers crossed. In the meantime, I was spending much of my free time up at Mom's, sorting through five decades of family stuff in preparation to put the house on the market. That house had always been an oasis for me, part of the world that I could count on to retain who I had been, and already I could feel it fading, slipping away between the cracks. I knew Molly didn't really like seeing me bring home boxes upon boxes of my old stuff, forced to choose to keep it or discard the many boxes of old baseball cards and comics, baby toys my mother had kept since I was too small to remember, plastic bags full of my lost teeth, handwritten cards from Mom for every holiday and special occasion, as well as countless other knickknacks loaded with memories and stories from precious times. Each of these relics, I slowly began to realize, as felt through Molly's eyes, only served to reinforce the attention she'd never had, and therefore provided a good reason to despise me where it hurt most. "I didn't like to see people caring about their families," she'd written in *Bandit*, "or insisting that their private family story should be meaningful to others," an aside I tried not to take too much to heart.[22] If I'd hoped to make new memories out of these old ones, narrating for Molly the significant events of my early life, I realized there wasn't much room there to share, and what room there was fit tight and tacky, not at all the space I'd long imagined I'd someday find in love—more like contraband now than holy totems, good for little else but feeling hurt and lost and old.

━━━

We started doing psychedelic drugs. Now that I'd been smoking pot for almost a year and liking it far more than I'd ever liked drinking, I felt ready to have my clock cleaned a little brighter; good, clean fun. Molly had done most everything already, and she felt excited I was

22   *Bandit*, p. 164.

at last loosening up, able to meet her in a place I'd shied away from. We set aside whole days to hang out and get high together, listening to music and watching films or hanging out in the backyard with the birds. On LSD, everything seemed to become clear, all the nonsense of everyday reality replaced with an overarching comprehension of the scheme behind all things. If only I could retain the higher sense that I acquired from the trip into my actual reality, I kept trying to remind myself, amazed by trees, the sky, the earth. On mushrooms, ideas had many edges, bulging layers, vast curiosity, though on a dime the vibe could shift to nausea, nails on glass. I remember wanting to rip my head off listening over a video of Glenn Gould, his sing-song voice over the piano pathetic enough in its compulsion to make me want to hide inside the bedroom with the door closed, head between pillows, while Molly sat on the sofa and wept alone. On ecstasy, the world around us seemed to brighten and grow warm, sealing us together in a moment where nothing much mattered besides cuddling and whispering of love, listening to our hearts beat through our chests. All the walls we'd built, the long, weird ways we'd worked around each other, would seem to fall away when it was no longer us there at the helm. It felt healthy giving ourselves space we needed to disappear for a bit, to feel something other than overrun. Even as a couple times a month became several times a week, without a care for how the higher highs might fund lower lows, the drugs felt good, and we could take them as we wished, whenever we wanted without regrets, unlike most everything else in the world. Now, though, when I hear "Molly" referenced in rap lyrics, I don't think so much about the glow. I think about how fast life moves, how brief the window. I think about the fact that she is dead.

■■■

During what would end up being our last summer together, Molly and I visited James Turrell's "Akhob" installation at the Louis Vuitton shop in Las Vegas, its title taken from an Egyptian word for "pure water." We were escorted with another couple into a darkened room where we were asked to remove our shoes, then we were led down a narrow hallway to where we were seated in front of a wide staircase. I remember not knowing what would happen next, feeling Molly there beside me, each aflutter, while we received instructions on how to move. We were asked to ascend the stairs to a pale alcove, like a cave, where two adjoining, sculpted spaces gave us a floor, at once warm and elusive, rounded and endless. There then began, without a signal, to appear a changing light—waves of shifting spectrum, spreading in and filling out into no space but of the colors. We were not allowed to speak. More than the light, though, I remember Molly—wanting to watch her, to try to see the way she saw, feel how she felt; to see her face and how it changed, too, and how she held herself, where she stood. She seemed so small there, and so brave. Sometimes if I close my eyes, I can go back into that moment, finding the colors now reflected against the flesh under my lids; I can imagine her posture and her size, her eyes wide open, taking it in; and then, whether it actually happened then or not, her shoulder at my shoulder, her left hand slipped into my right hand, forever there.

———

Molly started getting Botox and lip fillers every few weeks. She'd become obsessed with her looks more than ever suddenly, hating herself and talking shit only more and more as she got older, even though to me she was as beautiful as she had ever been. I felt caught off guard about her interest in something she'd normally have blasted off on as *bullshit for rich bitches*, but I also knew it didn't matter what I thought, nor did I expect it to. "I've been doing this for a while now, Blake," she smirked when I responded with surprise, "and you didn't notice until I told you." Now that the subject had been broached, though, Molly admitted she had bigger plans: she'd been to see a plastic surgeon and received quotes on breast implants and liposuction, an all-natural process moving fat from her thighs into her chest. She'd wanted bigger breasts her whole life, she sat me down to explain while going over the papers for the procedure; the one thing about her body she most wished she could change. It would work wonders on her self-confidence to fix that, which then would lead to bigger changes, too, able to finally feel comfortable in her own skin. Would I want to help her pay for it, she wondered aloud, maybe as a Christmas gift, coming up soon? $10,000 is a lot, I tried to say, rolling it over, trying to see it from her shoes while simultaneously confused by the impulsivity, a little extreme even for her. I wished she didn't have to feel compelled to change herself to stay desirable—easy for me to say, though, as a man, who didn't even feel the need to put on sunscreen to prevent wrinkles, which I'd seen Molly talking shit about online. The taking care was hopeful after all she'd suffered, I imagined, even if it seemed reactionary, not like her. My only worry about the procedure was the surgery itself, which required her being anaesthetized, under for hours. Slim chance that one should die, but still a chance. Molly of course didn't care at all about that aspect—in fact, it was part of the upside, she wryly joked. Anyway, she'd already decided she was going to do it no matter what I thought, she let me know, completely nonplussed by my reluctance, happy to take debt in her own name. She knew very well how weird I felt about the money I'd inherited after mother died; how I'd told her that I hated having it, how I wanted to put it to good use. At the same time, what I really wanted was for her to see her as I saw her, now and always—a force of nature; beautiful and brilliant because she was. Nothing much I'd ever said or done seemed to help her see that, but maybe this could. So, I agreed, "If you really think this is going to make you happy, let's make you happy."

The surgery, at least on the surface, did the trick. Almost immediately, Molly assumed a sort of glowing confidence she'd rarely carried. She'd stand at the mirror measuring her body, posing and strutting, taking countless pictures of herself. It felt funny to go with her for the checkups, sitting in the waiting room with Molly and all the other Buckhead bodies in the office, touched up and tightened, wearing Spanx and Gucci shades. Normally, Molly hated these types of people with a passion; now she was in there with them, though she did seem to be having fun. In post-op pictures, her grin seems saccharine, charmed but sated. Her slightly larger breasts looked good, sure, but so had her original ones, in my opinion, which I understood was not the point. I held my tongue and tried to help when she would struggle with the damage from the knives that'd sucked what little fat she had out of her thighs, wearing a suit to hold the tighter flesh in until it settled, eating painkillers. This was the best decision she had made in a long time, Molly already knew. I should go get work done, too, she added, for my love handles, which had always bothered me. Why not be exactly how you want? I even began to consider it, mostly conceptually: What would it feel like to have your body changed completely overnight? How much of you could you change before you were no longer really you? And who was counting? Molly's impulse-driven logic could be infectious in this way, especially as she continued to shed the decorum her teaching reputation had kept her tight with. Her newfound confidence appeared to alter other aspects of her behavior, too, flaunty and provocative in ways I'd never seen her act. I'd been sitting right next to her on our couch one night, for instance, when I saw she tweeted the offer of a photo of her left breast to anyone who had the guts to ask. "Really, Molly?" I asked, interrupting her strange reverie there on her laptop at my side. "It's just a joke," she reassured me, barely looking up, "and anyway, no one's ever going to ask." Another night, while I was away, she posted a picture of herself in her underwear with "Bernie Sanders" photoshopped onto her ass, clearly showing off under the cover of the way everyone else was acting nuts online, part of the political frenzy of the times—a little funny, sure, but also unusual for her. I felt confident enough in who we were to not let it bother me; Molly felt body-positive, for once, apparently, and she should be allowed to do whatever she wanted within the limits of our trust, which I fully trusted she'd never break. When she dyed her hair back to platinum blonde, like it'd been when we met, and even as I could remember how she'd told me point blank, speaking of someone else, that "when a woman dyes her hair, she's about to leave," I still didn't imagine it was her and me she meant, that I should worry. Had I asked, I already know, she would have only played it off or made me feel bad, though at the same time the fact that I didn't object directly only added to her idea that I didn't care about her either, like all the rest. She remained a pro at being able to shift the focus of a conversation off herself and onto me in moments like these, able to explain why I shouldn't be upset, if also slightly seeming to want me to be. Trained as a professor, and perhaps by her father, she spoke with an authority that made it feel like she knew more than I did about the situation, morally and existentially, and so I should really think about it more before opening my mouth. Quick twists of focus like that, able to make me feel uncertain of myself as on a dime, would lead me to retrace my steps and second guess my own behavior instead of hers, while also showing no restraint in shaming me for all the many ways I failed. The fact that I'd forget to get my laundry out of the dryer overnight would be a terrible, serial offense, one that she said proved that I never thought about her feelings, or that I wanted her to be my slave. If I asked if she wanted anything from the grocery store, she'd say that I should already know the things she likes, that I should be able to make a list without asking for her labor, though if I came home without any one of those many specific things, then that, too, must be a sign of how little attention I paid to her. At the same time, I agreed with her when she grabbed me by the arm and told me to stop walking in front of her when we left the house, and that my walking in front of her a few feet reminded her of Trump, and I changed my behavior to reflect that of a respectful man, grateful to have been corrected, so that I could be more aware of in going forward. This didn't mean I didn't get my feelings hurt or get frustrated, but instead of expressing how I felt, I'd bite my lip, swallow it down. Instead, I started ranting to myself in private, furiously searching for a reason why I felt so insane all the time, so stupid and useless when all I ever did was try to do things right? Why couldn't I be more ideal, more like Molly, underlined me in so many ways I started doubting things I felt I'd known for a long time, like who my friends were? I'd heard the term *gaslighting* before, primarily through Molly's usage of it, and I certainly couldn't have imagined she'd be making these things up. The problem, I knew, because Molly had told me, began with *me*—finding out what was wrong with *me*, fixing *me*. By the end, some of it would be so deeply embedded in my mind I could hear her in there, and even still, a voice masked in the vortex of my brain, feeding me with information whether I wanted it or not.

▬

One night, while on the sofa watching TV, Molly announced she'd like to have a threesome. But it had to be with another man, she said, because she didn't like women. She asked if I'd be into that, and when I said I wasn't sure, that I wasn't against it entirely but also didn't think I'd want to watch her having sex with someone else, she asked if I thought men were attractive. Sure, I knew when men were good looking, I said, had explored fantasies, but I'd never been in a situation where I felt the impulse to act. She asked me to describe a time when I'd found a guy attractive, and I thought about it and told her there'd been a guy at the poker table in New Orleans on a recent trip I took alone to play some cards and visit friends, but again, just a passing observation, no big deal. "The next time you find yourself in a spot like that," she said, "you have my permission." I said OK, trying to imagine what she meant. "You're probably bi," she suggested. "I think it's beautiful." I wasn't sure what else to say, or how to codify what she was saying in a way that connected with how I actually felt. If we did decide to have a threesome, I said, how would we find a person we both liked? Molly was quiet in response to that, eyes on her lap. Later that night, while making out to *Master of Reality*, she perched on top of me on my lap and said she wanted us to be wilder. She wanted to call me daddy, for example, and for me to be more aggressive with her. I said I would, but on the inside, felt something different, like I wanted to know why now, after so long; and why *daddy*, given all I knew about her dad. I found myself returning to the scene in *Bandit* where her father is driving her to her elementary school; how as they pass boys from her class on the sidewalk, he calls out through the window, "Molly loves you," laughing his ass off as she squirms. In her journals, when Molly writes about waking from a dream of being raped in prison, she finds it reminds her of her father, perhaps in the same way that made her go blank when we would argue, unable to hold in honest light the same love she'd felt in calmer times. At the same time, I felt dumb for lingering on her past, trying to convince myself I should just go with it and give her what she wanted in the moment, perhaps a form of therapy itself. Isn't that what discerning adults do? Wasn't I lame for having lines to draw, harboring preoccupations instead of getting off on it? Why did I need to understand? I'd spent so much time already worrying, wondering, projecting for the worst that might yet happen any second, and I couldn't see what it'd brought me but anxiety and paranoia. It seemed I'd caused more trouble for myself in being vigilant, doubting others, when in the long run the principle of Occam's razor held better court. What right did I have—as a man, a husband to a person who I saw as nearly flawless, if affected—to suspect anything else?

——

We skipped Thanksgiving in Michigan that year. Molly decided she'd had enough of traveling to visit family when she didn't feel like it, especially while recovering from surgery, and insisted that we should do whatever we want at home instead. She'd been cancelling her weekly phone calls with her mother, in the meantime, citing how Nora would only talk endlessly about herself. It really was all just the two of us now, I imagined, especially on my end, with no one expecting us, no concrete plans, which felt like a relief in a way even if I couldn't help but be aware of how much our lives had changed in such short time, at once more isolated and more ours. As if to sanctify this, chasing another whim, we flew to L.A. to go to a live taping of *Dr. Phil* on LSD. We'd been watching his show for quite a while now in the evenings during dinner, as a kind of ironic activity that became habit, strangely enthralling both for the parade of bizarre lives they put onscreen and for Phil's formulaic freestyle problem-solving, which Molly said made her feel better about her own life. That morning, while tripping ass waiting in line, Molly kept pointing out how much the scene reminded her of Auschwitz—held among numbered masses, without access to food and water, being judged by our looks for where we'd sit, brain-jarringly loud soundtrack while in holding, nosebleed bright lights, ritualized performance on demand. Our emotions swung from stunned astonishment to feeling ill, jarred in being surrounded by packs of strangers among the corporate bravado, all in the name of witnessing human pain. The primary story that day featured a woman who was stuck living with her agoraphobic sister and deranged mother, unable to feel free to live her own life in light of their refusal to seek help. Molly seemed very moved by the fact that no one paid much attention to this person, focusing instead on her ill family, trying to convince them to agree to therapy, eventually ending in an icy stalemate, resolving nothing. "No one actually loves anyone," Molly concluded on the drive back to our Airbnb, a statement that while still on LSD, I couldn't quite begin to imagine how to parse. It just felt true—true of America, in particular, and of people; how so little ever seems to reach us or hold weight; how hard it is to recognize who cares, without any definitive reason to expect that the floor won't fall out at any time. It made it only worse that this was my wife speaking, allowing no exception when she spoke so frankly, in a way that only made me laugh as I agreed, knowing how she'd react if I tried to counter with my own feelings about her; how no matter how hard or weird our lives together had become, I still believed in her beyond all else, loved her more than anyone alive. "Satan cries because he's the only one in hell who *remembers* God's love," she would write about the taping. "He had felt it. He was once there, right up next to it."

———

"If you ever tried to go to church, I would divorce you," Molly informed me out of the blue once back at home, as if in response to a running conversation in her head. She'd never liked that as a child I'd gone to Sunday School and been confirmed, despite the fact that church was as far from my list of interests as it was hers. That I wouldn't come out and say for certain that I believed the same as she did—that there was nothing after death, and that at best my experience of anything otherworldly was afflicted, brainwashed, or just dumb—remained an easy way for her to separate us, a bait I often took, when in a bad mood, ready to bicker. Few things could set her off as much as when I'd say I considered atheism an equal extreme, as righteously self-assured as the evangelicals. Why insist on labeling as *fact* what can't be proved? Why rely completely on logical rationale despite the course of human history, including science, having proved many times over how little we know? "I already know that's how you feel," Molly would interrupt, leaving the room. She'd already made up her mind and would accept no substitute, no conversation—instead, another brick laid on the wall, if one that I perceived as ornamental, part of the differences that gave our many similarities relief. I got the sense that there was something else there in her posture, a kind of shadowy refusal that thrived only more in zero light—impossible to comment on without a fight, but also screaming out in her own way for something like help. We had our whole lives to work these threads out, I imagined, to learn to better love each other as we were; to challenge one another, iron on iron, in a good way, at once safe from harm and against the world. I held onto hope someday she'd find a friend or a more steadfast source of faith that she could trust outside of me, but in the end it had to come back to a bitter baseline, knocked off its pedestal at any sign of uncertainty, as if no matter how she thought, she'd already learned to keep it at arm's length, to protect herself when inadvertently it failed. Who could ever really want her, even if they seemed to really want to? How long could true love last?

━━━

The last movie Molly and I saw in theaters together, *Uncut Gems*, tells the story of a degenerate gambler, Howard Ratner, played by Adam Sandler, who gets himself and his family into trouble because he thinks he thinks he's smarter than everybody else. Like Molly's father, he gambles with money he doesn't have, making larger and larger bets to try to cover up the past. Molly had assured me she could take it, sitting through a story so much like her own, but ended up having to leave the theater during the scenes where Ratner would shout and rant at games with so much money on the line. Of course, Sandler makes the movie, for someone without ties, fun to watch, likeable on the surface as he pursues his whims, living a double life, neglecting his wife and children, lying to everybody that he sees. Like Molly, the looming tension of a possible cancerous polyp in Ratner's body backgrounds the narrative, barely mentioned amidst the larger waves of chaos and distress. I wondered if maybe we shouldn't have come to see it together, clearly affected in much different ways, and perhaps I hadn't thought enough about the impact on her, I realized, whether she admitted it bothered her or not. I didn't get yet what trigger warnings were for, why anybody could be so hurt by the inanimate; I'd have to feel it for myself, many months later, when I realized the regularity of gunshot suicide imagery on TV, how the sounds of firecrackers in the distance could put me right back in the worst moments of my life, barely different in its feeling from the real thing. *Uncut Gems* ends when, spoiler alert, having gone too far, Ratner is shot in the face at close range, ending his life. The camera zooms toward the bullet hole, moving on through it, into the darkened tunnels lacing his flesh. "I'm glad they showed the wound like that," Molly told me, as we exited the theater. "Everyone should have to see."

———

Uncertain what else to do for work, Molly applied for unemployment. The visiting position she'd accepted after KSU—a two-hour drive south from our house—had just concluded, with little hope of a renewal after she'd ended up in another fight with the brass, this time due to a mishap with her contract, thinking the position came with health insurance when it didn't. She'd also just learned she wasn't going to get the other dream job she'd applied for, another hard blow to her ego that by this point just seemed unfair, as if there were no place in the world where she belonged. I felt it wasn't her fault things hadn't worked out in academia, the biggest suckhole of them all, and I identified with her unwillingness to settle. I tried to remind her there was no rush here, that I could cover our expenses while she figured out what should come next. Now that my mom was gone, I'd be willing to move most anywhere, following her lead. Clearly, though, the lack of traction for her own utility dragged at her soul; she'd been working her whole life without a firm lead, and suddenly it seemed like there was nothing left for her to do. Outwardly, however, instead of wholly giving up, she began brainstorming by making a list of her previous jobs:

Painter's assistant
Clerk at Greens
Clerk at Sydney Bogg
Pantry at Kruse and Muir
Pizza at Kruse and Muir
Maid
Counter at Dairy Queen
Intern at Orbit
Sushi Waitress Rochester
Sushi Waitress Auburn Hills
Waitress at that horrible shitty family restaurant I can't remember
Café (SoHo South) Waitress
Reading tutor for elementary students
Café (other Savannah Restaurant I can't remember name) Waitress
Books-A-Million bookseller
Barnes & Noble bookseller
Aid at Retirement Home
Babysitter for Teacher's Kids

Baker at Harvest Grains
Clerk at Oilily
Belgian brewery waitress
OU Bookstore assistant manager
CCS Bookstore assistant manager
College reading tutor
Cranbrook Art Museum store manager
Barnes & Noble (Morgantown) bookseller
Secret Shopper
Grad Student assistant to Comp Dir
Teacher at WVU
Teacher at ASU
Cashier at Fresh Market
Teacher at Emory
Teacher at (that other shitty school I adjuncted)
Kitchen help at Pie Shop
Cashier at Cacao
Editor at Digistrive
Teacher at SPSU
Teacher at KSU
Teacher at GSCU

What a loser, she decided. All that striving now for naught, void of a future. She'd given everything she had and look at where it'd gotten her—aging, ugly, hopeless, stupid. All other options outside academia felt like settling, relegating herself to a life she already despised, and even as she half-heartedly sent out her resume to as many opening positions as she could find, it seemed she did so inconsolably, going through motions in hopes something else good would appear in the nick of time—*as if.*

———

It'd felt like a glimmer of hope, then, when Molly approached me with the idea of manifesting her own poetry residency. She wanted to rent a room out in the desert somewhere, so she could search her soul and try to write. I happily agreed to help her pay for a 10-day stay in the Tucson desert, hopeful a getaway might be exactly the reset that she needed. The morning of her departure, minutes before leaving, she let me know she couldn't find her wedding ring, no longer there beside the sink where she would often rest it overnight—no big deal, though, it'd turn up. After taking her to the airport, never one for patience, I came home and set to frantic searching—going through trash, taking apart pipes, scouring the floors—still driving myself batshit hours later, once she'd landed. *Calm down, BB*, she tried to remind me, suggesting I just rest, do something else; until then, a minor miracle: the ring had been in her make-up bag all this time! What a relief! She proved it with a picture of her pinching the ring in her fingers in someone's bathroom, a gentle rejoinder to what now appeared to have been an overreaction on my part. Why did I always have to freak out so completely whenever something minor went awry? Did I maybe actually relish the strain a little, more an inherent part of who I am than I'd yet realized? When would I ever learn to chill? The revelation of an answer to any question could never be too far away, and maybe eventually I'd learn a patience, more like Molly, or at least how to sit with my discomfort without exploding, perish the thought. Who could say, and if they could, who would I trust to, if not my wife and not myself?

———

That evening, alone on the eve of my family's estate sale, I wandered throughout the house where I'd grown up, talking to myself with all the lights off. A marketing company had come in and organized our stuff, the many lifetimes of belongings neither my sister or I had room to carry home, all of it with what seemed completely arbitrary price tags attached: my mother's sewing trinkets and her jewelry, laid out on card tables in the den where we'd build blanket tents; the husks of old computers I had saved since a teenager, their hard drives full of files long since forgotten; piles of clothes my mother and father and sister and I each had once worn, outgrown or ragged; drawings and paintings we'd made at so many different ages; piles of books I'd read or not read, remembered or not remembered; childhood toys I'd never had the heart to throw away. In the wake of that, back at my own home, I killed the lights and lit some candles, as if to make the two houses connect. I sat at my desk in my office, prepared to work on what I hoped was my next novel, about a troubled woman living in isolation with her husband at an evacuated religious theme park after the fall of civilization—lonely, lost, abused, beyond her wits. I thought of the characters as Molly and me, each sort of a blur between the two as in certain ways I more resembled the woman and she the man. I put on headphones and blasted Aphex Twin's *Drukqs* so loud it made it hard to think, typing in rhythm through the darkness until I felt my mother's voice appear inside my head. The words I wrote with her in tow, draped like a curtain over my own drive, seemed somehow electric, even alive, like I could see the code beneath the language, what each sentence really stood for when logic stepped out of the way. Mom and I had a bond that could synthesize us beyond death, I heard her urge me; and though there were things outside the comprehension of the living she couldn't share yet, we could work together in intuition shaped by the sacred time we'd spent together on the earth. I felt a sort of joy I hadn't felt for quite some time then, typing in tandem and speaking aloud with Mom as kin and peers alike, able to communicate with who she'd been before dementia had worn her mind down, without remorse. We could collaborate in this way whenever I wanted, Mom acknowledged. It would be an open window. All I had to do was ask.

———

"And when you look long into an abyss, the abyss also looks into you."[23]

———

After the window with my mother closed, the channel remained open in my mind, as if something else, something more menacing within the undead energy had become aware that I was there. *You're not supposed to be here*, a different kind of voice explained, more like my own but displaced, aligned within the darkness of the room. Then, even more clearly: *You are rapidly approaching a point of no return.* It felt as if at once was being warded off and goaded forth, provoked by thoughts that meant to chide me for turning back. Beyond the edges of the candlelight, there at the doorway, I felt a lurking presence, spilling up like smoke from the long dark—demons, I understood, called online as a response in the line I'd opened between realms. I ignored it at first as paranoia, my imagination fucking with my vulnerability because it could, though the longer I ignored them, the more aggressive they became. *If you don't stop, we're going to hurt your wife*, I heard them hissing. *There's no limit to the pain we can create, so you should go away unless you're ready.* Feeling actually freaked out, I took my headphones off and turned to face the window, finding mostly only my reflection there against the outer dark, the world beyond. Through the headphones' leakage, now on my lap, I noticed how the music had shifted from its prior syncopated flow into something like an elevator music, as if my stepping off had only placed the situation on a temporary hold. *We thought you said you were fearless*, the demons goaded. *But really, we can see you're just another*

23 Nietzsche, Friedrich. *Beyond Good and Evil*. Translated by Walter Kaufmann, Vintage, 1966, p. 89.

coward like the rest. They knew exactly what to say to challenge me, to draw me forward, like they could see into my soul, seeking its cracks. I kept reminding myself this wasn't real; that I had worked myself into a frenzy, out of grief. I put the headphones back on, shocked to hear the soundtrack shifting back at once to how it'd been. The demons couldn't win if I refused to let them, I decided, determined to force myself on past them, no turning back. Who was I supposed to be if not brave now, at odds with my own imagination's very soul? What would it mean to concede here, to such an arbitrary-feeling form of fear—that not only were there forces beyond my control, as I had learned in losing Mom abruptly, but worse; that my own fate, the fate of my most loved ones, could be rerouted based on what I did or didn't do? Wasn't I strong enough to overcome that, to find some way to *win*? Wasn't this why I was here?

　　　　　　　　■

After the writing, Molly wasn't responding to my texts or calls. The last thing she'd said was that she was going to take a Percocet and have a bath, and the longer that I waited, the more my brain began to lace itself with bad ideas, traces of the demons' voices still live and loud inside my head, filling me with images of her falling asleep in the tub and drowning, or even worse. Eventually, I'd worked myself into a panic, pacing from room to room trying to analyze other explanations, reminding myself of the countless times I'd gotten worked up in paranoia only to discover everything, of course, was fine. She's just asleep, I kept repeating, trying to distract myself with TV until I finally decided to try to go to bed, laying with my phone on vibrate beside my head, still desperate for her response. I'd trained myself into a lifetime of insomnia worrying like this, so terrified by thoughts of ghosts or hidden lurkers that I'd tear my inner world down trying to avoid them, chase them off. I'd learned to dote and fret from my mother and her mother both, and both had ended up in forms of madness, after all, the lingering threat of what form of terror might appear most any second of any hour of any day, inside of an abstraction where every second the worst thing you can't imagine hasn't happened yet is an exception, beside the point. This very lack of actuality, its continuous expectation left unprocessed, had come to form the fundament upon which reality occurs, a roving, ambient window calling out for someone to come and close it, finally enclosing what exists on either side into its place. I was still talking to myself, shouting at God, tossing and turning, when finally, just before dawn, Molly replied. *I'm ok bb! Sorry I fell asleep! Everything is fine ☺ No worries, I love you! Go back to sleep.* Another great relief, see! Every improbable horror I'd tortured myself imagining the worst proved all for nothing after all, the removal of the possibility of tragedy somehow more fulfilling than an actual experience of joy, like the way a gambler remembers their greatest losses more than their wins. Later, on the phone that afternoon, we'd laugh about it—*same old hysterical Blake; he'll never learn.* Turned out Molly had been writing that night, too, she said, working on poems about a woman in the future, looking back on all the things we'd taken for granted, before they disappeared—mail and phones and medicine, for instance—an eerie parallel to what I'd been writing that night, too, as if somehow within the wake of what'd come open underneath me, we were connected through our ideas, past time and space; as if we'd been bound up in something else, beyond ourselves.

▬

I can't see around the corner, I'd find Molly wrote in her journal that same day, *so it feels like I am at the end. The idea that I had ever lowered myself into less that I wanted is now revealed to be a soothing coping mechanism. Actually I am shit, have always been shit, and nothing had been derailed. I was never meant to be what I wanted. I have merely bumbled into survival, unworthy of it, without original contribution, without creativity, without even an honorable love for those I've tried to love. I have never—not once—done a good job loving anyone. I am a failure. Paying a woman to tell me I'm normal. A vampire. Vampires simply don't deserve sunlight and they know it. It's not a real weakness. I belong in the trash compactor. I belong unassembled. Let some animals eat my body, which didn't deserve to take up space at any point. I have to find a way to make this ok. My fingers crawling all over these letters doesn't help. I have to find a way to help. I have to find a way to take my ugly, evil life and force it to do something right.*

▬

Welcoming her home, Molly received word that *Alone in Poland* had failed to be picked up on its first round. Though the editors' feedback was often positive, it hadn't been a fit for any one of them, uncertain how to frame it on their list. Molly sat beside me on the sofa crying as she read the comments aloud, skipping past the high notes for the hard blows—how the book "added nothing new" rather than how brave it was. Oddly, she didn't react cataclysmically, as I had feared; instead, she spoke about it as a confirmation of what she'd already expected: that she was a hack, could never make it as a *real* writer, never mind the past. The manuscript still had further rounds to make, I tried to remind her, but Molly was certain this was it—not only this book, but her career, her hopes and dreams, any possibility of having the life she wanted. She resigned herself to the kitchen after that, newly determined to finish up the several open orders already on her calendar, after which she'd put Kookie House on hold. Time to take a break for a while from writing and baking both, she let me know, and to instead start thinking long and hard about her future. Later, I'd find out she'd replied to several incoming queries from shared acquaintances that she'd received some "bad news about (her) health," forcing her to be unable to perform—news that somehow never made it back to me on either side. Whereas before it'd felt difficult to get a word in edgewise past her loathing, it now became next to impossible. What did I know about rejection or frustration? she'd demand with a feral fire in her eyes, running roughshod over any attempt at conversation. *You already have everything.* Instead, she began spending more and more time in the guest bedroom, ostensibly looking through job listings or working on poems, if clearly now from a position of total defeat.

———

"I'm afraid that if Molly decides to kill herself, no one will know until too late," I told our therapist at my next session. "Because she's shrewd enough and strong enough to pull it off without a word." Complex feelings surround the memory of such a statement, clearly, if in what felt like an abstract way at the time, unaware of the actual extent to which my worry had a basis in an approaching version of our reality. In a way, I'd grown accustomed to this feeling, having felt it from the beginning of our relationship; exacerbated, yes, by recent events, but still effusive, assuaged in part by Molly's appearance of caretaking: having owned up to her thoughts, going to therapy, and promising above all else she'd be okay, and she would say so if that changed. I was supposed to go to NYC soon, to read at a memorial for Stephen Dixon, an author I'd long loved, but maybe I should cancel that, I thought, stay home and nearby. Our therapist agreed I might be right but suggested that I wait until they spoke again so she could get a read. Several days later, she determined she felt certain it'd be okay—Molly was clearly struggling, yes, but things had levelled out a bit, and we could take her at her word. To help with my uncertainty, she suggested I ask Molly directly to make a promise she would tell me if she was feeling suicidal; that it was my right to ask this of her, as her partner, which in a way felt like news to me. I brought it up immediately, while out to lunch at an Applebee's on Valentine's Day, following our silly tradition of spending corporate holidays at corporate chains. I watched her face fall and her posture slump soon as I said it, the color rushing from her cheeks. "Yes, Blake. I promise," she mumbled, staring down into our basket of fried onions as if embarrassed that I'd ask. Afterwards, we walked across the strip mall parking lot to a nursery, where together we wandering along the aisles of potted plants and blooming flowers, together picking out several to be planted in our yard as a fresh start on the garden we'd let grow over since the first day we moved in.

━━━

My weekend in New York passed as a blur, spent mostly inside my hotel room, trying to rest. Just as she'd said she would, Molly kept up constant contact with me, texting back immediately and answering the phone when I called. At one point, she sent me a short list of "Things I have convinced bb to like that have made his life better," including *therapy*, *not drinking*, and *birbs*, to which I added several more including *tea* and *listening*, hopefully interpreting her gesture as a good sign. I certainly felt reassured, upon returning home, by the fact that my fears hadn't developed into anything more than fear itself. As if to emphasize that, Molly scheduled an appointment at the tattoo shop down the street. When we met, she'd just had one tattoo—a monochromatic gray-blue bird in flight filling the space between her shoulder blades, which she'd gotten young and come to hate, glad to not be able to see it but in the mirror. On either side of that, during a rekindled teen obsession with James Hetfield, she'd recently added a pair of Metallica tattoos—*Kill 'Em All*, on her left shoulder, featuring a hand in stabbing motion with a knife, and *And*

Justice For All... on the other, showing the same hand holding up a pair of scales. Not long after those, another dagger, huge on her right arm, swarming with clouds. Deep down, I wasn't sure what had inspired those choices—they didn't seem to fit her, really, besides the impulsivity; more so, they seemed to fit an idea of how she wished she was, at least to me. Now, she wanted to get a ghost, she said—the *classic floating sheet kind,* exactly the kind of morbid joke that she loved most, almost identical to the single sticker she'd stuck onto her laptop's casing, purchased on my birthday earlier that year. *Didn't I warn you how it'd go?* I can almost hear her saying in the pictures I took after, a little knowing wink hung like a buoy in the drowning of her eyes.

"There's nothing after death, and I will see you there," she informed me later, as I came to tuck her into bed, as I did most nights. We'd spent the evening actually cordially discussing the nature of the universe after a documentary about black holes, for once allowed to build beyond our usual stalemate. She'd stared right into me as she said it, *and I will see you there*, as if she'd solved a riddle with a paradox, at once poking at me and reaching out from some newly abstracted middle ground. I even felt relieved a little as I kissed her forehead, turned out the light and closed the door behind me, thinking of her pronouncement as a nudge toward some possibility of a point from which we might grow closer, if not philosophically then intellectually, emotionally—exactly what we both needed, maybe, in different ways than ever before.

███

Two days before her suicide, Molly and I went to visit the High Museum, where we'd been together many times over the years. There were hardly any other people there, blanketing the wide, bright white displays with vivid silence. Molly suggested we try counting how many images of chickens we could find inside the paintings, which quickly turned into a quest. We set our goal at ten, then upped to twenty after finding half a dozen in the very first landscape—a little flock so delicately rendered against the texture of the background we almost missed them. After that, we didn't see so many chickens and would never reach our readjusted goal. Instead, we wandered side by side around the showrooms as in a labyrinth, sharing our favorites and least favorites, until my head began to bleed. I'd been picking at my scalp too much, pulling my hair out, a nervous habit taken up from recent stress. I remember the color of my blood on my hand there in the antiseptic light amidst the art, at once embarrassed and enraged. Molly remained quiet, allowing me to rant and curse myself as we hurried back down to the first floor's bathrooms, where I stood at the sink with my reflection and blotted at my scalp. I barely recognized myself, I realized, always in such a rush I rarely ever took the time. Who was I, really? What did I want? Things to wonder over some other time, maybe, as the clock was ticking, and either way, it didn't seem to matter to me what I thought. After I'd cleaned my blood up, I hurried back out to gather Molly from where she stood with her back against a wall, lost in her thoughts. We headed back upstairs into the outsider art wing, Molly's favorite, where we split our paths when a patchwork quilt brought me to tears, thinking of Mom, while Molly moved on ahead without a word. Later, she'd ask me to send the photo I took of her sitting alone, waiting for me to finish, so she could tweet it, captioned solely with the emoticon an iPhone suggests when you type the word *home.*

The last picture I have of Molly and I together is of our reflection side by side in Anish Kapoor's *Untitled*, a concave mirror made of fragmented stainless steel. Our bodies appear shattered in the image, hundreds of vectors, barely distinguishable as complete selves. Molly's arms are tucked tight at her sides, cloaked in her black dress; her face obscured by the mirror's many fault lines, looking head-on into the camera with a wry grin. "Lately deciding between head or heart," she'd written in her journal three days earlier. "They say head, if to back of the brain/brain stem is most instant/painless. But idk. The heart, it's so beautiful. What's another couple seconds. I'm not scared anymore. Just the opposite. I'm scared of living."

Another picture, taken just before that, shows Molly standing on her own. Her smirk hasn't emerged yet; instead, she holds a broken glare, her jaw set in a straight line like wired shut, knowing what she knows. She barely seems to resemble the way I would have remembered her, without the picture, then or ever—my closest friend, my wife—far beyond reach. "I am sorry to have kept all of this planning from you," she'd already typed into a suicide note, saved on her hard drive for the last time earlier that same afternoon, under my first name—Blake. doc. "I wanted to have a normal time with you these last few weeks, just normal, nothing dramatic, and of course I didn't want to alarm you or anyone who might prevent my course of action. It was the most lonely time of my life, keeping my plans from you, and I know you'll be sad about it, and I'm sorry for that as well."

Leaving the museum, my memory cleaves to two things: how as we came along the concrete tunnel to the parking garage, we heard a familiar music, piped in from unseen speakers overhead as we walked together hand in hand, so much like the outro music from *The Shining*, but not quite—instead, anonymous and perfect, beyond time. The second is my road rage—furiously impatient to end up stuck in rush hour gridlock, shouting and banging my fists against the wheel. Molly sat beside me, hands in her lap, letting me vent until she'd joined in with equal vigor, raising her middle fingers and shouting insults at the drivers in nearby cars. A complex mortification in realizing I'd squandered those fleeting minutes, some of the last we'd ever share. Only once at dinner, sitting across from her sharing tea, everything in its right place, would I be thankful for the day. I looked her in the eyes and said how grateful I was to have a partner I could rely on so completely, who understood me in a way no one else ever had. I suppose I mistook her hard, silent expression in response as a mutual knowing, flanked by an existential distance I'd since grown used to not as a frigid thing, but as an earned part of the person I most loved. No matter what I might have said, they tell me, it wouldn't have changed anything, and even if it does feel sort of dramatic to imagine somewhere to begin, though my gut has an idea: *When I used to say it was all going to be okay, Molly, all I really meant is that I love you.*

━━━

The following morning, I drove to my parents' house, knowing it would be the last time before it went on the market. The rooms were almost completely empty now, with only odds and ends leftover from the estate sale, needing to either be discarded or taken home. My nephew, Lucien, kept asking me to chase him up and down the hall, conceptually understanding Grandma wasn't there anymore, dead like the fishes he'd seen displayed on ice at the grocery store. His happy cackle billowed through the evacuated rooms, a final layer over the five decades of sound and light my family had emitted there within it, sealing up the innumerable memories soon to be displaced. Soon I'd no longer be allowed inside here, I kept thinking as I took pictures in the many empty rooms, standing in places I'd stood so many times, just in case I needed a crutch in the future, if my memory started to fail like Mom's and Dad's. I felt at times as if I could sense the many versions of myself suddenly beside me, breathing down my neck, or around the corner in the closet where I'd hoarded sentimental objects since I was old enough to want time of my own. Everything had moved so fast—it seemed like weeks ago, even, that I'd draped white Christmas lights along the hallway so Mom wouldn't get scared walking down it in the dark, though it'd been months. It seemed like it'd been years since I'd been a child myself here, rushing around from room to room playing made-up games, though it'd been decades. This time, too, when I left and locked the door behind me using the same golden key I'd carried around since I turned 15, it'd be for good.

■

The last picture I have of myself before my life changed is of my reflection in the bathroom mirror in what'd been my bedroom throughout high school. Before it became mine after a remodeling, it was the master—possibly even the same room where I'd been conceived. After I moved out, it became my mother's workspace, where she'd spend hours sketching designs and dying fabric for her quilts, singing along to Arlo Guthrie and Willie Nelson, still partly audible in my memory even now. The room since then had been stripped, leaving nothing but the parts of a house you can't take with you. I guess that's what the picture's for, or why I took it, though I haven't looked at it much since until now. I think I'd been afraid that without the image, my sense of recall would disappear, taking what I'd lived right along with it. Now I know without the picture all I'd have forgotten thus far is how different the empty room looks, barely apparent as the place I carry with me in my mind. I do recognize myself, though—staring at the mirror basked in shadows with the midday sunlight at my back—perceptibly resigned amidst the process of packing up and moving on. From here, it might even appear I have some sense of what's to come for me tomorrow; that somehow I'm aware of the beginning of the end. Molly would mention that a few times throughout her journals during those last weeks, I think he knows, as if the expression on my face should seal her fate without a word. But he doesn't know. He has no idea—not about Molly, not about reality, not about himself. He's at the end of his rope, the picture reminds me in a way I could never on my own; hoping for more but knowing better, so he thinks. Maybe he can even feel how close he is to the edge, teetering blindly without a clue of how deep the hole will go, fearing the loss of control with only conceptual sense that when it hits his world will never be the same. I really only recognize him now as someone else, maybe my brother, for whom I wish I could intercede and take his place. In a way that I could never care for my present self, I feel for him; his glare, his posture—mostly defeated but still there, much like a ghost, going through the motions to do his duty, carrying a chaos in his head. When I zoom into his face, I see the pixels blur and break apart the way it had in Kapoor's mirror, somehow imprinted on his core. Closer still, it's like an elevation map, composed of gridlines and halftones in abstraction, allowing no apparent human form. As if to prove the point, I mostly can't remember what else became of the remainder of that evening, the last we'd shared—all clots and flashes, wisps of time locked out of sync. The final picture in my phone inside my childhood home is of my nephew, almost five, playing with his toys in the empty terrarium flanking the front door where all my life there'd been a slew of potted plants. He looks a lot like me when I was little, staring up at me with rosy cheeks in an expression I can't help but want to read now as discerning, as if there's something he can see that I cannot. The next photo I would take tomorrow is of the business card of the detective assigned to Molly's case so I wouldn't lose it.

━━━

After a while, feeling overwhelmed with packing, I excused myself and went outside to drive around and get some air. At a stoplight, I took my phone out, scrolling idly, and saw immediately where Molly had tweeted, then deleted, that she was surprised to see how easy and cheap it was to buy a gun. I felt my heart against my throat. I pulled over in a parking lot to call her, again relieved she answered almost immediately, like she'd been waiting. She sounded tranquil, far away. I asked her point blank, calmly as I could manage, why she was looking at gun prices, why guns were on her mind. She shrugged it off, the way she always would, said she was just messing around, making a point about the gun problem in this country, something like that. I no longer remember her exact words, slurred in my memory as silence, perhaps because I know now that she was lying, saying whatever she could think of to turn me off. Later, I'd find she'd spent hours reading through online gun and ammunition forums, screenshotting morbid jokes and taking notes on good techniques. In her journal she says the only reason she didn't take her life that afternoon was because she knew it'd be *too cruel*, that she didn't want me to have *to suffer any further* on my last day at my childhood home. On the phone, though, our final call, she knew exactly what to say, having repeated it incessantly to placate me all throughout those last few months: *Please don't worry. I'm okay.* What I find that I remember now in place of language was the striking brightness of the light that afternoon outside the Chick-fil-A where I had parked to make the call, the kind that glints so hard off of windshields that it leaves spots along the middle of your vision, tiny pops—almost exactly how the sky looks through the window in the room where I am writing this right now, 655 days later, 571 miles away from where I'd been. I'll be home soon, I let her know, just wrapping up here.

———

Meanwhile, back at our house, Molly's still alive, dreaming of death. Five photos in her own phone from the same timeframe offer little narrative—just different headshots taken from bed, facing the camera, the last of which is actually a video, five seconds long. *Some struggle isn't it*, she's typed in tiny black font beside her chin, near where the bullet enters. She might even seem bemused if you didn't know her fate yet, biding her time there at the cusp behind façade. "I know a criminal wants to be caught," she'd written of her father in closing *Bandit*, "because it is the only way of being known." With that in mind, she'd finally stepped up after a lifetime of playing mum and asked him over prison email about getting older, feeling different, if he ever thinks about his crimes. To her surprise, he'd even finally actually responded, several months later, with a 6-page handwritten letter sent through the mail, explaining his whole lifetime of bad decisions as if they hadn't been his own to make. "In the end, I don't know what I owe him," Molly offers before providing the entirety of the letter for the reader to examine on their own. "The layers of my feelings toward him seem to have no conclusion, however much I peel and dig. I don't want to say anything about this letter. It's the least I can do now, to let him speak for himself."[24] In earlier versions of this manuscript I'd imagined sharing Molly's suicide note could do the same, though as more time passed and the story shifted, I realized the letter wasn't really it. It's too much like her father's—full of half-truths and affectations, meant more for the world than for herself. Amidst returning time and again to this caesura, right where you're reading, I realized there was still more that she could say, in the only

24 *Bandit*, p. 291

way she'd ever found to speak her truth—through poetry, the very thing that'd saved her life time and again. In the end, I don't know what she owes anybody. The layers of my feelings toward her seem to have no conclusion, however much I peel and dig. I don't want to say anything about this poem, her very last. It's the least I can do now, to let her speak for herself.

Camp
By Molly Brodak

A child waiting on a thin dirt road.

A horse, bored, in a small stall.

A man with fingers laced into a fence.

A body at the foot of the fence.

A glamorous song, smiling, milky sequins, audience all in on the joke.

An empty dorm. Bunks slowly combed by wasps.

An empty dorm saturated with pigeon babble as if church.

Songs and long lines.

Collection of crutches.

A clarifying process, starvation.

A tin of embroidery thread transformed into little bracelets that soil and break.

A prayer at lunch, a rhyme about manners. Reluctance to bow. Keen to watch others instead.

No guards fluent in one's language.

A hug among children. Having witnessed it in parents.

A siren, inscrutable message.

A gratifying abuse, permanent.

An exaggerated set of eyes. Makeup as an insult.

A cookie saved for later, wrapped in panties.
A girl grinning, golden hair, all limbs in casts.
A day made just for leeches.
I wrote many letters, never received.
A sound of a train as if understood.
An emblem.
A single black day behind, a single black day ahead.
A song sung so low it stays.
Clean cold soft sheets.
The full moon.
Pine in sun.
Images of planets from the right distance,
this one too.

March 8, 2020 - 12:28 PM

I insisted on staying alone that first night without her—March 8th, its name and number marked forever in my mind like the password to hell. It also happens to be International Women's Day.

Several of my friends had come over to stand with me on our porch, hugging my body, all of us mostly unable to find words. I was somehow still doing the thing where I hold myself in and pretend I'm fine, despite how obvious it would be now that I was not. I *did* want to be alone, I thought, unable to imagine being forced to feel like this in front of others for much longer, holding out. I'd learned since boyhood, studying my father, that if you want something done right, you have to do it yourself, a principle I'd also put to work on my emotions, certain at all times, even in crisis, that no one could ever understand. How could anybody ever understand this? Why should they have to? I could see it in my friends' eyes that they wished there was something more that they could do, held at bay by the parts of me that would insist beyond all else to have my way, even now, irreparably fucked. I told my friends goodbye and closed our door and flipped the lock, then turned around to face the insides of our house, a bunch of rooms someone had filled with emotional detritus made to look like where we'd lived, my deceased wife and I, throughout the last few years of our shared lives.

I knew I needed to call Molly's family, her mom and sister, though I couldn't quite think how to begin. I sat under the half-window facing the gardens I'd just come from, in the goldenrod chair Molly had salvaged from a thrift store, years ago, and tried to imagine what words I could use to say what happened, as if I knew. Finally, I closed my eyes and dialed, waiting with my breath held until ending up in Nora's voicemail, leaving a brief, calm message asking her to call me back ASAP. I called Becca next, and she picked up quickly, clearly surprised to see me calling. I felt very far away there on the line, as behind glass, some terrible script rushing up from within me to be fulfilled: *I have bad news. Is now an okay time? Is your child there with you in the room?* The news itself was just one sentence: *Molly killed herself this afternoon.* Quick inhalation, her voice pushed high and twisted. We hung up quickly, barely sputtering, though not long after, she called back, more business-voiced now, asking for information; in particular, she wanted contact information for the police, which I provided, trying not to let what felt like iciness on her end irk me. I did get the sense of feeling shaken down rather than received. While still online with Becca, Nora called back, marked with a beep in my ear noting her presence, which I let go, trying to focus my attention still on Becca in the way one must learn from on-the-fly how to handle all the fraying threads of what happens in the human world just after a death. After hanging up with Becca, minutes later, I listened to Nora's voicemail before calling back, perhaps so I could hear what it would feel like to not know, her bearing chipper, curious. Already, I felt a little out-of-sync stuck in this spot, my memories of Molly's stories growing up neglected already burning through the netting of my brain, but also, more so, broken up to have to be the one to tell her that she'd just lost her child. More than most anything about the call, though, what I remember is how Nora didn't seem surprised; her nature flat, as if from a remove already—the shock of the words, perhaps, too much to understand inside the moment, allowed by language to address a thing but not conceive it. I kept expecting something else to break, a more unhinged reaction, something severe, but more so there was a deliriousness, a hollow wall there, as if our timelines were split off, somehow routed through a delay. I can intellectualize it now, but in the moment, the urge I felt was to vomit, get away. I'm sure I must have answered some other questions I can't remember, explained what happened, but soon as I could, I said I had to go, hung up. Our living room felt full of fog now, wearing something arcane hidden behind every hard surface, all I touched; like no matter where I sat or stood, it wouldn't come off me. Even the soft light through the windows like a shoehorn, pulling the fabric of the world up at its edges in my peripheries, everything fake. I noticed Becca had texted me asking for me to text her back a photograph of Molly's note. That note was mine, though, my body screamed; in what world could I stand to use my iPhone to upload digital files of pages of language the person I loved most in all the world used to convince herself she had no choice left but to take her life? Wouldn't I just rather disappear into thin air, never be seen again by a single other soul who ever knew me, anyone who'd ever seen my face or heard my name? What choice did I have but to comply, at the price of being some massive asshole, even a suspect, despite the fact the letter was clearly addressed to me, was mine, and in some way, too, all I had left? But I didn't have the strength yet to mince accountabilities, to stand up out of the rift in how I felt and grip the wheel. So, in the way one might a paycheck for deposit, I photographed the letter, one page at a time, and sent them off into the ether, pure information.

On our couch, sitting and staring in the same place I'd have been hanging out with Molly most any other day, time passed as if it meant to work around me, some broken bubble amid the normal shape of human time. I turned the TV on, for some distraction, an NBA game I placed on mute, feeling so much I couldn't feel anything. I watched the massive moving bodies rush around on-screen, most all a blur behind my face, their lives so far from my own devastation it was like the game was taking place on some far planet, one I'd never been to, not like this. I remembered I had a fantasy baseball draft scheduled for that evening, an auction that would take hours to complete. I sat there with my machine, hardly even thinking, and drafted a team, going through motions as if everything was just the same, as if any second the door behind me would come open, and Molly would enter, explain it all away as a huge misunderstanding, laughing like that night that I had first gone to pick her up. Suddenly that memory had such different architecture, plagued with images of our someday future now aligned, as if everything we'd ever done could not be stopped from leading to the image of the hole she'd put into her chin. Another night, another night now, dark as any other ever had been. My body was still my body, after all. I could lift my arm and see my arm move, could think back on the last several hours flashing past, but none of it seemed coherent with the center of where I was, who I'd become now—*Molly's widow.*

———

It must have been near midnight when my phone rang, an unknown number, and I answered it without imagining who it might be, hearing my voice mumble *hello.* Some woman on the line there, still not Molly, no one I knew. The coroner's office needed my permission for the harvesting of Molly's organs, the woman explained, trying her best to sound consolatory and delicate despite the task, a true professional. She'd have to ask me a series of questions, each of which required a specific legal format—did I feel able? Go ahead, I said, knowing I had essentially no choice; that this is what Molly would have wanted—a final way she could be of service to those less fortunate physically, no further waste, despite her ongoing espoused hatred of human life. One by one, she hit me with it, recording my voice for their receipt: *Do we have permission to take her kidneys?* Yes. *Thank you. Do we have permission to take her liver?* Yes. *Thank you. Do we have permission to take her pancreas?* Yes. *Thank you. Do we have permission to take her brain?* Yes. *Thank you. Do we have permission to take her heart?* After a point, no matter what she asked, I just said yes, wanting only for it to end, though also in a weird way thankful to be talking to somebody, anybody, about Molly, even like this. You can go ahead and take it all till nothing's left, I thought of shouting into the receiver finally, or simply hanging up because I could. Instead, I forced myself to play along and read the script, already unable to stop imagining the other people who'd soon be walking around wearing parts of Molly, never knowing who she was or what she'd done—just grateful to be alive.

━━━

Hanging up the phone, as the unstructured silence held over thereafter filled back in, suddenly I realized how alone I was. The illusion I had felt in keeping to myself, as if all I had to do to make things right was pretend it was okay, came crashing in around me, like a vice, to the point that I realized if I didn't get this out of me in some way, by telling someone else, then I'd be even more fucked than sitting still. Where to begin? Especially this late, so far from tomorrow morning that it might never ever come, all I could think of was to type "Help" into Twitter, sit and wait to see who might respond. I found myself on the phone, then, with one friend and then another, forcing the words out between my teeth to try to say what felt unsayable, like spilling poison into cracks. At least with another person's voice there, I had a bit in my mouth, a means by which to force the truth toward its form. I still didn't want anybody near me, I insisted, refusing to agree to being picked up, taken elsewhere. I still wanted to stay close to where it'd happened, there inside it, as if the next time that I left the house it'd be for good. *I just need to go to sleep*, I kept repeating, for lack of any other thing to say. I couldn't stand to touch our bed, where

Molly should have been tonight by now. The night passed in black fits from there, blank streaks surrounding any fragment of how I felt, like blacking out and back in with quick succession, zero dreams. I wouldn't have dreams for more than a year thereafter, I didn't know then; the black inside of sleep was nightmare enough, a feeding hole that succumbed to nothing I could give it, only floating, far from sense. It was only when the sun came up again, upon a new day, that I felt the silence in me break apart—the horror of the sound of cars outside in passing traffic on the way to work again; the birdsong stitching etches of a semblance of prosperity; the whole wide world right back in swing, as if everything was just the same except for us.

—

Finally, I texted my sister, *I need help.* She responded minutes later, saying she was on her way, no questions asked. Then suddenly she was in the living room there with me, alongside an ex-girlfriend she kept being friends with more than a decade after we'd broken up. I looked up to see them standing our dining room, scanning the area as if having been allowed into a crypt, and immediately screamed for my ex to get out of there, embarrassed to be seen in such a way. After she rushed out, some paramedics showed up, a cluster of them standing over me, asking if I was suicidal. What the fuck, I shouted right back at them, seeing red; I'm not going to kill myself, I just didn't want to be alone. They seemed confused, almost deflated, and I heard my sister apologizing as they went out, explaining how she hadn't known what else to do. I turned over on my stomach and covered my head and body with the blanket Molly had helped me pick out months before, trying to hide, not wanting to respond to anything else that might be said. "I'm so mad at Molly," my sister said, kneeling near my face, trying to comfort me, but which only made me buckle, turn to glass. This wasn't Molly's fault, I wailed. No one but me would ever understand, it seemed, how long she'd been in pain, backwards, mistreated, lost in the blood of her own mind. To be touched at all, by anyone but Molly, felt like I might melt beneath it, turn to mush. To not be touched felt like there was nothing left to tether me to earth. I'd already been halfway living in a version of this shell for many months now—how after my mother died, my body hurt no matter what I thought or did, flooding heavy with what I'd described as waves of acid, a sickened feeling underpinning every breath, but after Molly, in comparison, even those waves of acid might have felt like a relief in comparison with the high black wall inside my brain, so full of inexplicable emotions there was nothing left to do within them but exist. Any effort I might make to stay alive felt at once compulsory and impossible, like all there'd ever be let to expect at best was treading neck-deep in blood that looked like water, with a black bag over my head, its fabric lined with mural-style dioramas of the scene of Molly's suicide inscribed into them, interlaced with miles of smoke. In this way, I would relive the instant of her choice to die over and over, filled out in each returning image with new detail to try to make it hurt as much as it had the first time, and the underlying yearning to change the story only growing stronger with every infernal repetition, beyond flesh. The rest of life felt over now, to the extent that I could imagine it at all; or even worse: longer than ever, boxed in on all sides with bile and gunfire, open sores that squealed with Molly's cadence, as in her last breath, just before she pulled the trigger, forevermore.

———

From this point forward, I was no longer left alone. Faces of friends I'd known for years materialized as if from thin air all around me, orchestrating into efforts I knew I couldn't read the full effects of from underwater, stuck to the sofa. I'd open my eyes, coming up for air, and hear someone speaking what felt like a foreign language, impossible to annotate with my own sense. Every second felt like it would last forever, like all my life was just one day. I already felt the beginnings of a rising anger in me, then and there, something clinging desperately to righteousness amidst the endless sprawl of mass putridity God had allowed to persist in the same space as his supposed lambs. Even the heavy, selfless work of my friends to try to help me felt like pity, marked only more so by the distance I perceived deep in their eyes, like more than anything they had to be relieved to not have lost so much, to still have ground. I felt so much more alone in being cared for somehow, nowhere to hide my face but in my hands. Did we really have to accept that life is full of hell and those who can't withstand it are defective in their brains, too strange to live? Was there really no choice but to persist in the face of so much virulent egoism and insatiable gluttony, as if nothing could be more valuable than life itself; that nothing could be worth fighting for or dying over, as I insisted Molly had? I was alone, besides the cops, in having seen the bullet hole she'd installed into her neck, a desperate message sent to prove that she was worthless, a feeling only deepened by my remembrance of the fly already feeding on her blood. I could feel her still lurking in my peripheries, at times, too, a secondary kind of silence agitated by the ongoing commotion of all else, or worse, the constituent silence deriving meaning in her absence, filling our house. She'd appear sitting there across from me beside our fireplace, dressed up as an undead Raggedy Ann, her flesh all rotted, caked with black blood, staring out from the black sockets of her eyes. I could hear her voice laced in my thoughts, repeating *someday you'll really love me* over and over, or laughing at me for thinking I could have ever had a chance to save her life. *My dear, sweet Molly*, I moaned and moaned. *My poor baby. Would you just look at what she'd done? Please make it stop.*

I no longer recognized my world. Everything I thought I knew or felt or wanted had been shredded, stomped out, drowned, and it hurt to even have to try to see another way than how I'd seen it at her side. It would take my whole life to get back to anything like even ground, I thought, and even then, it'd be nothing more than a charade, mortgaged against the absence of her love, God's love, much less anybody else's. What else did I have left to look forward but bullshit answers to half-blind questions I wasn't even sure where to begin confronting, in midst of mourning, toward any form of explanation that would make the story even slightly easier to bear? What good could living do me now but as pure work, a job I hadn't even signed up for but in the process of fulfilling the expectations placed upon me in having been forced into a self, only to see all the work I'd done, my years of living, ripped out from under me, destroyed? My wife had been the only one who really saw me, my soul insisted, and just look how that'd turned out. Even her insistence that I not follow, written right there into her suicide note, as a plea— *Please listen to me. Stay alive.*—felt like an insult in its own right, like holding someone's head down underwater and asking them to learn to breathe. It felt dishonest, somehow, to not give in, to want to be dead. All my thoughts, my drive, my dreaming, constrained to circle the same scene, wanting, without any ability to undo it, to at least try to understand. There still seemed no certain reason she'd chosen to do this, without me knowing; how it could have gotten so bad there was no better way out, much less a word. "I knew from the first second I saw you that it was going to all be ok with you," she'd texted me while in Tucson, just weeks before. "I knew no matter what I had to fight for you and wait for you. Because you are made of gold." Her suicide note expressed the same, attesting amidst her resignation to the warmth and love that we had shared: "You were the only one in the world, it seemed, who could make me happy…The marriage we had was a place like I've never known. Safe and good. I am very grateful to you for the ways you tried to help me, and I will always love you." No matter how many times I read the letter, over and over, trying to piece together the underlying message in her voice, like seeking truth from sifting sand, something still stayed missing, hollowed out, or otherwise forced off its tracks by force of will. I thought of how, upon return from Tucson, she'd said we should go back some day together, stay in the same place she just had. I thought of what it must have been to be her, living her denigrations and doing everything she could to keep them close, no one's but hers, as if that alone meant more than being real. "I tried so hard to do so many things," the note continues, "and it was not even the failure of their outcomes that one might imagine led me to such disappointment and heartbreak. It was that the straining itself, the work, couldn't save me. It solved nothing. Every future goal I set for myself passed through me like a ghost." Could that really be the breadth of it, the final logic of the ending? Could she really not have seen the forest for the trees, even if all of it was burning?

━━━

When I could stand to stand, regardless, I put myself to work, searching through the rooms where she'd last been, as after any form of evidence that I might use to try to better understand. Everything seemed newly supercharged with meaning, and also absent of any measure or significance besides how it had been inscribed now with Molly's death. In the guest bedroom, on the bed where Molly had spent her final morning, I rummaged through the pile of books she'd last been reading: William Vollmann's *Rising Up & Rising Down*, Volume 1, bookmarked at a section in his "Moral Calculus" titled "ON THE PLEASURES OF MAKING AUTHORITATIVE

STATEMENTS"; Dante's *Inferno*, a longtime favorite, of which she'd recently written: "I wanted to hear him talk about the dark wood, the crisis, but he's spending all this time on nationalism and gossip about people he doesn't like. He was a fool."; the galley of my novel that we'd last talked about, its ending perhaps the last words she'd ever read. Alongside those, she'd left a few of her most recent journals lying out, which she told me she'd been reading through them throughout those last days, sick to her stomach by how sad her life had been—the sort of thing she'd say and not want to go into more than that: the feeling in the fact, to be observed, never explained. I'd seen the journals crop up here and there around the house over the years, but only allowed myself to look inside them once or twice, stealing a peek against my decision to no longer be paranoid, a snoop. Also, I'd learned my lesson from that first time; how mostly what Molly wrote about her life was angry, hateful, or depressed, like having bile spewed in your face. Few friends or family, including me, were ever spared her wrath, all references to family and friends revealed only for their baseness or their bullshit, but most of all, as always, she lashed out most cruelly at herself, her living world. Descriptions of a stark sky or a sweet animal must be surrounded by depressive rundowns of all the worst parts of her hard days, scornful diatribes against most everything. Now, cracking open her navy-blue journal that begins with Jan 1, 2020, I found the story Molly had been hiding from me all this time, outlined and archived in broad daylight, available to anyone who bothered to intrude.

———

Over time, reading the journals once and then again, over and over, as I would obsessively, like an addict for information, I began to see a timeline of our last months, if circumscribed completely by the same uncertainty as I had felt without them, given the many different kinds of truth they entertain through Molly's very splintered POV. She'd begun the year on a high note, I read, happy about how close she'd felt to me, what fun we'd had on New Year's Eve. "This year I'm taking back my energy and I'm going to use my days," the opening entry closes. "I wasted a lot of time last year. I feel rested and ready to step up and stop waiting." On Jan 5, she tells our therapist—unknown to me—that she needs to stop coming in for a while, that she needs rest, and that she feels bad for not being there more for me during my mourning for Mom. On Jan 12, she laments not getting the job she'd wanted, realizing at the same time it is an opportunity to "think radically" about her life. "I also keep thinking I just want to kill myself and be done with it already, but I know that's just me being cowardly and tired." The entries thin out between then and the end of the month, when she goes to Tucson, from which she comes home having decided that she can't think of what to do about her life but die. On Feb 17, the day she learns her book had been rejected: "The last balloon I was holding onto—snip—and it was gone. There's nothing left in my future. I know then that I was at the end of my life." Everybody dies, she says, but she feels better knowing when and how hers will arrive. She starts throwing things away, to "help Blake out." On Feb 27, while I am out of town in NYC, she buys the gun. "And now that I have the gun, I don't know how much longer I can hold out." Feb 28, she realizes the clerk at the gun store sold her the wrong kind of ammunition, and she goes back to two different locations to get the right kind, then she comes home and practices firing the empty weapon into her chest. "I'm even still exercising, ha ha." She tries to write a poem, aware it is the last writing she'll ever do, then watches Tarkovsky's *Stalker*, which she says makes her feel "<u>taken care of</u>" for the first time in her life. Feb 29, she says she knows how awful it is, how "evil" it is to inflict me with her pain, taking her life, but that I will be "better off in the long run." March 1: "When I have tried to tell people I'm having a hard time, they just say 'yeah me too' and turn away." She mentions reading Plath's *Ariel* "here and there, predictably, and it's extremely accurate, predictably. *This is what it is to be complete. It is horrible.*" March 3, she gets her hair done, describes how much harder it is for her to feel the way she does with me nearby; that when I tell her that I love her, it only hurts. "I really don't know what I'm waiting for now. Just any day Blake goes to the gym, that's enough…Doing things because I want to now rather than saving them. Choosing the jadeite bowl to eat strawberries out of instead of the boring ones." March 5, she makes a huge batch of cookies to send to writer friends who respond to her on Twitter, hand-painting and packaging them individually to go out just in time that they'll be delivered after she's dead. She doesn't have the date picked out yet, however, because if she did, she'd just "go crazy." March 6, after our trip to the museum: "There's just nothing left. I'm ready." March 7: "Need to stay in touch with reality. A leak of terror hits me sometimes and I panic…It seems so very very easy now. And I will just put it in my pocket one day and walk off and do it almost without thinking. Almost." She describes a constant underlying drive to want to tell me, to tell anybody. "I swear someone really could save my life right now if anyone reached out to me in any sincerity at all. But no. It's all jokes and vague fear." She throws away more stuff, unseen, wishing "you" could have seen her in the classroom, at her best. "Everything tastes weird lately, like aspirin. My hair finally looks beautiful again, what a shame. Nothing feels real. Nothing reaches me." March 8, in full: "Woke early, around 5:30, to the sound of one bird. Dreamed last night about going to class with a wagon full of cookies for everyone—gingerbread men. I spent the whole day just lying in bed yesterday, crying a lot. Stared out the window at the bees on the tiny flowers in the lawn. I guess I needed to despair for a while. Took a bath, said goodbye to my body. We ate grilled halloumi and made love after dinner and watched our favorite things on TV. Feel like I can see everything with such clarity this morning. I've been pretending my entire life. It's still so early even now. There's nothing left to do but wait for the window of time to slide over me. It's very quiet. I feel utterly paralyzed. All I can do is stare out the window. I am very sorry."

███

All of this left out half in the open, right under my nose. All I'd had to do was break her trust, turn to a certain page, and everything would be so different. A certain kind of torture in knowing how the lack of a violation you'd employed so many other times, in other relationships, could have been the way that saved her life, if maybe only for months or years—no way to say for sure, but still, it burned. I stood there in the bedroom where we'd last sat together and felt all this washing over me, part of a massive subset of our story I'd had almost no idea of besides the flood of signs that now appeared in looking back, the endless ways that I could twist most any moment into the straw that broke the camel's back. "And of course there is nothing to 'get,' nothing to 'really grasp,'" I saw Vollmann had written on one of Molly's earmarked pages in his compendium's *Moral Calculus*. "Atrocities leave only wounds, and a wound is a cavity, an emptiness. Am I belaboring the obvious in claiming that one reason for that emptiness is *helplessness*...The lesson of the catacombs: *No matter what you say or do, we skulls will see you underground*."[25] Like finding a new door in an old house you had lived in your whole life, which leads to a blood pit. Like seeing what you really look like behind your face. Suddenly I could see it all laid out so clearly—the looming evidence of Molly's plan—all so close, so real, for so long it'd made me blind. I thought of Molly's endlessly repeating how oblivious I was, how little I ever noticed details of my surroundings, in her mind meaning I should have been able to read her mind; that had I really

25 Vollmann, William T. *Rising Up & Rising Down*, v.1, McSweeney's Books, 2003, p. 126.

loved her I'd be able to see through her, cut her off. Even then, I must have walked past it countless times before I noticed the brown paper bag left lying at the foot of the bed, inside which I found the Smith and Wesson box, the opened pack of bullets, and the credit card receipt—a complete set of everything she'd need to end her life, acquired in a matter of hours, just like that. I thought about storming right out to my car right then and there, driving at high speed to the gun store where she had made her purchase, rushing in and throwing my body at whoever happened to be at work today, beating their face in with my fists for long as I could until they shot me, in *self-defense*. That would be at least a taste of justice, I imagined, itching in places I'd never felt, deep in my brain, certain that no matter what I might do to try and scratch it, short of bleeding, it would only continue getting worse.

▬

"I want you to know first of all that I thought about what this would do to you," Molly had written in her suicide note's second paragraph, front and center, which I continued to read over and again in shifting context with all the rest, "and I know how painful it is going to be for you, and I'm very sorry. I don't want you to follow me. Please listen to me. Stay alive." Why shouldn't I follow, though? What could ever again seem to make another second worth holding onto? Moreover, what made her think she got to say what I should do once she had left me without choice but to accept that this was what the world had made her do? I could see it all through Molly's eyes now, clearer than ever, all of our efforts stretching ahead to some distant horizon in our future where at last we crashed into the edge of damnation itself, with nothing but misery left to await us, one and all. Any form of consolation offered up in due time only came back to feeling more like water on a wound, something I thought I understood conceptually but would never learn how to accept, would never even want to have to. Even as I spoke on the phone to friends who had direct experience with suicide—their own attempts, or successful attempts by loved ones; as I listened to them tell me how it wasn't my fault; that my lack of intervention, then or now, didn't equate to participating in the cause, or even a failure; that she'd done this on her own, of her own will; how even if I'd caught her, taken her to get help, it wouldn't have changed her. In some ways, leaving it all out for me to find like that, on top of how she'd made sure I'd be the one to go and find her body, was another kind of violence all its own, not so different from the early feelings I'd had around her that made me fear for tipping her too far, the abstract threat of death and suicide spanning all the way back to that first night she'd showed me who she was, her MRI. I felt glued to these survivors' voices, even as I also withheld from my own experience any lasting confidence that this was true; that no matter what anybody said, I was her husband, her first and last line of defense. I felt surrounded by my friends whether I wanted to be saved or not, burned up inside only more the more they tried to help as I lay with my face covered on the sofa, hating the sound of my own breath. What difference did it make what I thought or said or did now that I'd lost everything? What now could ever be enough? Regardless of what I thought, when I could think, I couldn't help but feel grateful, with so many people showing up to help me out: people who stayed there with me, night after night; who, within their own grief, brought me everything they could imagine I might need; who brought over food, sent cards and emails, sent their love; who embraced me in their arms and said *I'm sorry*; people I hadn't seen in far too long, flying in; who managed all of the arrangements in memorial, down to every last detail, with a depth of grace and understanding that words themselves cannot provide; who stayed up through all hours on the phone, letting me wail, beg, gnash; who offered their own experiences of depression, suicidal thoughts, and broken faith; who listened to every word that I could muster trying to define, refine, explain the blinding story spreading out, surrounding; who reminded me to eat, to rest, to breathe. In some ways, the more they helped, the more it hurt, as in place of accepting my own need for love and care, I only wished that Molly could have seen it: how much so many had to give, given the chance. They would have done the same for her, I knew, had they known, despite the distance she projected against all. But they hadn't, and I hadn't either, I told myself, coveting her viral logic, desperate to stand beside her even still, to hold on with her through even this.

All language loses meaning in the flames. You feel your body being burned, numb in parts and crushed in others, with no clear way to make it stop. No one else can feel what you are feeling, you imagine, and you can read that in their eyes. You know that they don't know, really, what they're saying, how it feels to wear your skin. Even those who do care just seem to remind you there are still reasons to keep going, to hold strong, but often those reasons are all theirs, forged from their lifelines. Any logic of "the real world" no longer applies— just empty math. *It's no one's fault; it's everyone's fault.* Some part of me wanted everyone to have to feel what she had felt, testing out the gun against her body; to have to click around in the browser history from the last days she frequented gun forums; to see up close what she had done to herself, where the hole went, what came out, because it is a part of who we are, each and every one of us down here surrounded round the clock by the ambient depravity of man. Even then, it seems, some people come to show up in the specific gore of local tragedy in search of awe, some signal of what awaits them, too, if they don't play nice. You're the only one who can do the work your life requires, after all, and once you finally actually get sick of wading on through so much horseshit, day in and day out, you're the one who has to be willing to stay and look when others won't. So much of our lives we spend taking up measures to see to it that the worst possible things we might imagine never happen. We depend upon the hope that all those measures are only extra, that all our precaution might forestall or balance out some darker path, upon which, were we forced to walk upon it, our lives would split into before and after, then and now. Between the two, there is a silence, larger and louder than all the rest of it combined, which is the silence both that breaks us and combines us, in a frame we cannot see but from beyond. Giving into that imprisonment—reaching the limit of your knowledge of the world and believing it's the end-all be-all for everybody else too— that's exactly what the hollow soul of trauma wants; it wants more blank to feed the pain with, to fill the space up, retaining nothing but itself. It wants us all. What else might yet come for us, too, our friends and families, any stranger, if personal tragedy is the frame it takes to make us pause, and look, and see; if we don't start facing up to how we are, as to the fact that an unexamined life isn't simply *not worth living*, it's worse than death itself: the foundation of an empire of misery, and loathing, the boundaries of which begin and end with each and all.

———

I discovered Molly had been unfaithful in our marriage five days after her death, while looking through her phone for photos to include in the slideshow at her funeral. I already felt bizarre about peering in there, accessing images I imagined no one had been meant to see except for her. I wasn't surprised, at first, to find dozens of selfies in her roll she'd never shared, including many of her posing in the mirror in our guest bedroom, modeling clothes in various stages of undress. As I continued scrolling, though, I came to photos of her wearing lingerie I'd never seen, and many nudes, often staring straight into the lens—nothing so unusual, really, though strange to unearth for the first time with her already dead and gone. At the end of the roll, I realized there were many other photos in her 'Recently Deleted' folder that hadn't yet been permanently erased. There, among the many other random fragments, I found her posing on the bed, playing with sex toys, making faces like a doll. Then there were videos of her masturbating, moaning, sometimes narrating for the camera in a fawning, childish voice that hardly resembled her at all, saying the names of other men. Then there were photos and videos of the men, too, each presenting for her in their own way, leering into where she would have been beyond the screens, narrating to her while they jacked off, using her name. One guy in particular kept coming up more and more, a face that looked familiar in a way I couldn't quite place, a regular correspondence spanning many months. Stunned into an earth-splitting sort of silence, I went and locked myself inside our bathroom with her laptop, hiding from the voices of our friends in the next room who'd come to sit with me throughout the night, unable quite yet to understand what I was seeing, what it meant. This couldn't really be what I imagined, I kept thinking, despite the evidence deployed before my eyes, somehow compelled instead to hurt myself by looking longer, really letting it all in, as if somehow if I stared hard enough, my brain would break, and I'd go dumb. Maybe then the floor would fall out from underneath me, I imagined, and I could fall into the blank, beyond the edges of what had once already seemed the bottom, and yet was still not quite the bottom after all.

∎

Molly's affairs weren't simply photos, texts, I soon discovered. The evidence was all right there. Screenshotted on her desktop, I found a receipt for a flight to a city I'd never heard her mention, booked through the same dates I'd been in New York just weeks back. She'd hardly even left any space between our arrival and departure times, just narrow windows on either side, as if designed to get her caught. That trip had been cancelled, though, I figured out, tracing her emails for connections, tracing the trail. I knew I had to look, to know; the secrecy only redoubled the lacing shame and sickly pain wracking my guts, scraping its claws across my shattered plates of memory in their becoming redefined. Suddenly, our bedroom felt like a tomb, some brittle parody of what I'd thought it was those nights we'd slept together side by side, as perhaps others also had on nights I'd been away without a worry, thinking I could rely on what I knew. Two days before she'd died, in fact, I'd looked her in the eyes and said how grateful I was to have a partner I could rely on so completely, who I didn't have to worry over being safe with, with whom I shared such a strong bond. I'd mistaken the hard, silent expression on her face for mutual knowing, a bond requiring no language to extend; an empty glimmer somewhere deep behind her eyes, behind a kind of distance I'd grown used to, not as a cold thing, but simply as the way it always was. She'd been through more than I could ever imagine, and I knew this; it made her seem so strong to me, so wise, her hard edge only a product of neglect and isolation, how much she'd always felt alone, no matter what. Now, my mind raced with bone-shaking anxiety, already filling in all of the blanks ripped in my mind with furious elaborations of what she'd done, my brain filled thick with floors of snuffy nightmares made even worse under my imagination's incessant elaboration, enough to make me want to bash my head in right then and there to keep from being forced to learn the difference between my experience of our reality and what had been really going on right under my nose behind my back, without any way now to go to Molly and demand to know the all of it, and why, to get to look really her in the eyes, beyond the mask. Every memory I'd been hanging on to for dear life felt different now, rugged out from underneath me like a field of fire, zero sky but all the smoke.

━━━

Finally, I couldn't take it on my own anymore and went out to ask a friend to come and see what I had found. To my surprise, they had an idea of who he was: a guy we both knew a bit, who lived in the city Molly had planned to fly to—I'll call him L. L. had been texting them all week, freaking out and asking for information about what happened to Molly, which had confused them, as they didn't know they knew each other. Pulling up L.'s Facebook profile, I verified it was the same guy, someone I'd known from a remove for more than a decade, having met him after a reading once, awkwardly, and who'd badgered me continuously at various times to read his work, to blurb his book, to let him interview me, to send him work. I remembered once when Molly had even asked me what I thought of him directly, throwing his name out as some random writer-guy who'd been pestering her on Twitter, too, listening intently as I told her my general impression of him was that he was nuts, unstable, and annoying, to which she'd just nodded, said no more. Minutes later, after DM-ing him and receiving an immediate response, I found myself back in the bathroom on the phone, his voice like razor-wire around my neck. I came out shouting at him, trying to wish a way to force myself into the airwaves through the phone and come out on the far side so I could get my hands around his throat, while at the same time almost surprised to find how quickly I could calm down, on the surface, to try to coax him into spilling what he knew. More than anything I wanted to know the truth, so I could live it, and so quickly I shifted my demeanor from imploding to detective mode, demanding that he tell me everything he knew. He said that Molly had told him she was going to leave me to be with him. He explained how at first he'd refused to meet up with her after she'd invited him to meet her at a baking convention in Kentucky, which she'd presented to me as a possibility for her career, then changed her mind about attending, when he refused. He knew that we were married and was afraid they'd be discovered, a fear Molly had reinforced at different times by reminding him how furious I'd be, almost like gloating over the idea of retribution, jealous rage. She'd baited him by explaining how I never pay attention to her, how I'm lazy and I'm rude, how we act like roommates, grown apart—just the way she'd described her prior husband many times to me, after I found out she'd had one, as evidence for how the relationship had become doomed, all without a word offered directly, pretending all the while that everything is fine. She'd told him she wanted an affair because I'd cheated on her—never mind that we'd forgiven one another long ago, and since then gotten married, sworn our vows. Finally, not long after her plastic surgery finished healing, he'd finally given in and agreed to meet her for the first time in Tucson, the trip I'd paid for, where he claimed he'd fallen in love with her, head over heels. I listened to him explain their love to me in spastic bits and pieces, scattered between his battered affect, of a tone that seemed to range from cracked to righteous, holding the story she'd helped him piece together as the truth, despite also seeming aware to some degree, given her suicide, perhaps, that something vital had gone wrong. He said that Molly had told him several days prior to hold off contact until she let him know it was okay again, that she had to take care of certain things. He'd read this as that she was going to end our relationship and come to him. At the same time, trying to defend himself about the money that she'd sent him, he said he'd thought of his time in Tucson as *sex work*, as if he'd been providing her a service. At this, I finally lost it, unable to keep up the careful distance I'd put on to coax him into telling me his half. He just wanted to taste my dick, I screamed into the receiver, listening to him scream languagelessly right back at me, like an animal. Everything made so much more sense suddenly, in some bizarre way, at the same time bending my mind back even farther from the myth of what I'd felt I'd known. There was nothing left on earth now I called sacred, and nothing left of all I'd loved. The following afternoon, while sitting in the waiting room for therapy, I'd find he'd "accidentally" send me an email containing a video of Molly masturbating, then another email right after that calling it an accident, begging me not to open it, claiming he'd been trying to delete it.

———

At first, I decided to keep this information to myself. I didn't want anyone to know what Molly had done to herself, to us, to me, nor could I even think of who to tell, how to begin. I didn't want to have to put shame upon her after all else, choosing instead to bear it, no matter what the incipient damage of covering over her lies might do to me. I already had so much else to sift through as it was, framed the loudest by the arrival of Molly's family in Atlanta. They'd driven down soon as they heard the news and were texting me over and over to be invited to our house, already talking about going through her stuff together, taking things of hers they wanted. I couldn't help but feel spiteful about it, not yet ready to begin to go there, much less to sit up and put my face on, when in truth I saw their presence as a sort of dagger in my back all its own. I'd heard so many stories from Molly, read so many attributions to the trauma she'd incurred by growing up amidst these people. I didn't want them to come over yet; too much, too soon; and yet I felt guilty not responding, trying to delay the inevitable. How would I even look them in the face? Why did they need me to mourn their daughter and their sister, here and now? I already felt like I'd been smothered many times over in the wake of everything combined, and now here they were, on either side of me in our living room, grabbing onto me, a shapeless desperation in their eyes. Immediately it seemed less like they wanted talk about what happened, who Molly was and how and why, much less how I was doing or what I wished, and more so wanting to me say it wasn't their fault, that there was nothing they could have done. But I didn't feel like it wasn't their fault, in an even different way than how I wanted to blame everyone, including me. It felt partly true and partly a lie that they, too, were only victims of Joe Brodak, and yet I felt sad for them, both for the loss we shared, and for the way Molly's suicide must have made them feel about their own lives, their broken family. I couldn't stop thinking of how they'd left Molly feeling like an outsider, like they'd never wished to know the real her, only the parts of her that they could read, and at the same time I felt a brush from Molly's ghost to be the bigger man, to not be cruel. As much as I understood that, wanting similar relief myself, redemption didn't feel like mine to offer, and either way it didn't seem to matter what I said. Instead, I held their hands and let them cry in front of me, holding my own breath. They didn't ask me if I was okay or how I'd been surviving, or for more details on how this had happened. Instead, it was as if Molly had already been underground for quite some time but for the electric desperation now awakened in them. Nora had brought a photo album with her, a narrow volume containing maybe twenty shots of Molly over the years, infant to adult. We huddled over it together for a few minutes, listening to details Nora offered about Molly as a baby, trying to make light, while inside I couldn't help but think of my own mom had a whole cabinet full of albums of me and my sister at every age, a difference I felt etched in my chest in a way I'd never really understood before. I thought of how Molly told me she only had one copy left from the many zines she'd written during her teenage phase producing zines—*The Flabby Arms*, full of her strange drawings and funny one-liners, the kind of jokes only Molly would ever tell; the rest had been thrown out, along with a bunch of other stuff, by her mother one day on a whim, cleaning up house, never to be seen again, no remaining copies, like simple trash. I felt a desperate aching to tear through the photographs' slick surface, reach into the image and deliver the sweet, smart child Molly had been from her own past. Against these background textures, right or wrong, I resented them showing up here, now, pressing at my will to give even more, hungry with need. *You're still our family*, they kept repeating, staring so hard back through my eyes they might soon burst. I didn't say that I wished they'd tried harder to reach Molly on the grounds of who she was, not who they wanted her to be—how unfair it'd be to cling to such things now. I tried not to hold against them how it didn't seem to matter how I felt or what I said into what felt like an unfillable wanting suddenly exposed by Molly's actions, her rigid silence broken only quite too late. It itched my head to have to bridge the gap between us, to wish too that there was more to say or more to share; if nothing else, a pair of arms who knew Molly even longer than I had who could embrace me in a way that made me feel anything but only further gone. Instead, an acid rain, right in the pit of the holy land. A hole.

The day before the funeral, people tell me, Molly's father showed up at our doorstep and asked to be taken to where she shot herself, so he could see. I'd been in the shower at the time, and my friends made sure to hurry him away without me knowing. "Whoever you are…. fuck you!…… Molly is my daughter and I will visit her remains when I wish….no one will stop me! (sent with Loud Effect)" was his response, via text message, to my and Molly's family's insistence that he not attend the services. We provided pictures of him for the funeral home's security, asking them to call the cops if he appeared, even as some screaming part of me wished that he would pop up so I could beat his brains in, or even worse—tell him what I thought of him. In the end, of course, he hadn't shown—why show up now, at the end of a lifetime of not showing up; of refusing to face the direct effects of all his lies? Even after two long sentences in prison, he still blamed the world for what he'd done, full of excuses for his choices, never his—a willing victim of his own life, just free enough to continue to his grave believing he really was as wise and sharp and guiltless as he'd made out. His last association with her, after her death, would be another sad headline bearing his name, for her obituary in the New York Times: "Molly Brodak, Poet and Memoirist of Her Father's Crimes, Dies at 39."[26]

▬

Whatever else might have been coloring the water on the afternoon of Molly's funeral would, for the moment, fall away. Anything meant to distract me from her honor, the larger person that I'd always known her to be deep down, I set it all on pause, outside my mind. I'd find a way, someday, to forgive her for how she'd wronged me, all the ways she'd twisted us, demeaned us, and in the absence of that, I latched on to the feeling leaking out between the seams, the unconditional love I'd always felt for her no matter how off course or out of sync it sometimes felt, how hard I'd fallen through the hole she left behind. I stood before the congregation, packed end to end with friends and family, so many lives who'd witnessed Molly and I trying to love, and I spoke of Molly like the love she'd been to me all throughout the last decade of our lives. Whatever else she'd done, how far she'd gone, it seemed, to destroy everything we were, was absolutely nothing compared to what I felt in trying to put myself in her same place, to grapple with her absence here and now. I read aloud from the sun-yellow notebook full of forty poems, one for each year of her life, which I'd been working on for months as a surprise for her next birthday, just weeks away. I hadn't written much poetry since my late teens, a fact that Molly continued to regularly lament, as if that part of me were gone. I'd thought the poems might be enough to finally show her how much I loved her in a way she could finally allow; a

26 Slotnik, Daniel. *The New York Times*, 19 March 2020.

reason to believe me once and for all when I said I loved her more than everything. If only I'd given them to her earlier, I imagined, I might not be up here reading them aloud as for her ghost. After that, I read *Folk Physics*, her final poems, in its entirety, like a cipher all my own, forced with a hole in my guts to uphold honor in front of all these people I could feel seeing me at last as who I really was unmasked, if only now in the time of such grief that I couldn't bear to hide my feelings any longer, while at the same time, on the inside, split into halves—one half marked by the past, brought forward through it, to the edge of being, with no idea of what could come next; the other, side by side, more just a blur framed by the rolling wheel of fortune you've spent your whole life learning to frame against the terms of who you imagine you might be. And there you are.

———

Back at our house, after the funeral, I watched the rooms we'd lived in fill up with more people than we'd ever had over at any time in Molly's life. Children of friends played together in our yard, learning our chickens' names, each unaware of what it meant to be there. I let Molly's mother and sister go through her office and the bedroom, finding items they could hold on to in her memory, fragments that had once just been things left half-forgotten in desk drawers or on side shelves. I tried my best to speak to everybody individually, to get to listen to what they might have to say, or to remember. When I couldn't stand it, I went into the bedroom and closed the door, laid down on our bed and covered my head up, seeking unknown solace. Someone else would come to fill our space here, I knew well, just as we had done to those before us, all hidden history. In no time, it would be as if we'd never existed except in memories now mostly only mine, full of hours half-corroded, shared with people who were gone. Without her there, any keepsake or practicality dissolved its essence, a decoy for the way it'd felt to be alive there at her side, mere mortal evidence of some foreshortened event I'd once imagined from within it as everlasting and eternal, now wholly relic, rendered dust. I felt relieved other people could find any connection in the wreckage, most all of which just made me ache: handfuls of pictures of her with her sister or her mother, wedged in between the rarer shots of her alone, or of her and Joe; a construction paper heart-shaped card, addressed to "Daddy" in early grade school script, apologizing to him for being "bad," hoping that he won't stay mad at her for too long. Her closet full of dresses hung side by side in silent stillness, each aligned inside my mind with hours we'd spent, how she had moved, what she had said. Her row of aprons hung on hooks along the hallway from the kitchen and her coats hung in the armoire, missing only the last one she'd been wearing. All these windows where she'd looked out, the muted sunlight shining gently against the pastel green and gold wallpaper she'd hung herself, affixed in me alone as memory of how proud she'd been to get it done, over the table where she'd sat so many hours in our last year, hunched over hand-painting cookies hours on end, the echo of her laughter somehow still hanging there among the stillness having settled upon her tea kettle and her aprons and her plants. The random strands of her long hair loose on the floor, strung in her brushes, caught in the drains—all of it leftover like the grist within a mystery, newly reloaded, striped with blank. Her laptop and her school bookbag and her hairpins. Her purse, her shoes, her books, her shampoo. Her pile of shoes beside the door, the pile of mail already accruing with her name imprinted front and center, undelivered. Out in the driveway, the battered black Pontiac hatchback she'd been driving since we met, just a few days short from my unannounced plan to trade it in for her birthday, soon to come. Over the fence, out in the yard, our last three chickens in the yard, each still wanting their routines, their eyes wide in their head the way they'd get when picked up, knowing nothing of what had been changed, their eyes big in their heads when I picked them up one by one and told them Molly wasn't coming back, the language of it somehow different in its contour than how it felt to tell the other humans, their darting, feathered heads the only nearby family I had left. All of this stuff, this life, left lying out there in the apparition of what had once been our household as if this and all the rest of it were nothing more than a charade, or even worse, just one new layer of a nightmare from which we'd never actually wake up.

——

The day after the funeral, they closed the city in pandemic. We were no longer supposed to leave the house without good reason. When we did, we wore our masks, covering our faces to stop the spread of COVID-19, which was already claiming thousands of lives. The streets grew still, businesses and restaurants closed indefinitely, and many people were afraid to go near anybody else, much less touch, a perfect mirror for some fraction of how I already felt inside. It made so much sense, in a way—like Molly had exploded into microbes, all over everything, to prove a point; like we were finally getting what we deserved. "I don't love people," her suicide note had stated. "I don't want to be a person. Helping other people stopped making sense to me since I don't think people should exist at all. It seemed to me, in my logic, that removing myself would be the best thing I could do...I know you will understand why I did this more than anyone else." I did understand, at least to some extent, knowing well how hard and long life could seem to suddenly become, with no clear way to fix it despite the mass awareness, at our core, that we've gone wrong; that the reasons one could even want to live are often the place we feel that heat the most, short of sticking our heads back in the bag and hoping that somehow it will all just get worked out; as if there's really some central steering wheel somewhere that only the work of God can bring to pass; so that it doesn't really matter what we do, despite how clearly our behaviors have effects, ones that last long beyond our sheer impressions, over centuries and beyond time. Rather than asking for forgiveness, her death in me demands we take a deeper look at *how it is*, not *how it seems*, both in our instincts and conditioning, the hate and fear prolonged in those who haven't learned another way. It's in the air we breathe, the walls we raise up, the locks we turn, the work of bitter competition, born from hate, and no matter what you might believe, if left unchecked, unchanged, unanswered, it's only going to grow. The words alone are not enough. The limits of our world begin with *you*.

▬

"Love someone back," I hear her voice repeat inside my head like a mantra, as if right back where we started. "You just begin."

▬

Before I'd even had to begin imagining where I'd end up, two longtime friends, Amy and Adam, invited me into their home. They had a guest room I could stay in for as long as I needed, they let me know, including space in the basement to store my stuff, which after giving away or throwing out so much I no longer wished to ever see again almost exactly fit into a 10'x10'x10' cube. Because I was allergic to their cat, they said they'd already found a place where she could move and hired a cleaning crew to come in and sanitize the space from top to bottom. I could bring my chickens with me, too, as there was space in their backyard for the coop. Other friends, Nick and Carrie and Caroline and Caroline and Cyrus, volunteered to come over in the afternoons and help me pack, taking immense care with every object that they touched, making sacred work out of a wreck. They saw to it that Molly's dresses went to people who needed them, would love them; they itemized every single box with exactly what would be inside; they gathered fragments others might throw away and catalogued them, called them precious; they organized and oversaw and gave and gave, bending over backwards attending to my every need in ways I couldn't often even see, taking so much stress off my back without me asking, as if my life was also their own. These and dozens of other people who I can list out in my head like credits to the reason I'm still here created space I could fall forward into, as I needed; made me feel loved and like it mattered whether I made it through, like I was someone worth saving, even as at times all I could do was put my head in my hands and pray that I could go ahead and disappear, get boxed up, too. I remember like the back of my hand Adam explaining that it was a pleasure to have me there, that it made their lives fuller, too, during this strange time with everyone around us in the world all pulling back, leaving each household unto their own just at the same time as my whole life had come apart. I had my own space, my own chair at their family dinners every evening, requiring no commitment to the process, no explanation when I'd defer or disappear into my room, too sick to speak, or so confused with who I was that I could hardly separate the feelings of love and hope from pity. They stood beside me while inside I was screaming, violated, up to my neck in death and rage, taking me seriously when I said I might need to be checked into a ward, trusting me when I decided I'd changed my mind, wanted to stay. Their generosity reminded me of watching Mom give all she had to take care of my father through his mental illness, unwilling to sacrifice her faith for her convenience, no matter how hard the road ahead might prove: trust, compassion, inclusivity, direct access, honest faith, together forming a single thread dangled down into a bottomless pit. An actual miracle—I can think of no other proper name for it—offered as simply as the word *friend*.

Secretly, however, deep in my heart, I'd reverted to something like the plan I had when I met Molly—that I would run myself into the ground, filling my hours with drugs and fucking, spiraling out. It'd take my whole life to get back to where I thought I'd been, I kept reminding myself, borrowing the same suicidal logic that'd ended Molly's life: *it's all downhill from here.* This strange duality, stretched across spaces, made it hard at times to imagine how to display gratitude for being helped while still surrounded by miles of horseshit, fields of pins. No amount of generosity or love would ever make up for what had happened, I thought, no matter what; it could only make it that much worse, really, to be forced to face myself in some sadistic attempt to reclaim my life. Though by appearance I was taking part in my recovery—resting, going to therapy, handling paperwork, taking calls—I didn't actually feel like it was me there, only the part of me that remained too scared to just give up. I put on enough of an outward face to display the feeling I was hanging on, while on the inside all I really wanted was to be knocked out, waiting for the floor to crumble underneath me anytime. I had no appetite, not even a palpable discomfort no matter how long I forgot to eat, having already lost 15 pounds in two weeks. Some nights, locked in the bedroom, I'd sit on the floor in front of the mirror and stare at my face like it was someone else there behind the glass, someone I'd forgotten how to get near, how to touch. In that way, I wasn't so different from anyone I felt betrayed or overlooked by, like some latent part of how I was had been waiting for me to slow down a second, to look and listen, instead of trying to control everything before it fell. It had taken almost total annihilation to bring me to this point, to even just look right back into my eyes and ask what I wanted, what I believed in, only to find it felt so fucked that I could still want to, given everything I'd lost. Like how only when we're sick do we appreciate how it is to not be. Like how the very wondering of why we're here and what else there is itself becomes an essential part of the experience of life. I could see, though, phased in my eyes there, a frightened boy, at my behest, hoping against hope that I might withhold from bashing my head straight through the mirror glass, as I might have liked to, using it to cut my throat and kill the both of us at once. Instead, I held my breath and closed my eyes. I scrolled out into the blackness lining my insides to feel the streaming dark there holding tight, waiting for whatever else there might still be about me to take the wheel, steer back to light. No matter how long I could hold that, each next new breath echoed a reminder of all the other air denied by Molly, every cell and action auto-connected to the nexus where she'd put the bullet in her head. Impossible to pay attention to anything but that for very long; to meditate or read or watch TV, much less to write a coherent sentence, and yet all I had left as mine was time. When I'd go running, desperate for motion, I thought of stopping to lie down in the street or jumping out in front of SUVs. I'd stop and stand on this one bridge against its rail and imagine how it'd feel to fall into the water below, convincing myself it wouldn't be enough to kill me, and wondering where a better bridge might be. Each time, instead, I put my head down and kept running, screaming my lungs out to feel the rush, or punching myself in the head to shut me up. Instead of dying in the way that she had, I began thinking, I'd go out with a bang, at least—not death directly, but degradation first, meant to match the way I felt inside.

Coupled with the thoughts I'd had already about returning to the gun store, a ferocity for vengeance scourged my mind. I didn't give a flying fuck that she'd been the one who made her choices—I wanted blood. How could I take it lying down? This was a massacre, a travesty enabled by wicked men who'd plied their wiles upon her during her darkest hour, and every second no one did anything to stop them was a second wasted. Why should they be allowed to see another sun? It felt like truth and fiction fused together, intolerable to have to sit with, and impossible to overlook. I worked myself into such a frenzy thinking this way that I scared several friends ranting on the phone of violent plans, unable to stop antagonizing my desire for vigilante justice, never mind the consequences. If I ended up in jail or dead, who fucking cared? In the back of my mind, though, the same part of me that knew I still wanted to live also knew my reactions were in redline, and in the meantime, instead of a weapon, I bought a shitload of weed, ecstasy, mushrooms, and LSD. I began self-medicating to pad the impact in a way that at least would give me space to go away, to even make the safe suburban home where I'd been allowed to lay my head feel like a relic from another world. Soon as I could, I thought, once the pandemic lessened, I'd get in my car and drive away, spend the rest of my life wandering, with little care for what became of my behavior in due time. My wife was dead. My parents were dead. I was still here, but who would ever want to touch me, and why would I want them to, except to simulate a new experience of numb? I'd never used dating apps before, but I downloaded several of them, making profiles and maintaining conversations with several different strangers all at once. I tried out Grindr, to see if Molly's pronouncement that I might be bi had any merit and got kicked off for uploading pictures of my dick to a guy who got pissed that I didn't actually want to meet. I think I was seeking any connection I could find, any possible signal that could distract me from the onslaught of endless grief, but nothing stuck. People I'd never met, as well, came out of the woodwork on the internet, wanting to reach out to me in tragedy, to share a word that they were there, even if there was nothing else to say beyond just that. Every time I touched my phone or checked my email, there'd be new messages waiting, either in sympathy or reaching out to start a conversation about memory or death—a blessing and a curse, in that it hurt to be reminded over and over, though even worse imagining everybody was already moving on; that soon Molly would be forgotten by the few who'd noticed. "If I were you, I'd be doing so much heroin right now," a random woman from Twitter told me on the phone after listening to me spill my guts for hours during an interaction that seemed to walk the line between consolation and romance. It felt confusing to be approached by other people in this manner so close after the fact, battering my brain back and forth between impulses to indulge/destroy myself and to preserve any dim reminder of the feeling of having been a husband. Still, I found great comfort speaking on the phone to friends and strangers alike, and many nights I'd schedule a call so I could feel another person's voice there in my head in place of mine. I'd turn the lights off and put my headphones on, trying to hide my body from the idea of direct communication with something alive outside myself with someone else's voice there in my ear. Whereas for so long I'd felt idiotic in conversation, expecting no one would ever really understand me, now I felt all this wind in me come pouring out, all these feelings and ideas I might have otherwise hidden. The more I spoke, the more there was; like I'd been unlocked somehow, forced by the conflagration of my greatest terror come to life to look again, in search of threads within me that still hadn't snapped, even if I didn't quite know why yet.

———

But a phone, an email, even a letter has no touch—nothing to bridge the gap between the feeling of having been erased, gone from my mind. As if to find out what I was even capable of, but really just needing a warm body to remind me I was alive, I hired an escort from a website, a thing I'd never thought I'd do but now no longer caring what it meant. In a small, dingy room at an Extended Stay Holiday Inn, I stripped in front of the only person I'd been naked with besides Molly for many years. I told her I didn't really know what I wanted but to be held. Minutes later I found myself telling her what had happened to me, to Molly, to our lives. The escort held me close and stroked my hair and let me cry against her chest. She told me how so many of her clients were men like me, who needed warmth, an open ear in midst of grief. Then she recited from memory a long poem about her own struggles too, with drug addiction and with violence, her own suicidal ideation. We laid and embraced until the timer buzzed, then put our clothes on, said goodbye. *This is how my life is now,* I heard me thinking as I walked back out along the hotel's darkened halls, the endless doors, half waiting for a cop to pop out and arrest me. *Who I used to think I was is dead and gone.*

━━━

Alongside Amy and Adam, my other new roommate was their two-year-old daughter, Grace—a sweet, clever girl, who for some reason took a liking to me from the start. She'd often call my name out through the house during the day, wanting to play and run around. It felt complex, at first, to have to figure out how to disguise or suppress my mental anguish in her presence—inside, I'm screaming; outside, I'm playing Balloon Party and Hide 'n Seek. It felt hard, too, in another way, to spend time with such a charming child, so clearly loved and cherished by her parents, a live and up-close reminder of everything that Molly never had, if also an embodiment of hope that there could be something good left to the world. I wished I could somehow spread all that pure love and attention back through time and into Molly, too, to transform her through the walls of her neglect, another chance. I loved Grace at once, her breadth of pure imagination, gleeful play. I learned to lean into her imagination, her funny games, to find a different strength in the unknown joy a child provides in how they've not yet been tamed by thick reality. She seemed to be aware of something else there in me, too, of a kind of understanding that, unlike its formation in adults, I couldn't deny. "You need to rest, Blake," she'd sometimes announce, as if she could see straight through me, to my heart. She'd lead me over to the sofa and insist I lie down so that she could cover me with an afghan, take my temperature and listen to my heartbeat with her toys. "Be brave, Blake," she'd shout in giggles, trying to convince me to get up and continue playing Spin Around in Circles Until You're Too Dizzy to Walk. "You've got to be brave, Blake." At last, here was a voice impossible to want to deny; an innocent soul that made so much else surrounding my mourning fade away, a space within which I could laugh and see and feel again. Some summer afternoon there in the blur, collecting eggs from the chickens in the backyard, Grace asked to hold an egg, hearing her father's voice remind her it was delicate, to be very careful, before running off with it as quickly as she could. "What if that egg was a detonator to the universe," I said to Adam as we watched her veer and stumble across the yard, giggling unbound, "and if it breaks, that's it: The End?" Adam looked at me through the side of his face, eyes still on Grace. "Then that's exactly where I'd want the egg to be," he said and smiled, and we looked at each other, and we laughed.

Behind closed doors, however, I couldn't keep myself from digging deeper into any shred of evidence of Molly's secrets: her journals and her email and receipts and social media correspondences, all of which intwined to form a very different picture of her than I had ever known. Oddly, her personal writing never mentioned her affairs in any way, the same way that her suicide note had steered around them, too, along with so many other traces of the truth. Some details had very clearly been cleaned up, such as the automated messages from dating apps and porn websites that showed everywhere she'd had accounts, while most of the ongoing correspondence performed within them had been erased. Other times, there were whole extended threads she'd left behind, such as her emails back and forth with L., which spanned at least the last six months. I learned she'd saved his name under a friend's wife's name in her phone and kept in contact continuously, at first as friends, just sharing writing, which eventually turned into flirting, sexting, sending nudes. She'd made numerous videos for him performing for the camera, telling him she loved him, wanted him so bad, using a voice that didn't sound like her at all—childish and glow-eyed, like a doll. She'd sent him money multiple times, ~$1500, to help him avoid being evicted or to buy him food—money that was mine, essentially, given her struggle to ever keep a balance in the bank—until finally insisting that he stop using her for money, which still doesn't stop him from continuing to ask. At that first balk, he pleads back at her, making incessant entreaties, hollow promises, eventually attesting that he's in love with her, having just met her once, and will put his life on the line to prove it. He expresses fear about my finding out, claiming she's told him I would kill him, which she repeatedly reminds him isn't true, while in the same breath continuing to belittle our relationship, as she had her previous husband early on with me. I saw how they'd shared a little joke about the time I'd teased Molly for ordering the most expensive item on the menu at Taco Bell, twisting a decade-old joke into evidence that L. was big and I was small. "My baby can have anything she wants," he'd bragged by email, including a picture of the Taco Bell menu, even while the money he'd have used to buy it for her came from me. Meanwhile, to my face, Molly maintained level, making sure to keep me in my place as prior bedrock. "You are my best friend and deepest love of my life," she'd written to me in our texts while out in Tucson, likely with him there in the same room.

"Being with you makes me happy...I feel supported and loved by you in a way I have literally never felt before from any human being. You are home to me... I have so much respect for you...You know I love you so much no matter what...." She'd even texted me a picture of her grinning in half-sunlight outside the Airbnb where they got on, bearing an expression I had read then as on the cusp of breakthrough, finding peace out in the desert, near to nature. I realized, too, about the night I'd nearly had a panic attack after hearing demons in my head, threatening her life, that she hadn't been asleep, but instead was in his arms. The one picture I would find of them together, hidden in her phone, showed Molly lying on her stomach with her arms behind her back, her face completely hidden from the scene.

———

I couldn't sleep, and even when I passed out, I had no dreams. Inside my head, there was just black, like walls that meant at once to force my mind to stay together; though sometimes the edges would come open and I'd fall through, into an endless, open expanse of dense black, spreading out without an end on any side. The blank was waiting for me right there, any time, my reliance on my body all that separated me from the sort of space in which I'd imagined I would die since very young: by drowning in an expanse, like outer space or underwater, zero light. As a child, this terrified me, probably a primary cause of the decades of insomnia ahead. Now, though, I leaned into it, hoping somehow that its terror would be made true, and I'd been drawn into the same morass that'd taken Molly. Whereas before I'd asked for God to give Molly help, now I begged instead to be released from the same pain that she'd passed on. *Kill me, please*, I kept repeating, almost idly. *Crush my brain, destroy my body, make this end.* I'd stare into the abstract painting Molly had brought back from London, placed across from the foot of my bed like some 4D doorway to the past, trying to hypnotize myself or learn how to read between the lines where the paint obscured reality, an open node. One night I knew my body was on the bed with my head between two pillows, curled into a ball, while at the same time, in my mind, I felt a split, much like the time I'd left my body once before, though this time without a tether, any hope —as if the darkness, by my begging, had broken open into a landscape of immense encryption far and wide, exactly like my imagination of the transom between the living and the dead. I felt more afraid to open my eyes than to stay inside there, and so instead, I forced my consciousness to scroll ahead, falling forward through the nothing toward more nothing, as it seemed. It could go on like this forever, I imagined, no return. Just as I began to think I wouldn't mind staying forever there this time, left adrift, far ahead against some greater distance I recognized another impossible shape: a massive bulb or orb-like entity, bursting with color that refused to settle on my eye. I felt attracted to its pull; it called me forward, in a way that made the whole rest of the dimension come unwound. The closer I scrolled, the more intimately rendered its detail—pinions and pistons, humming silence, spindling out around some deeper point, like a black hole, but one where if you aimed into it, you could see through it, toward a kind of omnipotent space words can't relate. I understood, then, without knowing why, that the orb was the pure embodiment of *madness*; that all I had to do to be relieved of all my pain was give myself into its vortex, be swallowed up. So, once again, I had a choice: Give my life up and move on, or return to my body on the Earth. This time, I understood, if I chose madness, there could be no coming back. That sounded good, at least to some large part of me, just the ticket. I began to reach toward it with my mind, to try to feel within the pull its larger nature, what it could be like. In almost no time, I reached an edge: the final borderline between the states of sanity defined. A rising warmth, then, like hot bathwater; a tingling prickle rushing through my flesh back on the bed, enough to bump me up a level in my awareness that this wasn't just a dream, which carried over into *fear*. I remained capable of fear after all, part of me realized, suddenly back on the bed, funded perhaps by the part of me that still wanted to exist, discover life. My hesitation, right then, just a flinch, must have been enough to throw me back, like being scalded; this chaos, its impending transformation, wasn't mine. I opened my eyes.

████

I was still me. Still stuck inside the story I couldn't slow from unfolding even at dead end, continuously digging for even further information through any angle I could glean. I wanted to know it all, to hit some ledge where at least finally there could be no further to fall, and yet the more I looked the more there was. Not long after their meeting up in Tucson, I discovered, reading their emails one by one, things between Molly and L. grew hairy, tense. She accuses him of being in love with his ex-girlfriend, her tone unabashedly furious despite being married herself, scorned into self-loathing, chewing him out. He's only been using her, she writes, extorting her for money while in effect being too much of a drunk to really care, and the fact that he keeps referring to their time together as *sex work* makes her want to die. His responses to such accusations, over email, become manic on a dime, wildly steering between declarations of his love and backwards accusations of her cruelty, her greed. Suddenly, the strange and twisted idol she'd created of him all those months in leading up begins to fail to meet her terms. "You are not going to manipulate me anymore," she decides finally, after an ongoing back and forth. "Leave me alone." Across the next five hours, in response, he emails her over and over without reply, in a torrential diatribe of insults, accusations, threats. He repeats the same few things: how sorry he is he asked her for more money, how embarrassed he's been for being poor, how wrong she is about his character, how honest and true he's been, how he'll do anything to fix it if he could. At the same time, he tells her multiple times, in various manners, that he'll kill himself if she tries to cut him off. He asks if it would prove his love to her if he draws blood, that he won't eat until she responds, that he will never let her go, if it's the last thing he ever does. He says he'll come to Atlanta and expose her in our front yard or announce it publicly. He tells her she's insane, that her mind is ugly, that she's ruining everything, stigmatizing him for having had to ask to borrow money, that he has nothing left to lose. He's given her so much, he says, and is willing to go to "outrageous" ends to prove his love. "Stop threatening me," Molly responds, finally. "Threatening suicide, self-harm, dragging my name in public to get what you want—this is abusive, manipulative behavior and you need to stop. This is only making things worse." He responds to say his life is over, and it's her fault, reiterating how great it would have been if she weren't so tied to her bad memories, years of pain. Late into the second day of his emailing—92 in total, 72 from him, 20 from her—she responds one final time into the thread: "I don't really want to be alive right now and I honestly don't care about anyone anymore." He responds with four emails about how he is a good person and so misunderstood. The next morning, according to her journal, she buys the gun.

———

February 27: "Today I bought the gun. Drove there like any errand. Four old men inside who had no idea what they were doing, the judges in the *Passion of Jeanne D'Arc*." She goes on to describe the way they leered at her, a small, quiet woman in their store, never asking why a teacher would need a weapon, or noticing the way her eyes welled up when they spread the bullets for her on the counter. Instead, she writes, he tells her, *I've talked to doctors down at Grady*

about what these do to people. And they do a good job. They do a good job.
"That's what I wanted after all, a good job."

———

The *good job* that had required her destroying our relationship wasn't limited to the recent crap with L., so I discovered as I continued to connect dots. Her infidelity reached as far back as the early months of our relationship, including a fling with a student she'd hooked up with a couple weeks after our wedding. Then not only one student, but several, some over spans of years, all archived right there undeleted in her files. I could hardly believe what I was reading as I discovered email chains a hundred deep, reading back firsthand with her laptop burning against my thighs there on the bed as I traced Molly plying a strange, discursive method of seduction, clearly grooming. Early on, she'd praise the student for a job well done in class, a brilliant paper, then ask questions that led back into their life. She'd offer advice, asserting her position as their teacher, then tip her hand a bit, show some of hers. They'd become friends, meeting up under the auspices of office hours, where Molly would come on to them, sometimes quite to their surprise; later, these meetings turned into dates, into ongoing chains of desperation to continue and keep hidden both at once. This process was repeated several times, with several students, each of which she'd by turns worship, then deride. She focused on guys who seemed damaged, too, sometimes trading pictures of her tattoos, half-naked, in return for pictures of their own—often scarred, emaciated, or otherwise damaged, as she felt. "I'm your teacher. I just want to help you," she'd remind them, when there seemed to be confusion about the nature of the relationship, dodging the question "Aren't you married?" by insisting, "It doesn't matter. Anyway, I'm old and ugly. You don't need me. I'm just trying to be a friend." Each bit of correspondence that I read served a mere fragment of the larger whole—segments of the secret story, off the page, which only she and they could ever know. She'd speak around the aspects of her real life as if they hadn't happened, referring to me, in sharing how her day went, as a friend, often talking down about our memories as if she wished she hadn't been there—bored out of her mind on New Year's Eve, for instance, or irritated to have been dragged to a basketball game that had actually been her own idea, or saying she had a hen named "Water," too embarrassed to use the silly name I'd given Watermane in front of someone else. The students seem to trust her, too, surprised to find such intimacy with their teacher, which led them into divulging secrets no one else knew except for her—suicidal thoughts, for instance, which Molly recast by reminding them that they were smart and sharp and good; that they shouldn't hurt themselves, please; that they still had so much life to live. *But I still don't know why you like me*, they might mention, most every one of them in turn. *I'm confused.* Molly knew just when to pivot from those moments, so it seemed, changing the conversation back to simpler things, just making friends. She bonded with them about video games, anime, memes, intermixed with ongoing conversation about how hard it was to be a person in the world. Radio silence on their end makes her hysterical at times, clearly at once paranoid she's crossed a line and will be caught, while also incessantly intrigued with seeking contact, sometimes even begging them to come by office hours, or after class. At any mention of bad blood, she turns at once to self-defense, reminding them that this is not the way that she behaves, that this was something different, and they are special, and their future is so bright. She remains aware enough of getting caught that when real trouble comes, she's already prepared her exit façade, never mind the damage rendered. The relationships most often end either when the student pulls away, uncertain how to handle her intensity, or when Molly beats them to the punch, assessing any whiff of reluctance on their end for the telltale signs of lost desire; how it is.

Between the gaps, gleaned by the receipts from adult websites and meet-up apps, I realized Molly had often maintained regular crushes, meetups, and flings, filling in most any time I'd been away with who knows who or where or when, how many times. She stayed vigilant, too, in maintaining caution against most any window through which she'd be found out, one step ahead, ready to curse me out for any questioning of her hard lines. One day, for instance, she'd come home and said her doctor told her she might have an STD, and was there something I should tell her, preempting her own exposure with a jab, blowing up with weeping even as I attested that I'd been faithful ever since those early dating days. I realized she'd known exactly how to shift the story off herself and onto me when needed, changing the details as she saw fit, and she'd controlled me and abused me in this way. I don't mind admitting it, now: the word *abuse,* which I would have never imagined saying about her when she was alive. I can't even fully fault her for it, despite the knowing looks I get when I've tried to suggest she'd learned to wield her story as a weapon after having had no choice as an abused child, the extent of which I still believe that no one will ever know. Abuse is passed on through more abuse, of course, and who was I to want someone to be able to withstand that, to foment change. I realize, too, in listening to others who've been abused in much more immediately paralyzing ways, that this is a crucial part of the problem—that from inside it, under the influence of both the effects of the abuse and the related higher feelings that were used, expanded, by the abuser to fund their influence, keep you close. While I can hear a friend tell me their experience of gaslighting, love bombing, stalking, terroristic threats, and want to go and demolish the abuser, bring them to justice, in my own shoes I even still want to find ways to remain loyal, to relativize my own experience as just another part of the job of what love is; wanting to embody the belief that everybody deserves love, especially those in preternatural distress, and simultaneously unable to separate myself from that, to underline that the strange webs we weave in love shouldn't need to override the safety of the relationship, its sense. Trying to imagine Molly in these moments—what was really going on within her and how she maintained her firm surface; how stolid and replete she was in relying on her practices of maintaining control from within a chaos all her own; how there could be the Molly who knew right from wrong, theoretically, and the Molly who walked face first into the latter, baiting pure pain; how I can hardly even imagine her reaction if I'd ever said anything like this directly—probably laughing in my face, saving her real reaction for her journal, or not even there, just for herself, or maybe even twisting it back on me, changing the story, knowing how little I could do, how ready I would be to accept her analytical perspective as my own—it all becomes like trying to trace the image of a full person in flooding sand while drowning in the same sand. Very soon, there neck-deep in it, you almost can't remember a way out. Eventually, you might even start to think the only way out is further in. As for myself, lost in the aftermath, finally, I'd had enough; I didn't need to see anymore and couldn't bear to, so much so it made me want to laugh in the face of any extant possibility of truth. Beyond the shock of her adultery, I realized I had little articulable idea left of who she was, or how to parse the values she'd outwardly upheld, burned others over, against her own opposing actions and obfuscations, without any direct path to conversation, much less resolve. I logged out of her accounts, closed her computer.

▬

I've despaired over sharing these darker parts of Molly, the parts she hated herself for, and used against herself like cutting. Even writing it feels like transcribing a secret meant for silence. Should I be allowed to make this said? To bring to light a part of Molly's story she covered over at any cost? At this point, I feel I hardly have a choice, given the way the story, bound up inside me, feels like frying in a slow electrocution, with nowhere else to set it down. Is it wrong for me to even want to, to have the will to, outside the bounds of my own self? Shouldn't I be burying it, too, along with everything I thought I knew about her? In some ways, though, discovering Molly's infidelity at least made her story clearer to comprehend, seeing how she had trapped herself in endless lies; how her idea of love again remained unsacred in the wake of recurring deceit; and all the more impossible to have to live with or unpack, no longer being certain what about her had been true; where she had really been when she said where she was going; who else knows more about her that I don't. It seems to say a lot that she didn't destroy so much obvious evidence more completely; the correspondence and receipts still right there archived in her inbox, the feed of nudes left only half-deleted in the trash, the back half of her bottom drawer full of sex toys she kept while throwing out so much else without my knowing—as if she wanted to be caught, and maybe even understood, despite the absence of any signal in her last letter, any word straight from her mouth. In her journals, she writes of setting her estate in order, making it "easier" for me in the aftermath, while entirely omitting any mention of what was really going on in secret in her life, as if, should she fail to write it down, it wasn't real. "I know, rationally, life choices are fueled on fires of passion, emotion, principles, impulse," she wrote. "Looking back I don't know that I allowed these impulses to be loud enough in my head. Besides running away, that has always been a consistent impulse. So what then? Keep running? Quit this, start a new thing? Keep starting over again and again, forever, never done, never settled, one foot out the door. You would think maybe I like it—like running away and starting over constantly. But, no. It's horrible. I'm tired of that sick, churning feeling in my chest of uncertainty, of worry. I busy myself to avoid it, I just put my head down and grind. Then, time is wasted, years disappear." Other times, she makes allusions, as in her poetry, to things she's gone through off the page, talking around the central issue while also speaking up for what she's either buried or repressed, much like her leaving out the journals in hopes I'd violate her trust. "Last night explaining to Blake and Jamie why rape fantasies are appealing to women," she writes, of a night I no longer remember on my own, "that it's a moment of being so strongly and purely desired that nothing will stop him." Suddenly, her ongoing resignation and distortion of our shared reality made sense; the false fronts and dummy floors, in desperation, trying to juggle several lives at the same time; the unshared thoughts, emotions, expectations every single person ever has little choice but to learn to share or bury or carry on. Each of us, in every moment, having spent our entire lives in leading up to stand precisely where we are, without a way to ever say it but in fragments, fading fast. It's enough to want to believe in God, or at the least to feel affected in the shadow of his absence—to think that all of this exists in such a way that you could never experience it in the same way as another, much less describe it; as if your life is somewhere only you could go, against the tide of wiles and whims that flood our senses, too wild to read. Isn't it, perhaps, the seeming chaos of it all, the absence of compassion of a creator, that makes it inevitably exactly what we can't imagine it might be?

▃▃▃

What ends up being the greater wonder, as I see it, is less the idea that there's nothing essential to the narrative, but that we're not allowed to see beyond. Subjected to the will of that which we can't, by definition, ever capture—like a parent's love, perhaps, or like a fire in a memory, long since extinguished as what it was—we wait instead to be remanded into a version of the story where, for once, at last, the story of our life might be no longer all we have; that some person or some power could finally demonstrate how much they love us in such a way that all the terror and depression melts away, allows us, at last, to feel we have the strength to be the person we'd always wished. In the meantime, inside the silence, left to fester, trauma thrives. The gore of trauma pools inside us, colors over vision, breaks in waves that seek for land to crash and wear away until there's nothing recognizable. The deceit we weave ends up enclosing us, along with our idea of all the ones we meant to love, like a prison rendered out of the same bones we use to stand and walk around. In this light— regardless of how hateful Molly often was; how brutally insistent on failing to face her horror's most immediate effects; how impossible she made it for me to reach her despite her hunger; how much hurt that she recreated and played over in all the hiding from her pain—I don't think I'll ever give up the want to make concessions for her, to leaven in my heart the sorts of judgments from those who couldn't know her, or only knew her through the guise of her control; how though we can hear the hurt in the biographical facts of a *hard life*, a component part of all the pain and trauma in the world, and maybe we can even feel it burn inside our skin too, where the facts as facts do not congeal, but we can never, not completely, *understand*, each of us embodied front and center in our own perspectives, how real it is, how thick it burns. "Suicidological research has nothing to do with the concrete suicide," wrote Hermann Burger of the difference separating depressive madness and a survivor's drive to comprehend; "its psychological, sociological, and thanatological arguments draw it ever further from the *black room*, the pit grave of the universe, the non-Euclidean geometry and logic of death."[27] At my lowest, just like Molly, I'm filled with violent rage at absolutely everything and everybody, most of all myself, made only worse by recognizing that no matter what I think or feel, it can't change facts. When, through therapy and distance, the rage subsides a while, shifting back into abstractions much like myth, I find I often feel the aching binds of silence even more extremely, so much that I'd do anything to crack the seal and forebode anybody who might hear me that no matter what a person is or was or does, however damaged or deluded we might be, how pat it sounds: Nothing but love can shift the cycle. Nothing but love remains for long.

━━

27   Burger, Hermann. *Tractatus Logico-Suicidalis: On Killing Oneself.* Translated by Adrian Nathan West. Wakefield Press, 2022, p. 109-110.

Does this all seem like one big mess? A vortex of betrayal and bad faith? I know it must, but it didn't at the time, at least to me. It felt like life alongside someone I believed in more than anybody, and who I knew struggled deeply in herself, who I tried to fill with confidence against the tides, as the days went by like days do—full of sorrow and expanse, joy and creation, all moving past so fast sometimes it's hard to remember anything at all. Do I seem like a fool, an ass? That's fine. I got to share a life up close with one of the most brilliant and singularly stunning people I've ever met, good times and bad. I got to walk beside her and support her as best I could, as best she'd let me; to offer love where love had so long been denied. I don't regret it, never will, no matter how much pain it's caused me, all the mental damage. I refuse, when at my clearest, to simply demonize Molly for her struggle, her mental illness, her deceits, even her continuous abuse of me and our relationship; though sometimes it's difficult to know where else to turn amidst so much conflicting information bursting open in my soul now that she's gone. It overwhelms and overrides—the lies, the violence, held up against the tender parts of my best friend, my love, my wife, clouding in like ambient rubble over everything I thought we were. All of the thoughts she never shared, hidden behind her face in every picture; all the hate and anguish she pressed down, tried to exhibit pure control over her story, all it touched. "Blake has an idea of how I am that isn't me at all. I don't mind it of course," she writes in her journal near the end—quite well aware, at least in part, of such a difference, if still somehow unable or unwilling to name their parts. At the same time: "It might be too much to ask, but I hope your memory of me will not become bitter," she writes in her suicide note, at once seeming to ask for my forgiveness while simultaneously attempting to control her story from the grave. And the thing is: I understand. Past all the wreckage, I still refuse to pull my heart and mind away from the Molly that I knew despite all else, no matter how large the difference might have been at times between her modes. Someone told me that rather than thinking of having lost Molly so young, I got to spend the last decade of her life standing beside her, in a place that for at least a while gave us a home. Try as I might to override that, to dwell instead on all the tendrils of the tragedy, in pure defeat, I know I am so grateful, always will be, for what time we did have, how in my heart I feel, despite her illness, we really were. Most precious to me now are the moments when a passing glimpse of something like satisfaction might cross her face, however fleeting—times when she could almost see herself as others did; how proud she was the first time she pulled off baking a wedding cake for friends, the glimmer in her eye as she went over and over the minor details like a sculptor at the wheel. "I can't believe I could actually do it," she'd announced, for once victorious in her own heart, however brief. I'll never forget the cat-that-ate-the-mouse smile she let slip onto her face at a nice restaurant when she would order every dessert on the menu, like a shy and solemn kid allowing herself at last to speak up and have exactly what she wants. We'd had such fun then, going over each and ranking them in order of our favorites, where Molly would always be jubilantly ruthless, but also accurate, fair. I loved to watch the face of the wait staff when they would ask us how things tasted as Molly outlined in great detail her critiques, also generous with praise over a job well done, unlike she'd ever offer to herself. All she really needed was a couple more friends, I thought, who really saw her the way I did, just as I needed more of her, of the depth of drive I knew and felt behind her eyes, of her precious desperate want for peace and beauty despite the sick reality she often insisted was the only truth, consuming all.

———

Molly's first marriage had also experienced similar troubles with fidelity, I'd later learn from her ex directly, once I was able to utter any shred of this aloud. She'd still been married when we met, a fact she'd continued to conceal even after coming clean that night in Michigan, pretending there'd been a gap between. Our relationship had begun as an affair, then, unknown to anyone besides her, providing direct inspiration for her to give up on their decade-long relationship and move away. *None of your business anyway*, I can hear her saying in my head, had I known enough to press her further while still alive, to not only wonder why she had to act so coldly when I got too close to certain parts of her life story, but to confront her. He understood very well my experience of the ways she'd use to manipulate most any story to her favor, and it had taken him years to see more clearly, to think for himself. She'd put him through the ringer, to the point that after years of fighting over her continuous cheating, they'd come to an understanding—that there were things that Molly needed that her husband could not provide. She craved attention compulsively, to the point of wanting something more visceral, unsafe; someone who'd hit her, who'd do hard drugs with her, who'd make her scream. Even that, though, while on the table, came with furtive aspects, things that Molly would allude to but not say. She'd come home with a black eye and bruises and blame it on falling. She'd leave her journals out full of trace details so as to provoke a fight, bait she knew he would take, wanting both to be confronted about her bad behavior and to be given grounds to lash right back, unleashing all the faults she'd counted up until she burst. Once, he said, she'd gotten sick and only eventually admitted it happened from doing heroin for the first time in forever, returning to a habit she'd acquired during college. In their couples therapy, she claimed to not know who the person in her brain who wanted violent sex was, who sought out thrills that jeopardized her life, and yet somehow, she couldn't stop. Maybe the sex and violence, he suggested, had given her an outlet, some means to serve those she saw as wounded in the same way—a space where even if nothing became solved, it had traction, space to breathe, even if what she was breathing was laced with blood.

—

Please speak up. The world is clouded, but we must try, if not for ourselves, then for those who hardly even had a chance. I still believe that, at least at times, even as we continue to persist within a culture where it's been accepted that women are abused, that children are abused, that the most vulnerable among us are abused—and within that, that those who've been abused should often keep it to themselves, cope on their own, survive on their own—all part and parcel with *how it is*. We've become so accustomed to our culture's violence, the massive force with which the lines and laws of social living combine to ensure we have little time for anything but keeping up, that many can't remember how we got here, what we'd once thought lay ahead. Even many once well-meant phrases of awareness—"systemic violence," "safe space," "trigger warning," "wokeness"—have become more like placeholders, something mocked; like we're not even able to talk about what we're talking about but in code. We hear each other tell each other what has happened to us, what we fear, and we still stay stuck to what our mere survival demands. Get up, go to work, come home, eat dinner, watch TV, go back to sleep. It's not even a secret; any fool knows this. It's written in our mortal souls like time itself. Sometimes it's like we're down here smiling for the camera, thinking the eye behind the camera is the thing that's going to save us after all—never mind how life feels in the meantime; and never mind who pays the cost. Judge all you want what Molly suffered and inflicted on herself as both a liar and a cheat, much less the myriad ways she might have owned up any moment, taken steps to regain control of her own life. "This whole language I'm using is wrong," she wrote of her upbringing, how much it hurt in ways she couldn't face. "I hear survivors of other traumas say similar things when asked to discuss their experiences. Language itself just derails over certain topics. This is demon number one in this book."[28] Is she so wrong for holding out, for wanting more, even while refusing to figure out how to reverse the damage? How about us? Are we going to simply brush this under the rug and make excuses, turn away until it returns sevenfold, this time too wide and overwhelming for anybody ever to imagine? Some people turn to God in search of peace within that absence of understanding; others, like Molly, turn even further still away, reinforcing their desperation for relief with an even deeper bonding to its inverse, as if nothing else could ever be so true as pain. *Maybe someone will want to love me if I'm sexy, if I'm rich, or if I win.* Somewhere not too far down the line, perhaps, having reabsorbed enough of our own consciousness, we become blinded to the path itself, inviting instead of consolation or forgiveness, only more and more of the same grief, taking relief in lamentation, or degradation, or fast attention, boxing out the conscious possibility of even looking

28 *Bandit*, p. 88.

deeply at our own wounds—much less the wounds of others, much less their lives, much less our lives. There's simply not enough time to gather any else, we think, in the wake of all the worldly glory we can't help but want to covet in our hearts, no room to offer harbor to anybody but ourselves, too long a day; when really the glory is all little more than bitter decorations on a ship that, without some better intervention, has nowhere to go but down.

———

"Belief is one thing," Molly wrote of the role of the church in the history of Poland after her visit. "Belongingness is another." To what did Molly ever feel that she belonged? Although she emphatically framed herself a nonbeliever, references to "God" or "gods" appear regularly throughout much of Molly's writing—in *The Cipher*, the final book that she'd find a publisher for, released during the winter after her death, it's there nine times. From "Otto Dix": "God's back is black fog. // I know. He, we guess / means to do it. / To do all of this. // The brute center part / of an iridescent moth. // The carnation / against the man." From "The Cipher": "And a nonbeliever accepts / that God is very, very likely. // Nothingness is just not / how brute facts work." She'd even considered joining a convent, she admitted one night, unable to imagine any other way to get some distance from the absence that she felt spanning all things, if also another way to make me feel her blankness as a threat against the dearth of love she often felt no matter what I did or said. When speaking of her family, her friendships, her work in academia, the world of baking, the world of poetry, social media, Detroit or Savannah or Morgantown or Augusta or Atlanta, even our own relationship, there always seemed to be a wide gap between the space where she imagined a possibility of belonging and how she wore it in the chaos of her soul. "Imagine if I felt this way knowing people did care about me!" she wrote the day before she died. "If I belonged to a community, some respected unique terminal? It would be torture. As it is, it's all perfectly easy to just go." Terrifying in a completely different way, then, to see the world through Molly's eyes after the fact, to hear from so many people who did love and admire her, if from afar. Searching backwards through her feeds, I read through countless threads and notifications of people reaching out in praise: recognizing her poetry, soliciting her baking, letters from students and from admirers and friends. "Of course I am grateful," she writes in her journal about *Bandit*'s publication, the many positive reviews. "But I'm also resentful. Because none of this is mine. It's all Dad, all Blake, all everyone but me. I am still just a hack, a poser, and would have none of this if it had come down to my actual talent, because there is none."[29] It remains forever uncertain whatever else might have been done to try to reach her in the face of her own voice, insistent as she was to stand beholden to the darkness of the world; just *how it is*. Given years and years of further therapy, one narrative conceives, she might have broken through and come around; instead, a prior narrative contends, in never having thought herself worthy of love, she spends her life trying to convince herself instead to deny it, cleaving onto navigable ground the only way she knows, by how it hurts. Either way, no matter which narrative, what did it matter how she behaved if she felt no one cared enough to find her out?

███████

Maybe part of the problem is there's something self-fulfilling in the attraction of the wounded to the depths. How we hurt ourselves because we hurt, and we think that no one else could understand, even the people we have to pay to actually listen to us, which is a complaint Molly would use to decry the same therapy she'd talked

29 Brodak, Molly. Unpublished diary entry, 16 Oct. 2016.

me into starting, once she realized she had to stop therapy so she could die. She seemed surprised when I reported having cried for the first time during a session, slowly learning to let my guard down and open up. She cried every time, she told me; always had. Our therapist, however, describes it differently: *I don't remember Molly crying even once.* Not a word, either, of all the struggling to piece together her hidden life, *her actual life,* the stress of keeping a whole half of herself secret, nothing much that really touched the deepest edges of her lies. She'd even stopped showing up during those last months, while still pretending to go to her appointments, even reporting back on how it went, knowing I wouldn't press her if she didn't want to tell. When I ask why someone would go so far as to attend therapy and still withhold, our therapist shrugs. No one will ever really know. She's gone. There are things the brain divides, pushes back down, thereby creating blind spots in your awareness of yourself, and from in the blind, life perhaps becomes a kind of game sometimes, at least a little, *all in the mind,* the familiar world finally revealed as nothing more than soundstages, actors, scripts, each somehow walled off in the same stroke that identified them as significant. How, then, does anybody ever know they're loved? How might you help them to imagine, any hour, any day? Do you ask people how they're doing? Do you wonder? Do you really want to know? No, really: Do you care about anything as much as you care about yourself? Could you ever? Why must we allow the battered frameworks of our lives to be guided primarily by our ambitions within the system of replication and advancement? Why should it take a death to know a life? Even after all of the outpouring after Molly's death, I can't say I've felt any more certain that I understand why we are here, but I do know how often it goes missing right from underneath our noses, drowned in the wake of all the other ways we seek to glorify ourselves. I can't help but wonder why we're so rarely looking back until there's no other way to try to comprehend. In the end, no matter what it all adds up to, who's taking notes, it seems we leave very little time for the work of living, to stop worrying why we are here and just be here. Trauma's strange like that—from a remove, it has a face, a name, with an awareness of the fact that others just like you have already survived similar, but never the same, as your pain is only ever yours, a part of you that has already happened, no way back; and nowhere lonelier on all the earth but in that feeling, like being damned. Over time, they say, it flattens out, becomes ground that you have figured out how now to stand on, then to walk, as back at the beginning of your life, though also older now than ever, every moment. So, what's the point? Why suffer all this, go through all this unto death, just to take part in the same system that created the anguish in the first place, while in the meantime, the Earth is dying, assuring only further trauma yet to come? You can get so far into this form of thinking, walled in on every single side without a word, that you forget what ever made life worth living in the first place; how far you came to first have anything to lose, what made you yearn to have enough time to do the things that move you, why wake you up. The lack of any direct answer for *why* creation, *why* the roaring hoard, *what else awaits*, creates a vacuum within the experience of experience itself, simultaneously opening the door to mass delusion and to the fulcrum of creation, beyond the blank.

———

"To lack infinitude is despairing confinement, narrowness," Kierkegaard wrote of the intellectual in *The Sickness unto Death*. "The worldly point of view always clings closely to the difference between man and man, and has naturally no understanding (since to have it is spirituality) of the one thing needful, and therefore no understanding of that limitation and narrowness which is to have lost oneself, not by being volatized in the infinite, but by being altogether finitized, by instead of being a self, having become a cipher, one more person, one more repetition of this perpetual *Einerlei* [one-and-the-same]."[30]

———

cipher: "(1) a secret way of writing, especially one in which a set of letters or symbols is used to represent others; (2) a person or thing of no importance."[31]

———

I'm so sorry, Molly. I really tried. I know you tried too, as best you could. I love you forever.

30 Kierkegaard, Søren. *The Sickness Unto Death*. Translated by Alastair Hannay. Penguin, 1989, p. 63.
31 "cipher." *Oxfordlearnersdictionaries.com*. 2022. https://www.oxfordlearnersdictionaries.com/us/definition/english/cipher (1 Dec 2022).

In this room where I am writing, I finish writing the prior sentence, then I blow out the candle on my desk. I watch the smoke rise through the room, filling my senses with its odor, both from the burning and the tint of artifice, bred by design. Less than a minute later, the smoke has cleared, if not the smell yet, and I'm the only one who's here. They say silence can ring louder than any sound, but it's the sound that makes the silence ring, to the point it hurts, like grasping on to something no one has a name for. Through the window, just beyond the screen filled with these words, the sky is gray, wholly opaque beyond the premise of pending rain, as if there were something there beyond it worth hiding, until maybe someday.

Is death the end? No one really knows the answer, no matter what they'll try to sell you. You're not supposed to know yet, are you? Life is experience. It just keeps happening. You change, then change again, just like the days. Who you are, on paper, remains not quite who you ever were once, who you will be tomorrow and beyond, and yet something essential remains continually transferred and transformed throughout it all, a baseline we'd love to think of as our soul—the essential part of how you are that can't be separated from you no matter what else about you becomes changed. Could death, instead, then, be a beginning, like realization? Or is the beginning at the crux of every day, with every next second at last possible the one that shifts the whole thing, and at last we learn to see beyond the local trauma of having lived so long without clear shape inside ourselves—until at last, perhaps, there's no longer still such a thing as *now*. In the meantime, it requires a form of faith in and of itself to carry on, to open one's best mind to tomorrow, and maybe find there, strewn like seeds among the rubble, the possibility of possibility itself. Many of us learn to explain away the miraculous phenomenon of beauty, majesty, improbability, with logic, science, coincidence, converting any direct experience of the unknown as shadow play or desperation, reading between the lines of our own pleas. But if all we are is organisms in an exploded cosmos, the sum of our biology, then what is love? What is forgiveness? What is that faculty that, as if from out of nowhere, shows up in some unnamed way and provides a kind of feeling you couldn't have asked for on your own? Is the fact that we must suffer really only evidence against the knowable within the realm of human intelligence, which time has proven wrong over and over? Molly might scathingly insert something here about delusion and desperation, cruelty and chaos, other such forces that appear to solely guide the cold, hard truth of our lost world, of a logic system she'd created based on evidence as fused from affect as any other vice-grip worldview. But just because Molly was mentally affected doesn't mean she wasn't in the room, and just because we want there to be a meaning to it all, doesn't mean there is, or at least not one we as humans could ever comprehend clearly enough to state and make all the rest of us believe. I can't claim more than anybody else to understand how anything like hope or justice could ever find a way to outpace the countless teeming tragedies that seem entwined with human life, but here we are. Part of me doesn't want to have to acknowledge the effect of any hope or kindness ever, so often hardly offering even a speck of grace within the reigning sum of so much suffering and fury, all the damage we have done given the chance. At the same time, I'm only even partially aware of what it is that keeps me getting up still, from underneath; from holding back from acts of revenge and retribution, as if waiting still to be called out, to feel the click of something larger all around me, like a mask pulled off my face. In spite of—or perhaps in light of—so much unknowing, so much anguish, so close up, I find the deepest reaches of my person hanging on, as if I do know that what I don't know shouldn't stop me from imagining the possibility of something more—of change, if not of the whole world, then of myself, without a word to even frame it in my mind. There remains something that elides, its continuing absence the very fundament of the same mystery that drives so many to the grave, broken by the very same pain that girds the ego, demanding only, *right here* and *right now*, to know *why*. One step after the other, the bit forced in my mouth reminds me, like a pill against the illness of *myself*. One breath at a time.

———

The first time I felt Molly's presence beyond death was in the pantry of our half-evacuated house. Soon, the walls would all be painted over white, as recommended by my listing agent, given how little imagination people had, she said, for living amongst someone else's choices. I too found it difficult to stay there for very long now that all my friends who'd come to help me through the last weeks had returned home, back to their own lives. Already the house felt like a shell of somewhere else, barely recognizable besides its bones and the specter of malformed memories sunk on the airspace—ways we'd moved, moments unmentioned, all the kinds of time that has no name. I'd never seen a rainbow inside our house before, though there it was, striped across the lock jamb on our pantry, almost exactly the same place Molly and I had been standing the last time we embraced, those final moments. "There were always rainbows there," the Molly I knew would have likely said as explanation. "You just never noticed."

Seconds after I took this picture, the rainbow disappeared.

———

Days later, on what would have been Molly's fortieth birthday, I decided to go back to the exact place where we'd been wed. The approaching streets were almost wholly empty now, like in a science-fiction film, wide open gray even in broad daylight. I could barely hold the wheel to drive, and yet I knew I had to go alone. I didn't want anyone to have to see me like this, know me like this; to be seen would mean I couldn't mourn. Back on the mountain, I sat beneath the same tree we'd sworn our vows in front of our mothers not long ago. I cut open the cardboard box of Molly's cremains, ripping through the inner plastic bagging with my nails. I felt surprised at how large the kernels of the ash were, how bright pale white, like heavy sand. I read aloud some of the other birthday love poems I'd written to give to her, then from Milosz, following along with the pages she had earmarked, one then another. The words in each felt strangely timed as I recited, as if prescheduled to have synchronized with here and now:

> What strengthened me, for you was lethal.
> You mixed up farewell to an epoch with the beginning
> of a new one,
> Inspiration of hatred with lyrical beauty,
> Blind force with accomplished shape.[32]

In the breeze-shaped silence laced thereafter, I held my palm up and let some of the ashes catch the current, then a whole handful, strewing it out in front of me like disintegrating rope. I felt an urge to eat some of the ash, too, and so I did, thinking of how what had once been part of her body now mixed with mine, a part of me forever, our new future. Overhead, the sky was strange, wide-clear in some parts, overcast in other, threatening rain. I felt very aware of all the other people there around me, families having come to share the day before

32   "Dedication" from Milosz, Czeslaw. *The Collected Poems*. Harper Collins, 1988, p. 78.

the storm, unaware of how her dust now imbued the air, laced in their breath. From there, I got up and walked across the curving edge of granite to where we'd sat holding hands after our vows, looking out together across the sprawling face of the world; how I had placed my head against her shoulder and listened to her whisper in my ear, gone from my memory but in their feel. We'd been alive then, I remembered, entwined together with the whole rest of our lives still to be gathered, our muddled past little more than a distraction, lost in time. I felt lucky to have had that, no matter how messed up in the thereafter. Something *ours*, then: pockets of memory, like open windows, once bound within us, now with the dust, to be worn down and recycled, over and over, long after both of us were gone; our memories no less vulnerable to wear than our bodies, I knew, having seen dementia change my parents into stand-ins, losing their grip on even the most essential elements of who they'd been. In some ways they were as alive as ever, though, I thought, knowing how I could still hear their voices in my fiber when I reached, by all we'd been through, all they'd taught me. I could feel them with me even still, for having loved them, seen who they were spread over time—even death could not change this, no matter who else might be able to remember once our bloodlines grew further out, obscured against the wide but finite backdrop of history. No one could take Molly away from me in that mind either, no way to undo what she had done, neither the sad parts nor the small things, no matter how far gone they felt from here. The future continued to be the future, for every one of us, each in their own time, right where we are.

———

I stood and moved across the mountain toward a lake. Overhead, a hawk crossed over the airspace of my path, intersecting with us in sets of points that disappeared against the sky soon as it passed, as if the landscape was alive, aware of every speck of will and stitch of breath within its bulk. As I reached the lake, a wind came up and rose across it, spreading out the surface of the waters grey and flat, a mirror image for the sky, held up, it seemed, by nothing more than the tines of budding trees surrounding at all sides. A light rain began to fall then, creating concentric ovals across the lake's face cascading out, blanketing my sun-warm skin with goosebumps and vanishing dew. I watched the clouds above me part; there behind them, the blinding sun appeared, a white, hot light so instantly intense I forgot the world—everything on pause in all directions besides the blinding, almost like being seen, no need for words. Then, as fast as it'd begun, the cloudbanks closed up, covered the sun back, and the surface of the waters became calmed. That's when I heard the birds begin to scream—dozens of them, then maybe hundreds, terrifying in their high volume from out of nowhere, far behind me, through the woods over the mountain face. Right then I turned and ran into the screeching din as I might have into a tidal wave, louder and louder as I hurried fast as I could toward a part of the mountain Molly and I had never been together during our walks. Every step I made felt like one further into a delirium, as if around the next edge I'd come to stand before some shining altar, or a black gorge where death began—I would have believed almost anything I saw at this point, certain that something inexplicable was being done; the hand of God tipping its cards for just a second now that I had nothing left to lose. Soon as I thought that, like at a bullseye, I reached a fence, lacing the edge of open land there with high wire mesh, the sound of screeching now so high in all directions it felt like part of me. Through the holes in the fence, sweating and shredded by where the trees had scratched my skin, I saw a panoramic sprawl of turkeys, hundreds of them, all enclosed, clucking and cawing without relent in the apparent absence of any other person who could hear them except me. Screaming like humans, I kept thinking, without a way to alter what or where or how they were, at the mercy of their unseen overseers, very likely awaiting nothing more than execution. I stood there with my fingers in the wire, scanning from one turkey to the next, imagining they could see me there, beyond their reach, a lambent glint flecked in the black pits of their eyes as a reflection of the pins of light from overhead, bathing us all. Without thinking, I turned around and emptied out the last of Molly's ashes right where I was, then bowed my head and thought a prayer. Heading back out the way I'd came, ready to leave now, I spoke aloud in conversation with Molly like I had all those other simpler times, passing by other couples heading in the opposite direction, to make their own experience of where I'd just been.

——

Back in my guest room, I felt a voice. It first appeared woven deep within the layers of Brian Eno's *Thursday Afternoon*, an album Molly and I had once laid entwined together on the sofa and let play over us in full. Our shared experience had configured a link between us, something told me, means by which we could communicate without the need of direct sense, easily explained away as hallucination; and yet I could clearly feel her speaking to me through my body just the same, could even see her wedged there in a vista of the darkness in my skull, part of another layer added to me through our purpose, beyond death. She'd made it to the other side okay, Molly explained, speaking to me from within what appeared inside my mind to be a phone bank, deep inside a massive library with countless floors. Our dimensions were still connected in this way, she explained, as only two among an immensity of layers semantically connected to every object and experience on both sides. Everything that happened in any of the levels could affect the other levels in direct ways, for the most part rarely seen in our world and still requiring intimate attention and dedication from within hers to call aware. She'd had to practice for what would be trillions of years in human time to be able to speak to me as such, to translate her experience back into a form of language I could parse. The boundary between our realities could bend but not break, she said, and the bond we'd found in sharing love in time, magnified through tragedy, allowed a certain form of intervention, a means to press beyond mere reason. She was very sorry for having hurt me, she uttered tightly, somehow still uncertain how to say it straight, still clearly clouded by her will but also having trouble reconnecting to what it might feel like to still be me. Any urge I felt to try to interrupt the ethereal with pressing questions about her suicide, the things she'd hidden, were met on her end with a rejoinder to try to focus instead on larger scope—how she could only keep this window open for so long, and there was so much more essential information she wanted to relay. This was the Molly I most knew, after all—steely and professional, determined to get work done, to forge forward where many others might balk. I found it hard to meet her in this condition, to correspond beyond the fuzzy edges of my mind, trying to set aside my own anguish, my drive for answers, and just listen, even if still focused mostly on trying to remember every detail of the experience so I could retain in my mind after the fact, despite how I could already feel it slipping through my fingers, fading fast. Then, just like that, as if imposed as a reaction to my drive to understand, the window closed, and I was right back on the bed again, if now another step removed from who I'd been.

Once I'd interacted with what felt like Molly from beyond death, I found it easier, more readily available, to return to. It was sometimes hard to tell the difference between what seemed an honest signal and one I strived for, finding that the more pressure I put on making sense of it, the less likely it would be to offer truth. One night, the painting on the wall in the bedroom where I was staying appeared to be "alive," the human-fabricated lines that formed the subject of its picture little more than a distraction from the actual purpose of the object, as if could I only figure out what to say or do, just right, it would reveal a window or a door. Turning from that, I felt sure that I could see my childhood home reflected in the standing mirror perpendicular to where I sat, such that if I threw myself into it, I would be transported back through time, to space I'd already lived and hadn't learned to let go, wishing to live like a vampire in the comfort of what I already knew. I could at once sense the gymnastics of my anguish creating purpose for me from in the maw of myth itself and simultaneously understand that were there really any way to transcend, it might have to come in such a form as this. The dead could not speak to the living in such a way that would disrupt our own reality, Molly had told me; thus, all our communications, much like miracles, should be able to be written off, therefore preserved, which is why so much of human experience feels like a mirage. The work of language and image could be a vessel, then, to negotiate the vast but tight expanse between those still online in human life and those who'd passed before us into the partition between realms. While staring in the shine of the reflection, scouring it for edges where my mother might appear there somewhere inside the mirror's bending world, I felt a ping against my soul, an icon popping up from out of hidden folds: a definitively infernal presence suddenly arriving from some purgatorial hotbed, like a window torn in time—nothing palpable, only a feeling, something soot-black and invisible, calling me out. The presence wore a mask, it said, that made it capable of mortal interpretation, for my safety. It could see I was in need, it said, and it could help me, if I wished: *Anything you want. Just say the word.* Somehow, I didn't need to think of a response, took zero hesitation in telling it, by simply thinking, that I didn't want its help. Even in the grips of my desire to rewind time, to fix my life, I knew as if by instinct that any such incarnation of a change would be alchemical, a mirage. Nothing, no matter what they said, could take away what'd happened, and wherever else I had to go to overcome that was my path. Even as ruined as I'd become, I could still see and feel my body and the floor right there beneath me, after all. I'd be a fool to think I couldn't take another breath, no matter what all else I'd been forced to sacrifice already. Just as quickly, soon as I thought so, the demonic presence disappeared, wasting no time in moving on to seek new ground, as if it understood I wouldn't budge. Wanting to capture the sensation, I grabbed my laptop, and started typing, feeling Molly's voice within me right there, touching my own: *Good job with the demon*, I saw us type, no thought behind the process but the feeling of passing notes. *All data has a purpose, even data derived from nonsense*, the typing said. *The only thing you can do that's going to really hold you back is be afraid. [There are] different modes of access across the spectrum of possible probabilities of programmed time. The idea that God is has no plan. It has infinite plans. They all coerce each other into amalgamations of local image, filtered through brains that manifest their own definitions of experience. It's not quite simply relativity. It's more like, as soon as you think something certain it's been captured. Like crossing lines off of a list.* Outside my mind, the world was still; everything in the place it had been granted; any other day. *Finite and infinite at the same time. Reprogramming its conditions on the fly. This is all instant one stuff. It could take the rest of your life to communicate the instant one stuff. I'm still dealing with it and I've been here for 150 trillion years already. It's not an upload. It's just there.* My breath in my chest, life in my fingers, making language. *It was always there. And then it's gone again. You die again. You don't die forever, but there are levels. That's part of the experience of finding a reason to stay alive. Thank you for staying alive.* Soon, there were pages and pages of the language, offering another way of being in the world; of seeking how to raise the blinds on all the surfaces within us and all surrounding, like in grave rubbing, or like the way a dream resembles life.

‒‒‒

In this room where I am writing, several years later, I realize I have no idea what to type. Nothing I can think of seems to fit the way I want to shape what happened, no words that don't seem confused, like black balloons. *What words might I borrow from someone else?* I hear me think, then turn toward the shelf where I've gathered some of Molly's favorite books, which in their silence sometimes seem to stare. Feeling tagged, I get up and go trace my hand over the titles, not quite looking, until I feel my finger stop on one book's spine. I see only two pages have been marked with stickers, like tiny flags only just barely visible over the lip of the bulk of the book—Brenda Hillman's *Death Tractates*. I turn to the first sticker and find a single floating stanza orphaned against an otherwise blank page:

> I had only to trace the pen
> over the words;
> the poem was already written—[33]

Suddenly, I am aware of how the skin around my arms feel cold, my center empty, like the spot of shock that fills the space before the blood arrives after tearing skin. I decide not to turn back to read the rest of the poem, leaving it hidden behind the far side of the page. Instead, I turn ahead, to the only other sticker, another poem "Quartz Tractate," and feel my eyes jump down the page, skimming past stanzas until suddenly they stop, let me go slow, and read as through a window:

> Baffled by death, I sought her in myself,

33   Hillman, Brenda. *Death Tractates*. Wesleyan University Press, 1992, p. 32.

sometimes—often—speaking to her.
Now that has faded a little—

But still.
Why doubt that she goes on helping?
We were both everything in this. It wasn't
that she was the crystal and I was the ashes.[34]

Today, outside my two small office windows held parallel, the sky is eggshell blue. The view through each, I realize for the first time ever, aims onto different stairwells: one bisected into flights, two distinct phases, and one a spiral, both at once rising up and rising down. I go back to my desk and light a candle, watch it flicker.

Some days I can feel Molly sometimes in the rustling of long tree limbs as I move past; or in the pecking pattern of a wren with whom my eyes meet, our paths for just a second caused to sync; or in the mesmerizing texture of a field of fresh buds poking through the soil toward the sun. Returning to Piedmont Park, where we'd walk together in the summers, I see her body grown to fill the size of a huge field, high as the sky but still unnoticed, struggling to breathe. I see her walking just ahead of me with another recently deceased friend, Gian, just far enough that I could never catch them, only able to see their backs, or maybe it's just her, in my periphery, or lingering at a distance in certain rooms, around a corner, any corner, watching what I'm doing, following me, lurking. Up late at night now, I might sense her presence rushing forward when I turn my back, as if to knock me down or stab me, or worse, to beg me to save her from herself, rewind the past. I hear her twisting and turning inside the mattress when

34 Ibid, p. 48.

I can't sleep, or I hear her hissing, wailing, inside silence, or I hear a gunshot on TV or fireworks outside my window and imagine her face strained with abandon right before she pulls the trigger, or I see a photo of her as a child and think of who she might have been before the pain, or any of a million other waking terrors, any hour, any day, as real and as disturbing as any other facet of reality. Maybe it's her there, in my periphery, or lingering at a distance in certain rooms, around a corner—any corner—lurking, watching what I'm doing, following me, or rushing up behind me through the dark on my way to bed. In dreams and nightmares, when they finally begin returning from total blackness, her presence is most often an absence: just out of scene, disappearing into nowhere through a hedge maze naked with I've men never seen, or already elsewhere, far away, texting me photos of creative ways she'd come up with to kill herself again, beyond recourse. Like all the rest of the story, it's hard at times to keep apart the tender feelings from the ill ones, to trust what might be true or false about the past and future both. I feel her there, too, in my survival, in my desire to find out who I am now, and how, and why, to seek understanding in the absence of a more cleanly fitting form of grace; why it had to come to this, what else might change and what it says about the nature of creation to take part; why I can't shake the sense sometimes of being watched. One afternoon, out on a run, I keep feeling something pressing at my heels, a windfall in my periphery, parts of the world I can't see, until finally I stop in the middle of a cul-de-sac and turn around. Of course, there's nothing apparent but the road, the feeling of a rim of smoke too thin for me to harbor, beneath the air. *Please show me your new face*, I say aloud into the silence and feel the tremor of her voice bright in my brain, saying without language that she can't show me what she looks like where she is, as it would destroy me. Instead, she urges me to close my eyes, go inside my skull, and look straight up. When I do, I see a faint shape, held in reflection, just barely there—the oval outline like an eye, its center so deep it seems to pull against the fabric of the world—then, just as quickly, like the rainbow in our house, it disappears. Later, while looking back over the pictures from the day I spread her ashes, I find a photo that I'd taken of the sky just after reading aloud from an earmarked poem by Milosz, a spitting image of the face she'd shown me:

"I also am other than what I imagine myself to be," wrote Simone Weil. "To know this is forgiveness."[35] It is sometimes a part of forgiving, too, my therapist reminds me, that the person being forgiven need not know, much less for what. Every story changes as it ages, after all, whether bit by bit or all at once, just as the fundamental *facts* in

35   *Gravity and Grace*, p. 54

how we thought or felt revise their forms as constituent parts of a continuously discontinuous reconditioning of what might have once felt like the truth. Truth arrives inside the mind, after all, and in every person there's a different way to see. Molly tried to tell herself that she and the world both might be better off if she were gone, but suicide doesn't decrease pain and suffering, as I have felt it—it passes it on, translates its trauma into the experience of others manyfold, reenacting the exact same mechanism of devastation as if it alone were the true thing to be beholden to. Though I understand the vast temptation to create pain, to inflict on others that which we already have had to suffer for ourselves, and though it rakes my brain constantly to think of the person that I loved so much and now is gone, it seems there's little actual justice to be had in trading damage, an eye for eye leading nowhere fast but to a gore loop. The work of the forgiveness, then, is mine—a moral faculty I must live with, figure out how to accept and hopefully eventually let go of how it hurts, clinging best as I can to any reason, day in, day out; to keep up trying to not give up on the mystery of life, all the things we wish that we could separate from all the rest we wish we never had to know, akin with the idea that experience itself is a gift we cannot yet comprehend from here inside it, hoping that maybe someday we'll be granted some form of retroactive recognition, some guiding light. In place of stolid, steadfast reason, in the meantime, I'm trying to learn to listen now, to hold a moment as it unfolds, to imagine that though the cards fall as they may, the essence of life is derived in its experience, of trauma and majesty alike, through boredom and brutality commingled in the same way as our drive for love and life's high walls. No matter what I think, or how most any day I try to compensate against the perceived deficits and surpluses that blur the hours, something else unspoken sticks within—the knowledge of how it feels to have loved and lost it all in one fell swoop; to have held out hope and been abandoned, cut in the gut for wanting more—a sort of semi-conscious spiritual limb no one can see or lift except for me. I feel it throbbing in me almost always these days, a desolate redness in the background of even new high points, like a fever that won't break, and instead wants me to spread it and project it not only on those who hurt me, but on most any person, place, or object in my path. It is a desolation, a desperate rage so many others harbor sight unseen, undergirding our social history so completely it's a wonder we haven't all already bit the dust. *There's no floor to human misery*, I've found myself repeating sometimes in trying to explain how at once we're supposed to take it and carry on, as if *it can always still get worse* might be enough of a good reason to be thankful we continue to survive. While it feels foolish to deny that, I can't help but want to challenge myself to continue to imagine the other side of that same coin, true or false: *The ceiling of one's joy is in the mind. It can always be raised higher.*

———

"Reason sets the boundaries far too narrowly for us," wrote Carl Jung, "and would have us accept only the known—and that too with limitations—and live in a known framework, just as if we were sure how far life actually extends…We must face the fact that our world, with its time, space, and causality, relates to another order of things lying behind or beneath it, in which neither 'here and there' nor 'earlier and later' are of importance."[36] Do I believe that? No and yes—no for most any time I close my eyes I still can see the color drained from Molly's face there in those gardens, an image I can't imagine any amount of love and kindness ever completely setting right; yes for how I find myself alive still, lined with a fire to keep going in spite of all the ways I might have long since given up. That I still have will to imagine anything, hellish or holy, itself becomes

36 Jung, Carl. *Memories, Dreams, Reflections.* Translated by Clara and Richard Winston. Vintage, 1989, p. 302-05

part of the faculty of continuing to live despite all else, caught in the roving maw of human history as how who and what and how we are continues to reveal itself through generations. It is, of course, one thing to think this way, and quite another to stand within it and open wide, much less to have the strength to the lift the veil over the face of one's own suffering and ask the void within, against its silence, *What do you want?* Even now, after all the work I've done to teach myself again to want to live, I've only just begun learning to accept that I'm still here—still capable of seeking something more, of pressing forward through the duress that comes with having a body, having feelings, getting old; that, in having been torn asunder from the fundamental aspects of all my prior reasons to be; at times even embarrassed to still feel hungry, to yearn for love: giving it and receiving it, believing in it, against regret. The fact that Molly never figured out how she might save herself, how to face her darkest fears, somehow makes it only more vital for me to try to turn it over, to lift her and myself up as best I can in who I am while I'm still here. Despite the countless days I want to burn the world down, to claim the heads of those who've done us wrong, I see now how that's the same urge that drove my wife to become dust in being convinced that anything but misery must be a lie—the kind of lie that wants nothing more than to sustain itself by making others feel the same. Of Molly's pain, where I can feel it writhing in me, I'm trying to teach myself how not to simply push it down the line for someone else someday to solve. The mystery is hidden right underneath us, after all, and all around us, in a way that makes it even harder to believe, a façade from behind which you cannot yet comprehend the path ahead because it hasn't yet taken its shape, less so a product of all the prior paths that came before it than of a nature all its own; of the same ether, maybe, as the essence of must have once been before the universe began. In the same way we can't know death, life remains equally elusive, still in discovery, laced with a voice like those we only experience inside our heads at the cusp of sleep, coming back from dreams perhaps less out of sync with our reality than we imagine. *This is going to be difficult*, a voice portends, there at the edge of the unconscious, awaiting the next leg of your life, *an experience unlike anything you've ever known, containing information accessible by you and you alone, of pure terror and splendor both, through which we grow. Do you want to go?*

━━━

I dream Molly and I are staying at an unfamiliar mansion. We have a large bedroom that opens out into a hallway by two different doors. We are sitting on the bed exchanging Christmas presents. Molly seems checked out, in a bad mood. She opens a framed image I can no longer remember now. She opens another gift I can't remember. She seems upset. She says the gifts I have given her show her that I do not know her. She seems to have already made up her mind about this and that the gifts are an excuse. I get upset and try to explain why the gifts made sense to me; why the framed image reminds me of her. I go downstairs into the kitchen to get space and find two old friends there in conversation, drinking coffee. I convince myself I am upset. I go back upstairs to confront Molly that I don't understand why she would react this way to gifts, that it isn't like her, and I find that she is gone. I frantically search the house to try and find her until I realize she is no longer there. Outside, the light is weak, and the plants seem like they're slowly dying from dehydration. The dream ends when I reach a certain distance from the house.

━━━

I realized it was time to leave Atlanta, the only place I'd ever lived. After more than forty years in the same place, it no longer felt like home. Both my parents' house and the house I'd shared with Molly had been sold to other families back-to-back, and each time I drove past them, circling over and over when feeling nostalgic, wanting more, I saw less and less I recognized with each return. Their familiar spaces seemed besieged, suddenly, overlaid with so many forms of memory all it once it felt impossible to separate the good times from the bad, how much it stung to see it altogether fading in the wake of future time. Every street and park and building had become haunted, full of traces of simpler days we'd been carefree, not yet knowing what would appear on the next page. Even the familiar faces of my oldest friends suddenly felt altered, locked into lives I'd once had clearer traction in before my own life got lifted up and shattered, a constant friction in my head reminding me how life would never be the same. Sometimes, in midst of weighing my desires, I'd find myself falling back into the static glitch of alternate timelines: how if instead of marrying me Molly had moved away and got the right job somewhere else; how if instead of ending her life, she'd broken up with me and moved away, started again. Walking down a street alone, I think about the child we might have brought into the world together, who'd be almost eight years old now, perhaps holding onto my hand as we make our way along the snowy street out to the park. Part of me wishes I could know them now, that child; that I could get the chance to see their mother in them, for the better— her imagination, her resilience, her strong will—how we could have taken the bad example of her own time and used that as a chance to do our best. Other days, all such transmission of brighter feelings falls under the thrall of spiteful fury, at her, at me, at God, at everybody still alive, grateful to have spared a child the chaos. Most often, though, in my most true heart, I just miss Molly as she was, would give anything to get even one last chance to hear her speak or match her eyes. In absence of that, I find myself thinking of my mother, how near the end of her dementia, one of the things she'd kept circularly repeating was the first line of the Serenity Prayer: "Lord, grant me the strength to accept the things I cannot change, the courage to change the things I can, and the wisdom to know the difference." Though I'd never found comfort in those words the way that she did, I find them sometimes weaving their way into my sense, a part of who I am no matter what I think about their meaning, or how that meaning might connect to other thoughts. Like how I knew my mother had learned that prayer from her own mother, who had taped a card to the window in her own kitchen in Kentucky; or like the wooden wall-hanging hung by my mother on the wall of our home's kitchen all those years, too, its handprinted inscription working its way in through my periphery as I moved past: "She asked me if I had kids & when I said I did she said make sure you teach them what's right. & I said how will I know? & she nodded & said, good point, just don't teach them any obvious wrong then."

———

I haven't spoken to Molly's family since the funeral. I've ignored their calls and texts, long since gone silent. I still have half of Molly's ashes I've been saving for someone in the event they ask, wrapped in a box in the high shelf in my office closet, beside my mother's, which I still haven't had the heart to strew. Perhaps once I'm finally finished with this writing, I'll drive to Michigan myself, to the shores of Molly's favorite Lake Superior and empty her last remainder on the shore, a place I've never been before and somehow as close to home for her as I imagine I can get. I haven't heard much from my own family either, after the formal cards and flowers, and though sometimes I find it jarring, I try to tell myself that I don't mind; that the fulcrum of my life is carried in me, a source of strength I still have yet to understand. Everybody has their limits, so we've been told, despite our better inner ideals and our somehow still burgeoning understanding that we will mostly only ever fail. *Fail better*, history begs us. *There is no there there*, the culture replies. Underneath the logic of the language, in the meantime, the inarticulable awaits.

———

I find myself sitting on a ledge above a stream in a new city on the one-year anniversary of Molly's death. Above, the sun is high and faraway and draped with heavy silver cloud, a little breeze warm in its patches as I watch the water rush beneath me over rocks into pockets, creating floods of bubbles in the flow that spread apart and reconnect, another network hidden right out in plain sight. "No identity but what has been lived," I see I've written in the black leather journal Molly gave me for our last Christmas, its pages full of manic scribble from my mourning, cryptic fragments that would mean nothing to mostly anybody but myself. No matter what I do to try to find the right words to describe what's happened, now or ever, they always seem to come rushing out from under me right as I've said them, never quite there but at the instant of being formed. Even still, I find myself trying to try again, to trust the silence that settles in around each word, as if it isn't at all what I've said or not said that actually matters, but who I am, who I have been, who I might be. Every day that I am older now I am one day older than I was when Molly died, and she becomes a younger and younger person in comparison with me. Only our souls can bear the difference, as in the form of some still fast-approaching future I'm only just beginning now to trace—the budding seeds in me bright like the flowers she might have someday planted in our garden. Strange sometimes how love fills in to surround our lives' atrocities, how from the ashes of one lifetime, another form of life will rise—or maybe it really isn't strange at all, at least no more so than a sunset, or an instinct, or a sentence. It isn't in me yet to know, which in itself must be a gift, if one I still can't see because I'm in it, caught in pending alongside everything else as yet to come. Just as I'm preparing to move on, as such, gathering my will, I feel a presence at my back, just faint enough, beyond mere shadow, to know that if I turn to look, it must evade me, take other form. Instead, I take a breath and close my eyes. I lay back on the dirt and feel its warmth there where it's been gathering the sun. We sit in silence for a while, barely breathing over the running of the waters, the whole rest of the world around us as behind glass. Reflected in that, breaking through the darkness that my head holds, I can trace her outline like a glyph; I see she's wearing the black dress from our first date; her hair pulled back in a bun, the way she would when down to work. We sit a while like that, just listening, as if we'd always known this day would come but never how. *I'm sorry*, I hear her think into me, like a pulse. I focus on the feeling of that, the looming feeling of her sense there at my shoulder, a column of air at an open window. Then once again my eyes are open, too, already in the midst of the prior moment's having passed, one then the next, each voluminous enough to house your whole life and every other's in the same expanse, and at the same time, too quick to ever grasp but by a thread. "A bit of wind brings down a bit of grass just as I write that," I see my notebook reads, both now and in the future. "I touch the grass and it responds. I hold it with my thumb so it won't blow away again." It's still there today, that bit of grass, stuck in the margin of the pages from once when, so thin a wisp it could be blown back out into the sprawl of the world again if someone came and opened the notebook to the right page, any time.

———

Dear Molly,

It's warm today, in late October. The sky is overcast, has been all week. Constant light rain that fills the air with bizarre smells and muted light. I've been feeling sick so haven't felt like working. I find it harder to write lately, probably because I'm writing about you, our lives together. So far away and all surrounding. I get a little dizzy when I open this file, feel my heart pounding at my chest. Like it's a window and a mirror both. A way of being with you when I no longer know quite what that means.

I often think about our trees—the ingrown pair you pointed out at the preserve where we would walk, how you said we'd be like that someday in our old age. Separate but together. Sharing our needs and hanging on. There's a boundary there, now, between the memory of that moment, who we were then, and how it feels to have survived beyond your death. I told you once that I didn't like trees because all I can think of when I see one is their roots, the strange, disgusting maze they grow from beneath the ground. I'd thought you wouldn't like that, but you smiled. I think that's when I started liking trees.

The last time I drove by there, on my way to our old house, I was surprised to see how much they'd let the gardens go grown over, so thick from the street that I could barely see the entrance. Someone had even put a sign up, claiming it as privately owned now: TAKE NOTHING / LEAVE NO TRASH & LEASH PETS / SCOOP POOP. Just perfect, right? Still, I wanted to go in there, walk where we used to, but knew I shouldn't, and for once I listened to myself. I know what it means now to want to poke an open wound; how it feels good even, for just a second, as a reminder you've survived, not yet ready to forgo the unnamable—just one more time.

I wish I could have saved your precious life. The world is less without you in it. Without your voice. Without your mind. At the same time, it works within me, entwined with history in the mystery of life itself. Isn't that where we came together in the search of from the start? Not a certain meaning or an answer, but a path through the unknown? I know you loved to knock us down, as you'd claim in poems, and yet I can't stop returning to pictures of you as a child with those big cheeks, the distant glimmer behind your eyes, full of wild dreams. I wish I could have known how to be there for you better. I wish a lot of things, of course. These days I'm trying to figure out how to lend my wishes patience, their own rooms. Weird how easily *one foot in front of the other* turns into *one step forward two steps back*. "There is no master of the universe," I remember you wrote once of men's emotions. "The universe is for *joining*, not mastering." Good advice. Maybe you were also talking to yourself. Maybe we're all just talking to ourselves. Maybe that's where God is. Maybe that's why two stubborn dicks like you and me have such a hard time with our own thoughts. What do you think?

I finally got to visit one of the Great Lakes, btw—Lake Erie. It felt impossible, at first, to be there without you, to the point that I could barely see it as it was. I kept running up against its endlessness; how the reflective face of the waters obscures the depths, forcing those upon it to hold an often-unexamined form of faith. Maybe you remember I've been afraid of the vastness of the ocean since I was little, the meat of nightmares ever since, though that feels less true today than it once had. Still, I had to sit for a while at the edge of the water, gathering my thoughts, letting them out as best I could— no longer alone but with a loved one, hand in hand. We watched the buoys across the lake's face bob in a light wind, surrounded by strangers' families splashing and chasing each other, which as you know would have usually annoyed me but now felt thankful, like a screen. After a while, I got up and waded out into the water up to my knees. I tried to imagine where you might have been once, somewhere across it, probably teenaged, on a part of land consumed by the horizon, between the flat gray water and the sky, overcast then as it is today. I closed my eyes and raised my arms over my head and stood and listened. For a second, it felt like the center of the world, a place where anything could happen. When I opened my eyes, I was right where I thought I was.

Before I left, I fished a small black pebble out of the lakebed. It's about as big as my middle finger's nail, extremely smooth and rounded on all sides, shaped like a hedgehog in profile. I keep it on my desk beside the keyboard, next to a tiny glass bottle with a blank note rolled up inside, a future wish. Sometimes, when I'm frustrated or just bored, I cup the pebble in my palm and squeeze it tight, or maybe press it between the pads of my fingers, feel how its smooth appearance is actually gritty, full of pores. I wish I could ask you what kind of stone it is, listen to you talk about it. I could look it up, but I like not knowing.

It's time to me to leave for therapy, so I will have to wrap this up. I hope you're having a peaceful day, or whatever they call it where you are now. I'll be around. Write back whenever.

Love,

Blake

———

The only way for me to complete this book is to live.

ACKNOWLEDGMENTS

Thank you to Megan Boyle, who saved my life with love; who saw me as I was and didn't turn; who reminded me there's more to life than meets the eye.

Thank you to Amy and Adam and Grace and Cleo Robinson, who let me share their home and hearts like kin; who treated me like family without judgment or reservation; who made me eat and laugh and dance when nothing could.

Thank you to Ken Baumann for your resilience and your faith; for hearing out my madness and my terror and for caring when I didn't care at all about myself; for how you are.

Thank you to Sabra Embury for your brilliance and deep honesty; for staying up all hours taking calls and sharing sense borne out of chaos; for understanding beyond words.

Thank you to Nick Sturm and Carrie Lorig, whose deep attention and intuitiveness made me feel less alone all on its own; whose care and craft renew my faith in human consciousness.

Thank you to Matt and Nina Benard, York and Ashley Henderson, Rusty Weidinger and Christiana Worth, and Brian Weidinger for always having my back, for being family, for being real.

Thank you to Gene and Jenny Morgan for your trust and compassion and passion and collaboration; for knowing when to grind and when to chill and when to party; for Glass Orchid; for your example.

Thank you for hours on the phone and checking in and friendship and conversation and other acts of boundless care: Joyelle McSweeney, Johannes Goransson, Mike Young, Mathias Svalina, Kristin Hayter, April Ayers, Lorian Long, Ella Longpre, Kristen Iskandrian, Chelsea Hodson, Cass Donish, Claire Donato, Lily Hoang, Janice Lee, Julia Jackson, Scott McClanahan, Wyatt Williams.

Thank you to my friends who showed up to lift me up and carry me forward; who gave and gave, no questions asked—Stephanie Dowda, Scott Daughtridge, Morgan and Justin Kendall, Lucien Kendall, Paul Boshears, Kory Oliver, Caroline Worth, Caroline Crew and Cyrus Parlin, Mark Leidner, LK James, Casey McKinney, Robin Brasington, Timothy Willis Sanders, Sarah Rose Etter, John Lally, Tom Bruno, Jordan Jeffares, John Michael Dietz, Truett Dietz, Chris Landry, Andrew Weatherhead, Jordan Daley, Gina Myers, Jeff T. Jackson, Eric Raymond, Gregg Murray, Heather Christle, Chris DeWeese, Tim Brown, Beca Grimm, Matt DeBenedictis, Brett Butler, Caroline Mask.

Thank you to many other friends in Atlanta, Baltimore, and elsewhere, for their friendship and their passion and support: Drew Mobley, Lee Tesche, Franklin Fisher, Ryan Mahan, Onyew Kim, Laura Relyea, Aaron Burch, Jordan Castro, Nicolette Polek, Joey Grantham, Ashleigh Bryant Phillips, Kendra Grant Malone, Calvert Morgan, Keith Peters.

Thank you to GianCarlo DiTrapano—my friend, my brother, RIP.

Thank you to Matthew Porter and Jerry White Jr. for sharing, for remembering.

Thank you to Nicholette Scofield and Katherine Heines for their work with me over the years; for their wisdom, and what they see that no one sees.

Thank you to Joshua Marie Wilkinson and The Volta for the encouragement and opportunity to memorialize Molly, which gave way to the essay that spawned this book.

Thank you to Megan Boyle, Claire Donato, Nick Sturm, and Carrie Lorig for their generous feedback on early versions of this manuscript.

Thank you to Bill Clegg, Simon Toop, Nik Slackman, MC Connors, and The Clegg Agency, for the edits and the advice, and the continuous advocacy behind the scenes.

Thank you to Patricia Lockwood, Michael Clune, Emma Cline, John D'Agata, Catherine Lacey and many others for their support.

Thank you to Archway Editions, Chris Molnar, and Daniel Power for believing in this manuscript and taking a chance on it when no one would.

Thank you to innumerable others for your passion, for reaching out, for listening in, for remembering, for thinking, for feeling, for hanging on, for being you.

Thank you for reading.

MORE FROM ARCHWAY EDITIONS

Archways 1
(edited by Chris Molnar and Nicodemus Nicoludis)
cokemachineglow: Writing Around Music 2005-2015
(edited by Clayton Purdom)
Claire Donato – *Kind Mirrors, Ugly Ghosts*
Gabriel Kruis – *Acid Virga*
Brantly Martin – *Highway B: Horrorfest*
NDA: An Autofiction Anthology
(edited by Caitlin Forst)
Alice Notley – *Runes and Chords*
Ishmael Reed – *Life Among the Aryans*
Ishmael Reed – *The Haunting of Lin-Manuel Miranda*
Ishmael Reed – *The Slave Who Loved Caviar*
Mike Sacks – *Randy & Stinker Lets Loose*
Paul Schrader – *First Reformed*
Stacy Szymaszek – *Famous Hermits*
Erin Taylor – *Bimboland*
Unpublishable
(edited by Chris Molnar and Etan Nechin)

FORTHCOMING IN 2024

Archways 2
(edited by Chris Molnar, Nicodemus Nicoludis, and Naomi Falk)
John Farris – *Last Poems*
Jasmine Johnson – *Infinite Potential*
Ishmael Reed – *The Conductor*
charles theonia – *Gay Heaven is a Dance Floor but I Can't Relax*
Lindsey Webb – *Plat*